Lewis Falley Allen

History of the Short-Horn Cattle

Their Origin, Progress and Present Condition

Lewis Falley Allen

History of the Short-Horn Cattle
Their Origin, Progress and Present Condition

ISBN/EAN: 9783337326449

Printed in Europe, USA, Canada, Australia, Japan

Cover: Foto ©ninafisch / pixelio.de

More available books at **www.hansebooks.com**

KETTON. 1st, (709).

CALVED IN 1865.—BRED BY CHARLES COLLING.

HISTORY

OF THE

SHORT-HORN CATTLE:

THEIR ORIGIN, PROGRESS AND PRESENT CONDITION.

BY

LEWIS F. ALLEN,

AUTHOR OF "AMERICAN CATTLE," EDITOR OF THE "AMERICAN SHORT-HORN
HERD BOOK," ETC.

BUFFALO, N. Y.:
PUBLISHED BY THE AUTHOR.
No. 1192 Niagara Street.
1872.

Entered according to Act of Congress, in the year 1872, by

LEWIS F. ALLEN,

in the Office of the Librarian of Congress, at Washington.

WARREN, JOHNSON & CO.
Stereotypers, Printers and Binders,
BUFFALO, N. Y.

PREFACE.

This book has cost me much labor. The material from which it has been drawn was difficult to obtain—much more than those not conversant with the subject would imagine—and many years have elapsed in its gathering. Short-horn cattle history, in a connected form, has never existed since the race has been known, and it is only through the scraps and desultory notes made from time to time by different breeders and occasional writers within the past seventy years that we learn anything with certainty, and then in such disconnected fragments that the toil of dissecting, arranging, and putting them together understandingly has been most perplexing and difficult.

Still, the work, such as it is, has been accomplished; and that a volume of this character is needed by the Short-horn breeders, of America, and other countries where the race exists, must be evident to every intelligent breeder. Many of the various writings relating to Short-horns, their breeding and progress, scattered through the agricultural publications of the day, both in Great Britain and America are of decided value; but portions of them have been intermixed with such partisan feeling, and sometimes so inaccurate in statement as to yield little of correct information to those who wish to arrive at the real truth of Short-horn history. The mass of cattle breeders have not been of the class addicted to scholastic pursuits, although they knew many *facts*, valuable and important. Many of these facts have been given to the world; but more of them have perished with their possessors who died and left no sign of their labors, other than the noble animals whose posterity have survived them.

The English Herd Books, from the year 1822, have recorded pedigrees of the Short-horns existing nearly a century back, and as they have since increased and multiplied, down to the present time; but they have given us pedigrees only. Had they been accompanied with historical matter relating to their breeders, and the distinguished animals of their times, they would have added much of both interest and instruction. Some such notes have been written by accurate observers, and preserved, from which we have gleaned valuable information; but the information derived from them is less full and complete than could be wished. Inference and guess-work have been measurably resorted to by some writers in past days to give color to various facts and theories of their own—some of them right, and some erroneous. In the examination of authorities leading to the present work many contradictory statements have been canvassed, and an effort has been made to separate the probable from the improbable; yet it is not denied that errors may be found in these pages, so difficult has it been to detect and separate fact from opinion, truth from imagination.

It may be asked: Why, with such contrarieties of historical fact and opinion, strive to write Short-horn history at all? The plain answer is: The Short-horns *have* a history, and a most interesting one. A hundred years ago they were comparatively an obscure race of cattle, even in the land of their nativity. For several centuries they had been considered of little value over other common neat cattle, until sagacious men discovered their capability of improvement; and through the persevering efforts of such men they have been raised to a degree of perfection, value, and popularity, far beyond any other of the known bovine races. The money value of well-bred Short-horns now in the United States alone, may be safely estimated at several millions of dollars. They are worthy of a history, and a better one, too, if possible, than is here presented; but there having appeared no other, this must suffice until an abler and more painstaking pen shall replace or supercede it.

This effort has been a labor of love chiefly, for in its limited sale—anticipated only among Short-horn breeders—no pecuniary profit can result from its publication. Having been for many years connected with the compilations of the American Herd Book, and so many questions continually arising touching facts and incidents in their previous breeding, (perhaps better known to the author through his several hundreds of correspondents than to almost any other,) he has been convinced that these cattle should have, as they well deserve, as full a history as can be given of their race. The book makes no pretension to *literary* merit. It is a plain subject, treated in a plain way, and in the hope that it will be understood by all who may look into its pages. Omissions, both of fact and date, there may be, on the detection of which fastidious critics may carp and condemn. If such there be, we advise them to go forthwith to work and get up a better. Without further apology or excuse for its shortcomings, it goes forth to the public.

It is proper to say in this connection, that both the first and second volumes of the American Herd Book contain considerable matter (written and edited by the author of this work) relating to Short-horn history, *as then understood*. But the present work supercedes all that, as further sources of information more detailed, and in some instances more accurate, have since come to light.

It is fitting here to acknowledge the several favors which I have received from many correspondents in various parts of the United States, also some few in England, and the Canadas, who have contributed valuable information and papers relating to various subjects of this volume, for which I hold them in grateful remembrance.

LEWIS F. ALLEN.

BUFFALO, N. Y., *August, 1872.*

ILLUSTRATIONS.

WE have thought it necessary to illustrate the work with a few portraits of animals of distinguished reputation in their times, and such as would show the comparative merits and improvements in the anatomy and style of the Short-horns as they progressed from as early a day as possible down to a recent period. The scarcity of portraits of the earlier animals has afforded but a limited opportunity to make selections. We have wished to present the best specimens of their time, irrespective of any particular tribe or family to which they belonged, and only regret that the portraits we have been able to obtain are restricted to the herds of so few breeders; yet they were animals well known in Short-horn circles, and whose blood courses in the veins of very many herds of the present day. They are given with no intention to claim superiority over some others that may have existed contemporary with them, but because other equally good portraits could not be found. We place them in the order of time at which they lived:

1. DUCHESS, red and white, bred by Charles Colling, calved in 1800, got by Daisy bull (186), out of ————, by Favorite (252),—by Hubback (319),—the Stanwick (original Duchess) cow, by J. Brown's red bull (97). At 7 years old, milked down, and thin in flesh. Drawn by Weaver. Plate after a copy by Dalby. Page 13.

2. COMET (155), light roan, bred by Charles Colling, calved in 1804, got by Favorite (252), out of Young Phœnix, by Favorite (252),—Phœnix, by Foljambe (263),—Lady Maynard, by R. Alcock's bull (19),—by Jacob Smith's bull (608),—by Jolly's bull (337). At 6 years old. Drawn by Weaver. Plate after a copy by Dalby. Page 74.

3. KETTON 1ST (709), red and white, bred by Charles Colling, calved in 1805, got by Favorite (252), out of Duchess, by Daisy bull (186), etc., as in No. 2, above. At full age. Drawn by Weaver. Plate after a copy by Dalby. Frontispiece.

4. THE WHITE HEIFER THAT TRAVELED, bred by Robert Colling, calved about the year 1806, got by Favorite (252), out of Favorite cow, by Favorite (252),—gr. dam, by Punch (531). At full age. Drawn by Weaver. Plate after a copy by Dalby. Page 84.

5. DUCHESS 1ST, red and white, bred by Charles Colling, calved in 1808, got by Comet (155), out of ————, by Favorite (252),—Duchess, by Daisy bull (186), etc., as in No. 2, above. At full age. Drawn by Dalby. Page 125.

6. BELVEDERE (1706), roan, bred by Mr. Stephenson, calved in 1826, got by Waterloo (2816), out of Angelina 2d, by Young Wynyard (2859),—Angelina, by Phenomenon (491),—Anne Boleyn, by Favorite (252),—Princess, by Favorite (252) [bred by Robert Colling, and own sister to his White bull (151)].—by Favorite (252),

—by Snowdon's bull (612),—by Masterman's bull (422),—by Harrison's bull (292),—bred by Mr. Pickering. At 8 years old. Drawn by Dalby. Page 127.

7. DUCHESS 34TH, mostly red, bred by Thomas Bates, calved in 1832, got by Belvedere (1706), out of Duchess 29th, by 2d Hubback (1423),—Duchess 20th, by 2d Earl (1511),—Duchess 8th, by Marske (418),—Duchess 2d, by Ketton 1st (709),—Duchess 1st, by Comet (155), etc., as in No. 5, above. At 11 years old, milked dry, and left hip broken down. Drawn by Dalby. Page 128.

8. DUKE OF NORTHUMBERLAND (1941), red roan, bred by Thomas Bates, calved in 1835, got by Belvedere (1706), out of Duchess 34th, by Belvedere (1706), etc., as in No. 7, above. At 8 years old. Drawn by Dalby. Page 131.

9. NECKLACE (twinned with light roan Bracelet), mostly red, bred by John Booth, Killerby, calved in 1837, got by Priam (2452), out of Toy, by Argus (759),—Vestal, by Pilot (496),—Vestris, by Remus (550),—Valentine, by Blucher (82),—Countess, by Albion (14),—by Shakspeare (582),—by Easby (232). At 6 years old. Drawn by Gauci. Page 111.

10. COMMANDER-IN-CHIEF (21451), roan, bred by Richard Booth, calved in 1864, got by Valasco (15443), out of Campfollower, by Crown Prince (10087),—Vivandiere, by Buckingham (3239),—Minette, by Leonard (4210),—Young Moss Rose, by Young Matchem (4422),—by Priam (2452),—by Young Alexander (2979),—by Pilot (496). At 4 years old. Drawn by Gauci. Page 146.

The red and roan shades in the colors of the plates show less conspicuously in lithograph than in the original paintings, for which allowance must be made. The artist, Mr. Page, has executed them with great fidelity and care.

Further notices of these animals will be found on the pages where the plates occur.

TABLE OF CONTENTS.

CHAPTER I.

First Period of their History—The Second Period—The Cathedral Cow—When began the Improvement—Progress of Improvement.................... 13

CHAPTER II.

The Early Breeders—Dates and Names of Noted Animals—The Colling Brothers—Hubback—The Stanwick, or Original Duchess—Lady Maynard and Young Strawberry—Foljambe—Charles Colling's Mode of Breeding—The Durham Ox—Robert Colling and his Breeding 28

CHAPTER III.

Were the Collings the Earliest and Chief Improvers of the Short-horns—Their Early Cattle—The Galloway Cross—Berry's Youatt History—Charles Colling's Final Sale—Robert Colling's Sales of 1818 and 1820—The Collings' Improvement 56

CHAPTER IV.

The Booth Family and their Short-horns—The Studley Herd—The Killerby Herd—The Warlaby Herd 95

CHAPTER V.

Thomas Bates—His Short-horns and their Breeding—The Duchess Tribe—The Matchem Cow—Mr. Bates' other Tribes—Colors of the Bates Herds—Sale of Mr. Bates' Herd, and their English successors—Lord Ducie's Breeding and Sales 118

CHAPTER VI.

Mr. Bates' Influence on the Short-horns—Did he Improve them 144

CHAPTER VII.

The English Short-horn Breeders contemporary with the Collings and their immediate successors 148

CHAPTER VIII.

The Short-horns in America—The Gough and Miller Importations of the last century—The Patton Stock—Various other Importations—The Kentucky Importation of 1817—Sundry Importations down to 1830 155

CHAPTER IX.

The Later Short-horn Importations into various States by different associations and individuals—Declension of Prices 178

CHAPTER X.

Revival of the Short-horns in America—Importations in rapid succession into several different States by individuals and associations — Canadian Importations—The Short-horns as Milkers — As Flesh-producing Animals — Vitality, Longevity, and Fertility—Colors of Short-horn Noses—Bodily Colors 193

CHAPTER XI.

Exportations of American Short-horns to England and Scotland—The Style, Figure and Quality which should represent a Perfect Short-horn 222

CHAPTER XII.

Pure Short-horns—Herd Books—Pedigrees—The English Herd Book—The American Herd Book 230

CHAPTER XIII.

Progress of Short-horns in America—Have they Improved—English and American Herd Book Pedigrees—Notes on Breeding—Thorough-breds—Full-bloods—Conclusion 244

PART FIRST.

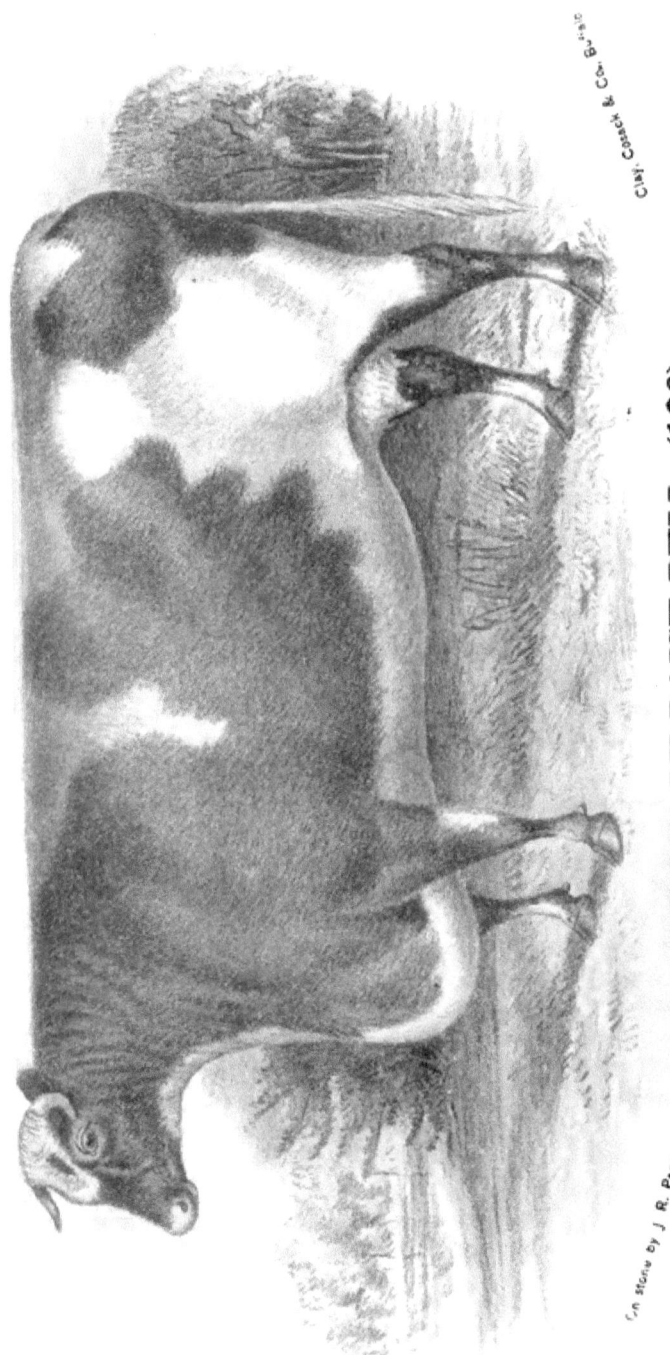

DUCHESS BY DAISY BULL. (186).
CALVED IN 1800. BRED BY CHARLES COLLING. 10 YEARS OLD.

HISTORY OF THE SHORT-HORNS.

CHAPTER I.

First Period of their History.

The origin of this noble race of cattle is obscure; but, that their lineage is ancient there can be no question. Modern records—say within the last hundred and fifty years, as tradition had already done for several hundred years previous—first recognize them inhabiting the counties of Northumberland, Durham, York, and Lincoln, on the north-eastern coast of England, and the country more immediately in the vicinity of the river Tees—the dividing line between Durham and York—as the locality where the more signal efforts have been made in their cultivation and improvement.

Why it is that the histories of nations, states, and peoples, usually so minute in what relates to conquests, government, laws, military and naval achievements, arts, and the general condition of the people, leave out valuable minor items to which the industry of the population is continuously directed, is difficult to say, other than the historians themselves have had no tastes or sympathies in common with agricultural pursuits; or perhaps the humbler subjects of agricultural industry were esteemed of too vulgar and menial a character to attract their notice. In short, domestic animals were below the "dignity of history," while the dirty intrigues of a lascivious monarch with a high-born wanton, or of a court favorite with an attractive wench of plebeian birth, were exalted subjects of record!

From researches through the various authorities in English annals from the time that England had a recognized history at all, we find no mention made of cattle, as distinguished by origin, race, or breed. They are mentioned as domestic animals, simply, furnishing a portion of the food of the people, and articles of traffic, and there all allusion to them ends. We know nothing further whatever of their existence, use, or varieties than we know of the foxes, hares and badgers, in which the outskirt lands of the nobility abounded. We have labored descriptions and illustrations of the costumes of the people, their amusements, games, tournaments—faithful chronicles of the times, no doubt—but not a word of their domestic animals, save now and then an allusion to the horses of the realm, but of them, even, no definite idea is given of either breed, conformation, or their adaptation to different uses.

In view of this dearth of information we have to resort somewhat to conjecture, and that conjecture drawn from collateral testimony, and incidents occasionally cropping out through historical events. Until, therefore, we can strike a vein of information with apparent truth and probability on its side, we must, as best we can, grope through the clouds of tradition mainly for an earlier account of the Short-horns.

For some centuries previous to the advent of the Normans under William the Conqueror, and while under Saxon, and probably the anterior Roman rule, the warlike Scandinavians of Denmark, Sweden and Norway, invaded the north-eastern coasts of England, comprising the counties which we have named, then called Northumbria, and held them for longer or shorter terms in subjection. The Scandinavians were skilled in the use of arms, bold navigators, pirates, both on sea and land, raiding upon all the weaker peoples which they could reach, and holding them subsidiary to their own power and purposes. With all these peoples, which, to a greater or less extent, they subjected to their rule, they established trade and commerce, and interchanged commodities, for they were as enterprising and sagacious in trade as they were daring in their conquests and robberies. They may not have carried away prisoners from England to their own lands, but more or less of their adventurous men settled themselves and made homes among the conquered people, married their women, and the children became Northumbrians in birth, habits and permanent abode.

At the time of the Norman conquest, in the year 1066, the people of Northumbria presented a mixture of ancient Britons, Saxons and Scandinavians, in blood, name and identity of character. Its climate was the most rigorous of the territory lying south of Scotland; its coast looked out on the bleak German ocean; its soil was moist, readily worked, rich in the natural elements of fertility, and eminently fitted for pasturage and the production of the better grasses; yet its agriculture, like all the northern English counties of that day, was in a low condition. Its laborers were inured to the hardest fare, and the rudest of homes. The invading Danes were not better in their own homes than were the subdued Saxons of Northumbria in theirs, and between them both, we may imagine that with the alternate struggles of invasion on one side, and defense or submission on the other, agriculture held but a meager opportunity for improvement.

Concurrent with their forays on Northumbria, the Danes extended their raids southward, taking possession for a time of Holstein, Utrecht, and the northerly portion of Holland. These countries they held, as they did north-eastern England, for purposes of plunder, trade and political advantage. As all these outlying provinces enjoyed a milder climate and a more productive soil than their own, the sea and land rovers profited largely in their conquests, and extended their commerce, not only with the peoples whose homes they had usurped, but with distant countries as well. Hence they waxed rich and powerful, as riches and power were then considered. Among the prominent articles of their traffic and interchange between Denmark and the provinces over which they held their fitful sway, was that of domestic animals, and the chief of these were neat cattle.

In north-western Europe, and all along the coast through Sweden, Denmark, and southwardly through the subjugated countries towards Holland, the cattle were a large, raw-boned race, of which we now know little beyond what the ancient chronicles say of them, and as they have been more lately known, only that they were useful beasts, strong for labor, yielding largely of milk, coarse in flesh, peculiar in color, and short in the horn. Such cattle, or those near akin to them, exist in those countries now. It may well be supposed that the continental cattle were frequently carried across the narrow sea separating England from the land of the Danes and their contiguous southern neighbors, and that they became a permanent stock of the country, as a cognate race existed in the Northumbrian counties, when the first dawnings of agricultural advancement opened upon the landholders and cultivators of that region some centuries after the victorious Norman had firmly established himself on the English throne, and driven the Danes from the possession of its soil.

For many years after their invasion and conquest, the Normans encountered much hostility before the stubborn Saxons and Danes (the latter which had settled among them now become incorporated with the others in a common nationality) peacefully submitted to the rigorous yoke which, from the moment he had secured his footing on English ground, the Conqueror had fastened on the necks of the ravaged people. Plundered in their homes, despoiled of their lands and chattels, subjected to ignominious servitude, and oftentimes struggling for life itself, the Northumbrian serfs, even when peacefully submissive to the iron rule of their new masters, could make but little progress in their rude agriculture, or rise to an improved condition of life, labor, or production.

To this subjection of the people and their lands to their new lawgivers, followed in succession through a long course of years, the foreign wars of the kings and rulers, heavy taxation, military conscriptions, the petty rivalries of the nobles among themselves, the rebellion of the barons against the despotism of their monarchs, civil wars, religious convulsions, and the almost numberless turmoils incident to a proud, brave, enterprising, warlike, yet ignorant people of divers races, such as England, by the intermarriages and social amalgamation of the higher classes of the Saxon and Norman blood, had now become. For several centuries the common people were little more than barbarians, and their rulers no better than despots. Agricultural progress either languished or barely held its own. The clothing of the peasantry and laborers was partially of the skins of sheep and goats, frequently undressed, or sometimes by a luxurious indulgence, of the coarsest cloth. Their habitations were covered with thatch, without chimneys, or floors, other than of earth or tile. Their beds were of straw or grass; their food of the coarsest of grains, and meat seldom. Their farm stock had little or no shelter beyond what the woods and frequent glens afforded, and of course were subjected to the inclement vicissitudes of the climate. Yet the barons, having monopolized the land, lived in state, indulging in sumptuous feasts and entertainments, although of necessity coarse in their kind, while the clergy and monks, appropriating to themselves the chief learning of the times, nestled in the choicest nooks of the territory, levied their exactions upon the surrounding people, and reared their vast Cathedrals, and spacious, comfortable Monasteries, while consoling them with their religious services and ceremonies. The royal courts, too, were more luxurious than either the barons or clergy, and although great in administration and powerful in arms, were more or less degraded in life and morals. Yet among all these adverse influences, great and bright men in court, and state, and church, arose through the degradation and ignorance around them, and gradually worked the people into better conditions of employment, progress and civilization.

The necessities of the great landholders began at last to lead their attention to the improvement of their soils. The country had progressed rapidly in population. The now constituted people of England, under a progressing nationality, had become a mass of breeding humanity. Human life had long been cheap in the sacrifices which had been made by the governing classes, as well among themselves as their serfs, during the wars, both foreign and civil, and also in the frequent executions at the hands of "justice," which then took place for even paltry offenses committed against each other by the common people. Yet the teeming workers at home filled these depleting gaps more rapidly than they occurred, and far beyond, furnished new mouths for consuming the products of the soil as well as hands to aid in its development. Along these times an experimenter and writer in agriculture occasionally turned up. "*The Whole Art of Husbandry,*" by Barnaby Googe, was published in the year 1558; "*Tusser's Five Hundred Points of Husbandry,*" in 1562; Sir Hugh Platt's "*Jewell House of Art and Nature,*" in 1594; Fitz-Herbert, Harrison, and some others, about the same time wrote and published limited works on husbandry. In addition to these more humble authors, illustrious minds, like Bacon, Raleigh, and an occasional compeer of noble birth or station enlightened the people with progressive ideas on soils, their management, and articles of production.

The English world still moved. Yet in all their agricultural advancement we hear nothing of improvement in neat cattle, until near the beginning of the eighteenth century, or shortly previous to the year 1720. It is true that great progress had been made in cultivating the soil; wide stretches of the marshy coast along the shores of Lincoln, Cambridge and other counties, had been dyked in and reclaimed from the sea. Considerable progress in science, in the arts, in trade, and various departments of industry had been developed, but with a strange indifference to the improvement of domestic animals, with the single exception of the horse—as he was indispensable in both war and luxury—little attention so far as public knowledge was concerned, had been given to either cattle, sheep or swine, except what was acquired in a few widely separated localities; and even those improvements, wherever they occurred, attracted little or no attention from writers on husbandry, or its interests. Yet we must suppose that intelligent and studious minds had occasionally been at work during the general progress in agricultural advancement, and some attention paid to ameliorating the forms and condition of neat cattle; for it is impossible that the Short-horns, like the fabled

Minerva, from the head of Jupiter, should have burst out in the full proportions of shape, color and condition, at the time we first hear of them—about the year 1700—from the coarse, unimproved herds of previous centuries.

Second Period of the Short-horns.

In the preceding rambling, desultory, and (as some of our readers may pronounce) irrelevant remarks, have been narrated the reasons why, if any progress had been made in the improvement of the neat cattle of England through past centuries down to nearly the year 1700, we have no certain evidences of the fact recorded until a comparatively recent date. We think the causes enumerated have been sufficient to explain. For the improvement which had taken place, tradition (uncertain, to be sure, when unaccompanied with sustaining probabilities) has done something to inform us, and recorded observation since, has done much more. A period of general quietude in England, with only occasional interruptions, since the expulsion of the Stuarts from the throne, in the year 1688, had given an unwonted impulse to the thrift and progress of every department of her industry, advancing her to a high position among the leading powers of Europe, both in commerce, manufactures, and the extension of her distant colonies. As a matter of necessity her agriculture had been largely developed and improved, and with that improvement no doubt much attention had been paid to the better quality and value of her domestic animals. To the various breeds of cattle which England possessed, down to about the period named, we shall pay no attention other than the Short-horns, the object of this treatise, argument, history, or whatever it may be called, being solely relating to them, as they existed anterior to their appearance at that time, and their condition through various stages of advancement to the present day.

The work we have undertaken, down to the period of our own memory and observation, must, of course, chiefly consist of a compilation from the writings and records of others, and from these will be given as faithful a transcript as possible, throwing out matter of doubtful authority, and admitting all which has the semblance of fact and probability. Exact facts, in all cases, cannot be ascertained; but an approximation to facts may be, and such we shall strive to give, without alteration or color. Yet, to give the semblance of probability to what may be said, the observant reader must at once admit, and yield to the theory that improvement from a defective organization to almost perfection in the development of their qualities in nearly all kinds of domestic animals, is measurably within the power of an intelligent breeder, who, by a sort of intuition, or through a long course of study and observation, is also a physiologist. Without such admission—that is to say—the capability of improvement by careful breeding, food and treatment of an inferior creature through a course of successive generations in its offspring into a superior one, all discussion of the subject is worthless.

The reader will observe that our first field of observation, for a time, will relate solely to the counties of England comprising the ancient Northumbria, once ravaged and occupied by the Danes. Let us start fair. We cannot, as we pass, well quote, in particular, all the several authorities from which we draw our earlier Short-horn history; for many of them are so fragmentary in their accounts that no continuous narrative in time or place can be made from either one alone. The principal sources from which we date our several items of history will be hereafter acknowledged.

A hundred and forty years ago, or about the year 1730, there was a tradition floating among the Short-horn breeders living in the counties of York and Durham, near the river Tees, that a breed of cattle had, many centuries back, existed within their borders—chiefly in Holderness, a district of Yorkshire—much resembling in size, shape and color, many of the cattle of Denmark, Holstein and north-western Europe, at that day. At what particular time they were first found in England, or who imported them, was unknown. They were of extraordinary size; had coarse heads, with short, stubbed horns; heavy necks; high, coarse shoulders; flat sides, the chine falling back of the shoulders; the hips wide; the rumps long; the thighs thick, and cloddy. Yet with all these undesirable points which rendered them large feeders, and late to mature, they took on flesh rapidly, and fattened into heavy carcasses. Their flesh, however, was coarse-grained, dark in color, and less savory to the taste, than that of smaller breeds. Their colors were light dun, or yellow red, deep red, pure white, red and white in patches, roan mixed of both red and white, and no uniformity in the laying on of either one of those colors, or their admixtures, the colors prevailing, as accident might govern. The cows were large milkers, yielding quantities, with generous feed, beyond any others yet known. There can be little doubt that these animals were the direct descendants from the cattle brought over from Denmark previous to the conquest. Some of that race of cattle existed in Holderness within the memories of men yet living, and we, ourself, nearly fifty years ago, saw several animals of a direct importation into this country from that district in Yorkshire, which were akin to the description above given.

But, to put at rest, so far as an illustration of art can do it, the question of the early existence of the Short-horn race in England, we extract a bit of history recorded in the eighth volume of our own Short-horn Herd Book:

"It will be recollected that in Vol. 2, p. 55, in narrating the ancient lineage of the Short-horns, a sculptured cow on the wall of one of the towers of the great Cathedral in Durham, is mentioned. The sculpture is that of a cow and two milkmaids, chiseled in light cream-colored stone, of nearly life size, from living models, and set up in a broad niche of one of the towers of the Cathedral. The sketch from which the engraving is cut, was taken at our request by Mr. John R. Page, of Sennett, Cayuga county, N. Y., when on a visit there in September, 1867. As to the reason for a statue of the cow and milkmaids occupying such a singular place, the following extract from a letter to us from Mr. A. B. Allen, in August, 1867, will explain. He was a few weeks in advance of Mr. Page in his visit, and was not aware at the time that the latter had crossed the Atlantic:

" I arrived at Durham, last evening, and have spent the whole forenoon of to-day, in and about the Cathedral. It is a magnificent old stone pile, and including the Lady Chapel, extending from its west end, is upwards of five hundred feet long and two hundred feet broad. It stands on an open place of several acres, the leveled top of a rocky hill, nearly encircled at its base by the river Wear. The building thus shows to great advantage; and, from its elevated site, you have extensive views on either side of the surrounding picturesque country. The quaint old city lies chiefly in the valley, a few only of its streets climbing up towards the Cathedral, and a large ancient castle—now converted to a University—also crowning the cliffs on the same plateau, several hundred feet north of it.

" The statue of the cow you desired me to inquire about when I left New York, occupies a broad arched niche in the north-east tower of the Cathedral, twenty feet or more above the level of the surrounding church-yard. The cow is an unmistakable Short-horn all over, the legs excepted, which the learned librarian of the Cathedral, the Rev. James Raine, informed me, were chiseled *unnaturally coarse*, by fault alone of the sculptor; otherwise it is a tolerable representation of a good animal. The two attendant milkmaids in the group are quite characteristic. The style of the cow is that of long-gone years, when the Short-horns were less refined than now. She is represented in moderate condition, with full udder and large milk veins, just as one would appear when yielding a full flow of milk. The present statue is comparatively modern, being a copy of the original, which was taken down and too much broken to be replaced when the tower was repaired, between the years 1790 and 1800, as near as I could ascertain. The Cathedral was finished about the year 1300, when the original design was probably sculptured and set. The figures, it

will be observed, are altogether disproportioned, the maids being too high and the cow too low in stature. It will also be seen that parts of the cow have been mutilated, a part of the tail and two of the teats broken off.

"In regard to the curious old monkish legend, of finding a peaceful rest here at last for the bones of St. Cuthbert, the patron Saint of Durham Cathedral, it is of such length, and so variously told, that it would exhaust your patience to follow it up in all its twistings and turnings. I will therefore give you the substance of it, condensed from what I am informed is the most reliable account:

"Know, then, that the mighty St. Cuthbert, famed for royal descent, and many and great virtues, died so long ago as the 20th of the calend of March, Anno Domini, 687, and was buried in *Holy Island*, a meet place indeed for so worthy and sanctified a man. Here his body rested in peace for the space of two centuries, when Bishop Eardulphus, and the Abbot Eadred, fearing that it would be disturbed in the terrible devastations which the Danes and other ruthless pagans began to commit in the neighborhood, exhumed the remains, and carried them, for re-interment, to Cuneagestre, situated a few miles from Dunholme, (now Durham,) where they remained one hundred and thirteen years, till the dreadful pagan war had nearly ended. Bishop Aldwinus then removed the holy body of St. Cuthbert to Ripon, in Yorkshire, to lay it by the side of another famous holy body, namely, that of St. Winfred, who was buried in the renowned Cathedral of that place. But after four months from this time, the Danish forays having entirely ceased, it was determined to carry St. Cuthbert back to Cuneagestre, and re-inter him where he had remained so peacefully before for upwards of a century. In bearing him thither, all at once, at a place called Wardenlawe, Bishop Aldwinus and his monks were stayed in their progress, and with all their force could not remove the body any farther, for it seemed fastened to the ground. At this strange and unforeseen accident, they were greatly astonished, and their hearts deeply exercised; whereupon they fasted and prayed three whole days with great devotion, to know by revelation from God, what to do with the holy body. At the end of this time it was revealed to Eadmer, one of the most virtuous of the monkish brotherhood, that St. Cuthbert should be carried to Dunholme, where he was to be received as his final resting place. But now came the great difficulty, for not one of the monks knew where Dunholme lay. Yet trusting to Providence to indicate it to them in some way, they took up the body again, and with confiding hearts proceeded on their journey. Presently they overheard a woman calling to another whom she met, that her cow had strayed away and was lost, and asked if she had seen her. 'Yes,' was the reply, 'just beyond, in Dunholme.' This was a happy and heavenly sound to the distressed Bishop Aldwinus and his brethren, who thereby had intelligence that their journey's end was at hand. Being guided thither by these women, they at once constructed a little church of wands and branches, wherein to lay their Saint till a larger and more solid building could be raised to enshrine him. This was soon done by the erection of a Cathedral of moderate size, which in the year 1093 was taken down, and the corner-stone of the present magnificent Durham Cathedral was then laid. After being finished, in gratitude to the milkmaids and cow, by whose means the final resting place for the holy body of St. Cuthbert had been found, their statues were placed in a conspicuous niche of the north-east tower, where it is to be hoped they will be allowed to remain as long as this mighty fane shall stand, whose foundations, in accordance with the instructions to us of scripture, have been laid upon a rock."

It is unnecessary to say more of the early establishment of the ancestors of the present Short-horn race in the north-eastern counties (Northumbria) of England, for some centuries occupied by the Danes before the conquest.

When Began the Improvement in Short-horns.

It has been asserted by some English cattle writers that it was early after the year 1700 that the improvement of their cattle was begun by the breeders, and that such improvement was aided by the importation of a bull or bulls from Holland. This assertion, however, is merely a conjecture. No *official record* of the introduction of any such bull or bulls has been found; and as no evidence of any such occurrence being even probable has been authentically recorded by revenue officials along the eastern coast of England in the counties where such importation would have been made, if at all, in a search extending near a century back of 1750, the conjecture or supposition of the introduction of the Dutch bulls may be not only doubted, but denied.* Indeed, no *positive* instance of any such importation is asserted by the cattle historians of that day, and the evidence of such being the fact was only hearsay. Aside from this negative testimony to the contrary, a statute of Parliament enacted in the eighteenth year of Charles II. (1666), positively forbade the importation of cattle from abroad into England, and that statute was strictly enforced until the year 1801, a time fifty years or more subsequent to the pretended importation of any bulls or cows from Holland. We might, from documents now before us, go into a

---

* "Youatt's Cattle"—American Edition—Article Short-horns.

labored statement of the *pro* and *con* assertions relating to such importations; but as nothing positive, beyond tradition, conjecture, hearsay, or supposition has been advanced to establish the fact of such importation, and the act of Parliament and the Custom records positively deny it, further remark is unnecessary.

To account for so many Short-horns being white in color, some of the cattle writers have asserted that this feature came from the wild white cattle in the parks of Chillingham in Northumberland, and Craven in Yorkshire, which had, almost from time immemorial, run in enclosures there, wild and untamable, as buffaloes. Aside from a likeness in color, these wild cattle had hardly a feature in common with the Short-horns. They were high-horned, black-nosed, light of body, long of limb, altogether opposite to the others. The supposition that the *white* color in the Short-horns was derived from the wild race is but pretension. On the contrary, there were, and still are, white cattle in Denmark. It is, and has ever been, a legitimate color in the Short-horn race.

Another fact may be asserted, even admitting that either the Dutch or the wild blood had been crossed into the original Danish blood, the period at which it took place was so long anterior to the time of the writers who claimed it, that even then scarcely a hundredth part of those bloods could be traced into the good Short-horn cattle of their day, and so infinitesimally small could it be now, that fractions can hardly compute it.

Thus, the claim of the Dutch blood, and the origin of the white color of the wild cattle in the Short-horns, by these writers, may be dismissed as apocryphal. So late as the year 1780, more than ninety years ago, as related on good authority, a tradition was then current among the cattle breeders of Durham and Yorkshire, that for two hundred years previous, running back to 1580, there had existed a race of superior Short-horns on the Yorkshire estates of the Earls and Dukes of Northumberland,[*] one of the most ancient families among the nobles of England. Their family name was Percy, and the Barony of Percy was founded in the year 1299. The family through its successive Barons, Earls and Dukes, was rich, powerful, and influential. Located near the Scottish border, and subjected to the wild raids of the northern clansmen, they

---

[*] Mr. A. B. Allen, in the year 1841, soon after his return from England, where he had spent some weeks in the Short-horn districts, informed us that in Durham an ancient record remains, showing that these cattle, in great excellence, existed four hundred years ago, say in 1440; but what the standard of excellence in that remote day was, is now difficult to know.

were brave by instinct, warlike by necessity, enterprising by education, rich by inheritance. Their estates were vast, and to their earlier grants from the Crown, they added largely both by purchase and marriage. They had the means to apply the agricultural improvements of the generations through which they had passed, and no doubt many of the heads of the family had the sagacity to adopt them. Among those improvements none were more probable, as theirs was eminently a grazing country, than that their attention had been turned to their neat cattle. In the earlier part of the eighteenth century the title of Earl of Northumberland became extinct by the death of the last male heir of the Percy family. The "proud Duke of Somerset," as history records him, had married the daughter then representing the Northumberland title and estates.* The issue of the marriage was only a daughter, and she a Percy on the side of her mother. This daughter married Sir Hugh Smithson, and having children, Sir Hugh, in the year 1766, was raised to the peerage, with the title of Duke of Northumberland. "So fond was he of his Short-horns that his peers quizzingly dubbed him 'the Yorkshire grazier.' He was in the habit of weighing his cattle, and the food they ate, so as to ascertain the improvement they made for the food consumed." Sir Hugh's active life was about midway and later in the years of the eighteenth century.

A hundred years earlier than the time of Sir Hugh, there existed fine stocks of Short-horn cattle in Durham and Yorkshire. "The Aislabies, residents of Studley Park, had very fine cattle in the seventeenth century.† The Blacketts, of Newby Hall, in Northumberland,

---

* An anecdote is thus related of the "proud Duke": His Percy wife dying early, he was again married to a lady of less rank in the peerage. The Duke being one day closely engaged in his room, looking over some important papers, his wife stepped softly up behind and tapped him familiarly on the shoulder. He suddenly turned around and with a severe expression exclaimed, "Madam, your familiarity is altogether inopportune. Recollect that my *first* wife was a Percy!"

† In a letter to us from our brother, the late Richard L. Allen, of New York, (a warm admirer of Short-horn cattle,) when in Yorkshire, Eng., August, 1869, he writes of a visit to Studley

"I spent a few hours at Studley Park, attracted thither by the ruins of Fountain's Abbey. Its graceful, undulating and massive old trees; one section of long, natural and now decaying oaks, of great circumference, and low but wide-spreading tops; another of immense beeches, which are of a different species from ours, tall and very wide-spread, and with drooping branches, which sometimes lie on the ground, fifty feet distant from the trunk; and then a stately chestnut in full bloom; double rows of the lime and elm, almost as fine as the beeches, and many firs of stalwart size, give to the park a great attraction. * * * * * *

"I asked the guide if there was any herdsman who could tell me about the cattle, and he said there was none. I presume the interest in the Short-horns on the estate died with Mr. Aislabie. His father was originally a private country gentleman, who became Lord Chancellor, and inherited the estate from the Mallorys, who owned it through several generations, his mother being the last heir. His son, William, who was in Parliament sixty years, was the great improver of

paid great attention to Short-horn cattle at the same time with the Aislabies. Portraits of these animals were occasionally taken and hung up to adorn the entrance of the hall; but when the noble residence passed out of their hands those pictures were sold. We should hope that they yet exist in some old curiosity shop, and if so, and can be found, we shall then have a definite idea of what *one* family of ancient Short-horns were."*

There can be no question, as our following narrative will show, that many valuable Short-horns, descended from and largely improved in appearance and quality over the ancient race, then existed in those counties, and were distributed in the hands of many different breeders. To what degrees of excellence they had then attained we do not know, nor do we know but a portion of the names of those several breeders; but at a later day, when their cattle had assumed a consequence and celebrity sufficient to attract the attention of agricultural writers a hundred years ago, they were chronicled in the books and agricultural surveys of their neighborhoods as of extraordinary value, and remarkable specimens of their race. The cows were described as large milkers, and the bullocks as attaining a great weight of carcass, and extraordinary productions of tallow.

Aside from the herds on the Yorkshire, Durham and Northumberland estates, we have a few names, of the then conspicuous Short-horn breeders in the earlier part, or before the middle of the eighteenth century, (1750.) Among them are Mr. Milbank, of Barningham, Sir William St. Quintin, of Scampston, Sir James Pennyman, of Yorkshire, and others of less noble rank, showing that the attention of some of the most respectable landholders was alive to the improvement of their cattle. It is recorded that Mr. Milbank bred and fed a five year old ox which, when slaughtered, the four quarters weighed 2104 pounds, the tallow 224 pounds, and the hide 151 pounds. Also,

---

the grounds and estate, and I presume was the one who did so much for the Short-horns. On his death the property went to his co-heir and relative, Mrs. Allanson, and on her death, in 1803, to her niece, Mrs. Lawrence, and on her death, in 1854, to the present Earl De Grey, now a member of Gladstone's Cabinet, who, although a man of mark in his way, I suspect cares very little for country life or the improvement of his estate, as he resides on it but seldom, and his neighbors have little to say of him in this respect, as they had of the Aislabies and their lady successors."

The above mentioned Earl De Grey was one of the late "Joint High Commission," who negotiated the treaty between the United States and England at Washington, in the year 1871.

It is to be regretted that the descendants of the once noble Short-horns which ranged over that lordly domain, should not still occupy the ground of their progenitors, which they long ago graced in their picturesque colors and comely proportions. A poetic charm still hangs about the atmosphere of Studley, coupled with the once aristocratic presence of its Short-horns.—L. F. A.

* A. B. Allen, in American Agriculturist, A. D. 1841.

a cow from Mr. Milbank's stock, afterwards belonging to Mr. Sharter, of Chilton, which, when slaughtered, at twelve years old, having produced several calves, her quarters weighed 1540 pounds. She was daughter to the celebrated "Studley bull" (626), he being calved in the year 1737.

This brings us forward to a period at which some intelligent inkling is had of the existence of Short-horn cattle in the hands of known breeders, and of an excellence in style, weight and quality commanding the attention of agricultural historians, and at about what date the *known* ancestors of our later Short-horn tribes, or families can, with a considerable degree of certainty, trace their lineage. It is possible that some errors, both of fact and inference, may have crept into the various accounts in those early days of Short-horn breeding; but we have sufficient evidence of the antiquity of the race, and the lines in which they had descended, down to the year 1750. Soon after that time records began to be kept of their lineage, as purity of blood was considered of vital consequence.

The colors of the cattle in those days were red, of different shades, red and white, pure white, frequently white on the body with roan necks and heads, and roan of red and white intermixed over the body, or in patches, with either more of the white or of the red prevailing, as now. What was their exact quality, style or symmetry, as compared with the choice Short-horns of the present time, it is difficult to say, as we have no accurate portraits of them; but that they combined the main points of excellence belonging to the race as now recognized, and in which still higher improvements over them have been made in the cattle of later years, we can have little doubt.

Thus, we have seen the Short-horns from the ancient race existing in Northumbria anterior to its conquest by William of Normandy—otherwise the Conqueror—within a few years after his landing at Hastings in the year 1066, brought down through a series of seven hundred years, steadily improving, with the progress of the English people in their agricultural advancement into a condition of excellence then unequaled, probably, by any contemporary race of cattle in the British islands or the neighboring continent, and that excellence attained through their own blood alone, uncontaminated by any foreign element, or if occasionally so, to such small degree as to be unrecognized in the predominating merits of the original race.

CHAPTER II.

THE EARLY BREEDERS—DATES AND NAMES OF NOTED ANIMALS.

ARRIVING at a point of time about the year 1750, or a little later, we find the Short-horns a recognized breed, and that great pains had been taken with their cultivation by intelligent landholders, as well as a dissemination of their blood into the hands of enterprising tenant farmers. Such we learn from the records of agricultural writers through the later years of the last century, and the earlier ones of the present. We now proceed to a broader field of operation, and a more intimate discussion of their merits in the possession of breeders, by *name*, as well as of noted animals, then individually known and recorded.

The field of operation is still the ancient Northumbria, the most active movements are within the counties of York and Durham, in and about the valley of the Tees. From the years 1730 to 1780, many eminent breeders are named, and among them, besides those already mentioned, are Sharter, Pickering, Stephenson, Wetherell, Maynard, Dobison, Charge, Wright, Hutchinson, Robson, Snowdon, Waistell, Richard and William Barker, Brown, Hall, Hill, Best, Watson, Baker, Thompson, Jackson, Smith, Jolly, Masterman, Wallace, Robertson, and some others. These names we find as breeders of the earliest cattle whose names and pedigrees are recorded in the first volume of the English Herd Book. It may be well to know that as this Herd Book was not published until the year 1822, (some thirty to forty years after many of the names we have mentioned had left the stage of active life,) tradition, and the memory of men then living, as well as written records of their predecessors, were the authorities on which the lineage of the earlier animals were admitted to its pages.

Confining the present relation to a period anterior to the year 1780, the earliest named animal on record is "Studley bull" (626), "red and white, bred by Mr. Sharter, of Chilton." This is all the Herd Book says of him. He was calved in 1737, and of the Barningham

(Milbank) stock, which came from Studley, in Yorkshire, where they had existed for many years. He is described, by one who often saw him, as having possessed wonderful girth, and depth of fore quarters, very short legs, a neat frame, and light offal. He was the grandsire of Dalton Duke (188). This latter bull was bred by Mr. Charge, and sold by him at the then high price of fifty guineas, to Messrs. Maynard and Wetherell, in whose possession he served cows at half a guinea each. From Studley bull came "Lakeland's bull," which was the sire of William Barker's bull (51), which was the sire of Richard Barker's bull (52), both noted as the sires of many of the best early Short-horns of their day. Studley bull was also sire of the cow Tripes, bred by Mr. Pickering. The dam of Tripes was bred by Mr. Stephenson, of Ketton, in the year 1739. From her originated Mr. S.'s Princess tribe.

It may be noted here that in the earlier recorded pedigrees—notes or memoranda, rather—only one or two crosses are given, with the name of the sire only, and but rarely the name of a dam given at all. In many other instances the name only of the recorded bull is given, without any allusion to breeder, owner, sire or dam; simply recognizing him as a Short-horn, from which other recorded animals are descended.

To "Studley bull" can be traced a larger number of the early recorded Short-horns than to any other one of which we have a particular knowledge. His blood was well known, and popular, and being of the Milbank stock, was probably as pure in descent as any then in existence. He may be termed one of the principal progenitors of the Short-horn race, as they stand recorded in the Herd Book from its first volume down to the present, although not the only one, as numerous others, no doubt, existed contemporary with him, sires to many noted tribes of a later day. We speak of him only as more is known of him than of them, he having a Herd Book record, and they not.

Another noted bull may be named into whose blood probably more of the later pedigrees can be traced to, and ending in him, than to any other, viz.: James Brown's red bull (97). The date of his birth is not recorded, but it was probably between 1765 and 1770. He was bred by John Thompson, of Girlington Hall, and got by William Barker's bull (51), which is all the Herd Book says of him. On the side of his sire, he was a great grandson of Studley bull. His dam is not named, and we have no record of his blood on her side. Indeed, there seems to have been but little care taken in those days to give the names of dams if they had names at all. We are to presume, however, that they were pure Short-horns, as there is no probability of bulls being recorded by the discriminating breeders of the time unless their lineage, as well as forms, was of the best standard; therefore the purity of their blood may remain unquestioned.

From all the accounts we have been able to gather, the cows of that day were good milkers, and capable, when retired from breeding, and the dairy, of yielding heavy carcasses of beef. These qualities were, of course, imparted to their descendants, and perpetuated as we find many of them at the present day.

We note many bulls in the first volume of the English Herd Book that lived anterior to the year 1780, but aside from their names and that of a sire, and sometimes a grandsire, little or nothing seems to have been recorded of their ancestry, and nothing beyond can now be known of them. Among these, in addition to those already named, are Alcock's (Ralph) bull (19), Allison's gray bull (26), Bartle (63), J. Brown's white bull (98), Dalton Duke (188), Danby (190), Davison's bull (192), Dobson's bull (218), Harrison's bull (292) [his record only says, "bred by Mr. Waistell;" the late Mr. Thomas Bates, in a private note to the record of Harrison's bull, states that he was got by Studley bull (626), dam Mr. Waistell's cow Barforth], Hill's red bull (310), Hollon's bull (313), Hubback (319) [of which more hereafter], Jolly's bull (337) [nothing but his name is recorded], Kitt (357) [nothing but his name is recorded], Ladykirk (355), Manfield (404), Masterman's bull (422) [got by Studley bull], Paddock's bull (477), Robson's (William) bull (538), Signior (588), Sir James Pennyman's bull (601), Smith's (Jacob) bull (608), Smith's (T.) bull (609), Snowdon's bull (612) [sire of Hubback (319)], Studley White bull (627) [got by Studley bull (626)], Waistell's bull (669) [the same as Robson's bull (558)], Walker's bull (670) [the same as Masterman's bull (422)].

The above named, of the 710 recorded bulls in Vol. 1, E. H. B., are all, probably, as near as can be ascertained (of record), that lived previous to, or about the year 1780, and a few years afterwards, and probably a great majority of the pedigrees of the present time, if their lineage could be traced, might run back into the blood of one, or the other, or several of them.

Of the cows, contemporary with the bulls we have named, few, if any, are recorded in either the first, or subsequent volumes. We can, therefore, only infer that the cows were equally as well and carefully bred as the bulls. Cattle fairs, (not *shows*, as our modern exhibitions are improperly called *fairs*,) where beasts were taken to market for sale, were then common in England, as now, and probably many well-bred cows and heifers were brought there by their breeders, and owners, and the breeders of choice cattle bought them, when their blood and quality were considered worthy of such use, and bred to their choice bulls. From such market cows descended the more immediate ancestors of many celebrated Short-horns since. It is no disparagement to those nameless cows that such is the fact, as very few pedigrees can now be traced by *name*, on the female side, beyond the year 1780, and but comparatively few, among a great majority of them, beyond the year 1800.

To show what was the general character of the Short-horns of the time above written, we quote Bailey, who made an agricultural survey of Durham, and wrote in the year 1810: "The cattle on both sides of the Tees have been known by the appellation of the Teeswater breed. About 1740, their color was red and white, and white, with a little red about the neck, or roan." In "Thornton's Circular," of January, 1869, published in London, in an account of "Ancient Short-horns," the writer remarks: "Mr. John Wright, born at Lowfields, near Catterick, in 1784, a well-known judge, and who was originally proposed as the author of the Herd Book, says, that his earliest recollections of the Short-horns were large, massive, expansive cows, with great width and substance, hardy constitutions, mostly red and white spotted, white bodies, necks spotted with red or roan, ears red and head white, frequently black noses, and rather long, waxy horns." Although these recollections may run down near or quite to the year 1800, it is probable that they give the features generally prevailing among the Short-horns of the time.

Although we might give further accounts from different sources—meager, however, at the best—of the Short-horns as they existed anterior to, or about the period of 1780, it is hardly worth while to cumber our pages with simply collateral testimony, (for that is all there would be of it,) and we proceed to a new era in their history, from which we are able to gather decided particulars of fact, irrespective of tradition, or common rumor.

The Short-horns at and after the year 1780—Robert and Charles Colling.

The reason why, in our previous remarks, we have made, and now again make, a point of the year 1780, or thereabouts, is, that near that period an era commenced by the action of a new class of men, or rather by a more intelligent appreciation of the value of Short-horns by those interested in their propagation.

This change of sentiment and action was partially introduced by two young men, brothers, just beginning active business life on their own account, Robert and Charles Colling. They were sons of a substantial farmer living in the valley of the Tees, who had many years been a Short-horn cattle breeder. He brought up his sons in his own pursuit, and no doubt aided them with an outfit, for it appears that they were each enabled to occupy a good farm in the year 1783, not a far distance apart, stock it with the necessary appliances, and commence in a spirited way the breeding of Short-horns. That they were intelligent, sagacious, enterprising, there can be little doubt, as their subsequent career was altogether successful.

In writing what follows, and saying much of the operations of the Colling brothers, it is not that we feel any partiality for them over other breeders of their time, but because more historical matter has been given relating to them and their proceedings than of other breeders contemporary with them, and further, that their course of breeding has been more freely commented upon during and since the time they were on the stage of action. It has been asserted that they were the chief and real *improvers* of the Short-horn race, and to them has been ascribed the great merit and glory of raising them from an obscure breed in a narrow locality, into the peerless excellence and popularity they have since enjoyed wherever they have obtained a foothold, and proved successful in their breeding. We say such has been *asserted*—sometimes by those who know nothing about it, other than by information through partial publications of incidents in the Collings' career, and sometimes by others who had a particular partiality for them through the stock descended from their herds; and the assertion has been as strongly denied by others. This question of their improvement of the Short-horns will be discussed hereafter.

We propose to state all the facts which have come within our knowledge relating to the Collings in their course of cattle breeding, and the results which have followed it. From such facts the reader may draw his own conclusions of their correctness, or otherwise. The results determined by the extended practice in breeding by the Collings have been too long discussed, both in England and the United States, by those who have considered themselves masters in the studies of natural history and physiology, to set up our own judgment in decision, either one way or the other. We have opinions, however, and may give them at a proper time as different subjects of discussion may arise, but knowing that different opinions may be as honestly held, and as freely discussed as our own, we do not choose to bias the judgment of others, or rule their conclusions. We aim to write *history*, and nothing else, in what relates to Short-horn progress and improvement.

Robert Colling, the elder brother, settled on a farm at Barmpton, and Charles, the younger, on another farm at Ketton, which latter one had been for many previous years occupied by their father, within a short distance of the Tees, and but a short way apart from each other, in the neighborhood of Darlington. *Practical* farming among the higher classes of nobility had become respectable. His Majesty, the third George, the first of the Guelph dynasty born in England, had become much interested in the cultivation of his royal acres at Windsor. He was a stock breeder too, as well as a farmer. Although intractable and pertinacious, as were his Guelph progenitors, in affairs of state, he was a sober prince, fond of country life, and a lover of fine farm stock. Placable in domestic life, with his cousin-German Queen, quite as domestic as himself, and their large family of children, he spent much of his time at the palace of Windsor, supervising and directing his farm. In his various attentions to stock breeding His Majesty had made the acquaintance of the celebrated Robert Bakewell, a stock raiser and farmer in Leicestershire, who had acquired a wide reputation in breeding up the "Long-horned" cattle of his district into an excellence of quality hitherto unknown. Bakewell had also given a new variety of long-wooled sheep to the kingdom, by a careful course of breeding from the rather scraggy-bodied, long-wools then prevalent in his vicinity. To such excellence and popularity had he raised these sheep that they afterwards assumed the several names of New Leicester, Dishley, (the name of his farm,) and Bakewell, as those who purchased from him and bred them chose to call the *improved* variety.

Bakewell was born in the year 1726, and died in 1795. He had pursued his vocation as a breeder long and successfully, became wealthy, was a man of large hospitality—for a farmer of those days—received many visits from noblemen of rank, who sought his advice in improving their farm stock, and among others George the Third had made him visits on the same errand, consulting him freely, and buying of his stock. Bakewell's system of breeding was his own, widely different from the usual practice of the English stock breeders of his day, and with him entirely original, as then considered. He was a good animal physiologist. He cut up and dissected various carcasses of his sheep and cattle, examined their flesh, bones and sinews, put them in pickle, and afterwards hung them up in his laboratory for further observation. He was a profound master of his business, and perhaps the originator of a new system of breeding by which, in his own hands, his success was triumphantly acknowledged over any other stock breeder of his time. It is probable that to his efforts and example England at this day owes her unrivaled breed of long-wooled sheep. His selection of the breed of cattle on which to exercise his skill was not so happy. Although of an ancient race, they were not generally popular with the farmers in and beyond the counties immediately surrounding Leicestershire; yet he raised them to a capacity for acquiring flesh never before equaled. Although now existing, and of excellent quality in limited herds—perhaps quite equal to those which Bakewell improved—the Long-horns have not attained wide popularity as a race.

Bakewell also bred the common cart or dray horse of England into enormous size and symmetry, which they hold to the present time; and all by one persistent course of breeding, good food, and watchful care. His system with all these animals was, first to select, wherever he could find them, and of the best blood, those as near a proper form for the purposes he needed as was possible, and then by breeding them to their own family blood alone, only going out of it for other selections when he could find a better, which was seldom, until he brought them to the points of excellence in form and quality that he wanted. This was "in-and-in breeding;" and although not concurred in by the common sentiment of humanity, so far as its own race is concerned, Bakewell and others who have since followed his example most closely, have decided, indeed proved, that *under proper selections of the animals so paired* together, the practice has resulted in the highest success. Such was Bakewell's practice. He may be said to have *introduced* the *modern* system of *improved* stock breeding—whatever may have been known to the ancients, and since lost—and as such improver, his name will go down to posterity with gratitude and honor.

The young Collings were sagacious men, Charles the more active and enterprising, although Robert was equally sound in judgment as a breeder; and they were admirably fitted to work in unison so far as their views in breeding were concerned. Forecasting, as well as thoughtful in laying their plans for future action, they had heard of Bakewell and his improvements—for he had been at work thirty years before the Collings began—his fame was abroad through the chief stock-breeding counties of England, and had long before reached the precincts of the Tees. At the outset of the brothers' career in breeding, they paid Bakewell repeated visits, closely examined his stock, saw the improvements he had made in them over the faulty originals from which he had reared them, and took many shrewd lessons in his manner of proceeding. They bought improved sheep of him, divided them with each other, and followed his practice in breeding them. The system adopted by Bakewell the Collings determined to pursue with their Short-horns, which they had now selected for their own breeding.

About the year 1780—perhaps a year or two earlier, or later, for we have not the exact date of their beginning—the Collings became stock breeders before settling at Barmpton and Ketton. "The best specimens of Short-horns of that time, generally, were wide-backed, well-framed cows, deep in their fore quarters, soft and mellow in their hair and 'handling,' and possessing, with average milking qualities, a remarkable disposition to fatten. Their horns were rather longer than those of their descendants of the present day, and widening upwards. The *faults* were those of an undue prominence of the hip and shoulder joints, a want of length in the hind quarters, of width in the floor of the chest, of fullness generally before and behind the shoulders, as well as upon the shoulder itself. They had a somewhat disproportionate abdomen [large bellies], too long in the legs, and a want of substance, indicative of delicacy in the hide. They failed also in the essential requisite of taking on their flesh evenly and firmly over the whole frame, which frequently gave them an unlevel appearance. There was, moreover, a general want of compactness in their conformation."* Of such material, mainly—although some of the Tees breeders had cattle with more of the good qualities, and less faulty than others—the Collings found the Teeswater, or Short-horn cattle, when they began their course as breeders. It is evident that the animals needed improvement, and that of a radical kind.

We have already recited the weights of some of the cattle anterior to the Collings. From them we know that they could be fed to an extraordinary weight, whatever the precise quality of their flesh might prove, or the amount of offal they threw off. Culley, after many years earlier Short-horn experience and observation, writing

---

* Mr. Carr, of Stackhouse, in his history of the Booth Short-horns.

in the year 1803, says: "The great obstacle to improvement was that no bull should be used to the same stock more than three years; if kept longer the breed would be too near akin, and produce tender, diminutive stock, liable to disorders." Bakewell, however, had upset all this nonsense by persistently breeding in-and-in his own cattle and sheep through all possible degrees of consanguinity, and the Collings adopting his theory at the outset, determined to put Bakewell's course into practice.

Here, then, were the two young breeders—Robert about the age of thirty, living a bachelor, and Charles a year or two younger, and married—settled in their vocation in the very home of the Short-horns, surrounded by a wide neighborhood of veteran breeders, life-long engaged in the business, in which their capital, pride and ambition were all enlisted. From the herds of those breeders the Collings could select at pleasure, without a heavy drainage on their purses, for prices in fine cattle had not yet taken a *fancy* altitude in that locality. The depression of agricultural values then caused by the late French and American wars had reduced them to their minimum. A pleasant time the young men must have had in ranging over the country, examining the herds and selecting their stock, with ample means in their pockets to command the best of them, and embark in a business so full of interest, expectation and profit. Educated to the pursuit by a shrewd, managing father, though possessing the same notions in breeding as were held by his neighbors, the sons had the sagacity to believe that improvement was within their reach, and their visits to Bakewell had confirmed it. What were the earliest purchases they made, who from, or the names of the cattle, history has given no record.

Robert and Charles were at first in partnership, but separated when going to their separate farms at Barmpton and Ketton, which took place some time about the year 1783. Still, they bred more or less in conjunction, frequently using the same bulls, alternating as they either chose, or agreed, but each having his own cows, and they drawn from the different herds around them.

HUBBACK.

Having early begun their course of breeding by obtaining several good cows, we now introduce another distinguished animal into the Colling herds, whose blood, coursing through the descendants of those cows and others in their hands, constituted an era in the Short-horn breeding of that day. This was no less than the famous bull

HUBBACK, in the hands of Mr. Waistell, of Ali-hill, and Robert Colling, about whose history there has been more controversy, guesswork, inference, and error, probably, than in that of any early Short-horn bull whatever; and for a part of this error the world is indebted to the *Rev.* Henry Berry, who wrote the brief Short-horn history in Youatt's "British Cattle," in the year 1834, and, as we think, from interested motives of his own, being a Short-horn breeder himself, and having an object in prejudicing the public against the purity of Hubback's blood. Of Mr. Berry and his history, more will be said hereafter.

We have investigated the subject of Hubback exhaustively, looked through all the authorities and controversies relating to him, which it would be tiresome and unprofitable to repeat at length, besides leading the reader into a labyrinth of statements and counter-statements, out of which he might not arrive, after all, at a very accurate conclusion.* His pedigree in Vol. 1, E. H. B., is here given:

"(319.) HUBBACK.—Yellow red and white, calved in 1777, bred by Mr. John Hunter of Hurworth, got by Snowdon's bull (612), dam from the stock of Sir James Pennyman, and these from the stock of Sir William St. Quintin, of Scampston."

This is all there is of the pedigree proper, although appended to it are references to the pedigree of Snowdon's bull through his different sires.

That Snowdon's bull may be understood, his pedigree (all there is of it) is recorded in E. H. B., Vol. 1, as follows:

"(612.) Snowdon's bull (sire of Hubback), got by Wm. Robson's bull (558)."

All the pedigree which Robson's bull has is, "got by James Masterman's bull (422)," and all that is said of Masterman's bull is, "got by Studley bull (626)."

Accompanying the pedigree of Hubback is also a certificate, as follows:

"I remember the cow which my father bred, that was the dam of Hubback; there was no idea then that she had any mixed or Kyloe blood in her. Much has been lately said, that she was descended from a Kyloe; but I have no reason to believe, nor do I believe, that she had any Kyloe blood in her.   JOHN HUNTER.

HURWORTH, NEAR DARLINGTON, *July 6, 1822.*"

---

* For a full and exhaustive discussion of the question see "Youatt's Cattle," American Edition; also its account of Hubback, by the American Editor, extracted and printed in Vol. 2, American Short-horn Herd Book.

This certificate was made by the son of Hubback's breeder, forty-five years after the bull's birth, and at the time he was recorded in the Herd Book. Mr. Hunter's recollection of the charge of Kyloe* blood in the cow was probably quite distinct. He had undoubtedly heard it talked over at the time when the bull's merits were ascertained and discussed, and from the very accurate description we have of the cow, there is little probability that she was any other than a pure Short-horn. At all events, the conceded merits attached to the bull as a getter of superior stock, in none of which do we find a cropping out of any other than Short-horn blood, (which would occasionally have been the case had he much of the Kyloe in him,) we may safely conclude that Hubback was as pure in blood as any other Short-horn of his time.

On the sire's side of Hubback all appears fair, and only on the side of his dam were circulated, by some parties, a suspicion of Kyloe, or Scotch blood in his veins, which seems to be fully set at rest by the certificate of Mr. Hunter. A like innuendo was circulated by others, that Dutch blood had crept into Hubback by the rumor (without anything like *proof*, however), that Sir William St. Quintin had, many years before, imported a bull or bulls, from Holland, and crossed them into his cows to improve their quality, and which blood had gone by descent into the stock of Sir James Pennyman. But, as in a previous page has been conclusively shown, we think, that no such Dutch importations had been made, these innuendoes, surmises and charges, all fall to the ground.

The history of the cow—Hubback's dam—is simply this: She was bred by Mr. Stephenson, who had lived at Ketton before Charles Colling's day, and the ancestors of the cow had been in Mr. Stephenson's possession for more than forty years, as he had long been a Short-horn breeder of the Pennyman and Studley stock. She was a small cow, of remarkably smooth and even qualities, and an excellent feeder. She had fine hair, a bright look, was a good milker, as were all the cows of her tribe, and no doubt imparted much of her good quality to her son, Hubback. How so much controversy could exist about her being of *Kyloe* descent, and thus damaging the integrity of Hubback—for it was only on *her* side that his blood could be assailed—is only to be accounted for in the jealousies and party spirit which was rife among the breeders of the time. The very fact, admitted by all authorities, that Hubback's begettings were

---

* The Kyloes are the "West Highland" cattle of Scotland.—L. F. A.

of superior quality—although from poor cows they were inferior to those of good ones—should be conclusive proof of his good descent, for if he had bad blood in him, it would, to a certainty, crop out in some of his progeny. Yet, aside from his meager pedigree, Hubback had a personal history—a plain, straightforward one, attested by several different accounts, all agreeing in the main, and as such we give it.

John Hunter, the breeder of Hubback, was a bricklayer, and lived in Hurworth. He had once been a tenant farmer, and bred Short-horn cattle, which, when leaving his farm to live in Hurworth, he sold all off, excepting one choice little cow, which he took with him, and as he had no pasture of his own for her to graze in, she run in the lanes of the town. While there she was put to George "Snowdon's bull," also in Hurworth. From him the cow dropped a bull calf. Soon afterwards the cow and calf were driven to Darlington market, and there sold to a Mr. Bassnett, a timber merchant. Bassnett retained the cow, but sold the calf to a blacksmith at Hornby, five miles out from Darlington. The dam of the calf taking on flesh readily, would not again breed, and after some months was fattened and slaughtered. Growing to a useful age, the young bull, in 1783, was found at six years old, in the hands of a Mr. Fawcett, living at Haughton-hill, not far from Darlington.

"Mr. Wright (a noted Short-horn breeder) says that Charles Colling going into Darlington market weekly, used to notice some excellent veal, and upon inquiry ascertained that the calves were got by a bull belonging to a Mr. Fawcett of Haughton-hill. This bull, then known as Fawcett's bull, and some years afterwards called Hubback, was, at the time, serving cows at a shilling each (about 22 cents). Charles Colling, however, as the merits of the beast were talked over between himself and others, did not appear particularly impressed with them. But Robert Colling and his neighbor, Mr. Waistell, of Ali-hill, who had also seen the bull, thought better of him, and more accurately measured his value. The two, soon after Good Friday, in April, 1783, bought him of Mr. Fawcett for ten guineas (about $52), and took him home, where he was jointly owned and used to their separate herds, Colling having seventeen and Waistell eleven cows, served by him during the season. In the following November (1783), Charles Colling having changed his opinion of the merits of the bull, offered his owners eight guineas (about $42) for him, and they sold him. Waistell had reserved, on his part of the sale, that Charles should let all his cows be served to the bull as long as the latter owned him, but Waistell sending a cow the following year, Colling refused the service unless paid five guineas for it.* The cow was driven home unserved, and Waistell had no cows sent to the bull afterwards.

Charles Colling kept the bull two years, using him freely in his herd, and then sold him late in 1785, at ten years old, to a Mr. Hubback, at North Seton, in Northumberland. "The bull had no name when Colling sold him. Mr. Hubback used him (the bull then being called Hubback's bull) until the year 1791, when he was fourteen years old, and he was vigorous to the last. Mr. Thomas Bates saw him, and calves got by him, in 1790."†

Thus, the story, written by Mr. Berry, that "Hubback was partly of Dutch blood, bought—when a calf, running by his mother's side in the lanes—by Waistell and Robert Colling, and both, including Charles Colling, using him but three years, when, by taking on so much flesh he became impotent, and was slaughtered," is all, but the three years' use, the sheerest invention. The facts, undoubtedly were, that neither Waistell nor either of the Collings, truly appreciated the merits of Hubback until after they had parted with him, and saw the excellence of his stock as they grew up and developed. He was a small bull; his dam was small—for a Short-horn—but a very handsome cow, of fine symmetry, with a nice touch, and fine, long, mossy hair. All these choice qualities Hubback took from her, and his hair remained unusually late in the spring before shedding. As good size was a meritorious point in Short-horns at that time, it is highly probable that the Collings discarded him for that deficiency more than any other. Yet the subsequent reputation of Hubback, among the breeders, stood higher than that of any bull of his time, and it was considered a great merit in any Short-horn which could trace its pedigree back into his blood, which, no doubt, could be easily done, as he was, both before and after the Collings owned him, open to the public at a cheap rate of service. Other animals than those of Waistell and the Collings, recorded in the English Herd Book, trace their pedigrees back to Hubback.

One more, and as we think, conclusive evidence may be added to the integrity of Hubback's Short-horn blood: "Mr. Charge, as well as Mr. Coates, and Charles Colling, always deemed Hubback a pure Short-horn; and neither he nor his descendants when put on cows

---

* From various transactions we have heard of him, with all his cleverness as a breeder, we incline to the opinion that Charles Colling had an especial eye to *his own interests*.

† American Edition of Youatt's British Cattle.

of the pure blood, begot any calves which denoted in their features or color any other breed than the pure Short-horn. His stock had capacious chests, prominent bosoms, thick, mossy coats, mellow skins, with a great deal of fine flesh, spread equally over the whole carcass, and were either red and white, yellow roans, or white."*

It is said that in the year 1784, after coming into possession of Hubback (or Fawcett's bull), Charles Colling picked up several good cows, among them some got by Fawcett's bull; but one of the most noted, as afterwards known in her descendants, was the "Stanwick cow" (the original of the "Duchess" tribe), which in June, 1784, was driven from the Stanwick estate of the Duke of Northumberland,† in Yorkshire, to be sold in the Darlington market, and Colling being present when the cow was driven in, took an especial fancy to her fair qualities, and bought her at the low price of £13 ($65). "She was a massive, short-legged beast, breast near the ground, a great *grower*, with wide back, and of a beautiful yellowish-red flaked color."‡ Colling called her Duchess. She was got by J. Brown's red bull (97), and no further pedigree of her was known. She was bred to Hubback, and through the produce of that coupling descended the since famous (through Mr. Bates' breeding on the female side) "Duchess" tribe of Short-horns.§

During the two seasons that Charles Colling possessed Hubback we may suppose that he made diligent use of him in his herd, but we do not learn that the bull made a strong impression of his value, or he would not so soon have parted with him. At all events, the merits of his stock were not fully appreciated until some time after he had disposed of him, and Colling had become in possession, through other parties, of cows of his get anterior to his own use of the bull.

---

* Thornton's Circular.

† We have since heard it asserted that the "Stanwick" cow was *not* from the Stanwick estate, but from the neighboring one of Aldbrough, also belonging to the Northumberland domain; but it matters little which of the farms produced the cow. She was of the Northumberland Short-horn blood, unquestionably.

‡ Mr. Bates.

§ The Stanwick estate was said to have then been in the occupancy of Earl Percy, a son of Sir Hugh Smithson, before related as being raised to the peerage with the title of Duke of Northumberland, under the Percy succession. This Earl Percy held a commission in the British army, and was one of the party who attacked the American Provincial troops at Lexington, Mass., in the beginning of our Revolutionary War, and was for some years absent from home. He afterwards succeeded his father to the estates and title of second Duke of Northumberland. The late Mr. Smithson, of England, who bequeathed the generous donation of $500,000 to found our National "Smithsonian Institution," at Washington, was a natural son of that second Duke of Northumberland, and grandson to Sir Hugh Smithson, the first Duke, previously mentioned. In his inimitable poem, "Alnwick Castle," our American Halleck alludes to Earl Percy, as having

"Fought for King George at Lexington,
A major of dragoons."

"Gabriel Thornton, in 1786, went to live with Charles, as farm manager, having previously lived, since 1774, with Mr. Maynard, at Eryholme. Some remarks of Mr. Thornton concerning Mr. Maynard's cattle, led Mr. and Mrs. Colling* to ride over to Eryholme that same year. When they arrived, a handsome cow, called 'Favorite,' that Miss Maynard was milking, attracted their notice, and Mr. Colling offered to buy the cow and her heifer. After some haggling on both sides, the purchase was made, and the cows, 'Favorite,' and her daughter, 'Young Strawberry,' went to Ketton."

As these two cows, "Favorite" (afterwards Lady Maynard, in Colling's hands), and her daughter, "Young Strawberry," mark the foundation of another distinguished family of Short-horns (aside from the Duchess already named), through the joint interbreeding of their own bull and heifer progenies, from which the bull "Favorite" (252) descended, and on which Colling's chief celebrity as an *improver* is based, a full history of the cows will be given.

LADY MAYNARD AND YOUNG STRAWBERRY.

Mr. Maynard had long been a distinguished breeder of Short-horns at his farm of Eryholme, then occupied by him, and for many years since by his descendants, who have continuously bred until a recent day first-class cattle. At the time of Charles Colling's visit to him for the purchase of the two cows, Maynard was in possession of an excellent herd, and Colling finding the things he wanted, bought them of him at the low price of £40 ($200) for the cow and heifer.†

The pedigree of the cow Lady Maynard is thus given under the name of "Favorite, or Lady Maynard," in the first edition of Vol. 1, Coates' E. H. B.:

"Red roan, bred by Mr. Maynard, got by Mr. Ralph Alcock's‡ bull (19), d. by Jacob Smith's § bull (608), gr. d. (Strawberry) by Mr. Jolly's bull (337)." ‖

---

* It is said Mrs. Colling was quite as much interested in cattle breeding as her husband, and having no children she had abundant leisure to devote to the stock.

† Mr. Bates' History.

‡ All the record pedigree of Alcock's bull is, "bred by Mr. Michael Jackson, of Hutton-Bonville, near North Allerton." A note of Mr. Bates' says: "A good bull."

§ Smith's bull has no pedigree whatever. His name only is recorded. A note to his pedigree, in manuscript, written by Mr. Bates, says: "Yellow red, white face, white back, and white legs to the knees."

‖ Jolly's bull has no pedigree; recorded by name only. Mr. Bates said, "he was bred by Mr. Waistell, of Great Burdon."

Mr. Bates afterwards wrote that Mr. Maynard gave him a long pedigree of the cow "Favorite," running back to the "Murrain" year, 1745.

Lady Maynard's produce is thus recorded:

SEX AND COLOR.	NAME.	SIRE.	BREEDER.
178-, cow calf,	Young Strawberry,	Dalton Duke (188),	Mr. Maynard.
178-, cow calf, red roan,	Miss Lax,	Dalton Duke (188),	Mr. Maynard.
178-, cow calf, r. & w.,	Phœnix,	Foljambe (263),	Charles Colling.
178-, bull calf, r. & w.,	Lady Maynard's bull (356),	Lame bull (357),	Charles Colling.
1796, bull calf, white,	Mason's white bull (421),	Bolingbroke (86), or Favorite (252),	Charles Colling.
and another cow calf which did not breed.			

Thus it appears that Young Strawberry, which Colling purchased with the cow, was her first calf, and she was bred by Maynard. As the pedigree of the cow Young Strawberry is already given under the produce of Lady Maynard, the pedigree of her (Young Strawberry's) son Bolingbroke (86) is found as her produce, under her record in Vol. 1, E. H. B., as calved November 12, 1788, red and white, bred by Mr. Colling, and got by Foljambe (263). Foljambe is entered in the Herd Book as bred by Colling; other authorities contend that he was bred by Mr. Hall, of Haughton-hill, got by Richard Barker's bull (52), out of the cow Haughton, by Hubback. Colling afterwards bought the cow Haughton of Mr. Hall. The pedigree of the cow Haughton runs thus:

"Got by Hubback (319), dam by a bull of the late Charles Colling's (which he bought of Mr. John Bamlet), gr. d. by Mr. Waistell's bull (669), g. gr. d. Tripes, bred by Mr. C. Pickering."

By other authority Tripes is said to be by Studley bull (626), and her dam bred by Mr. Stephenson, of Ketton, in 1739.

So it will be seen that Foljambe was of stranger blood to the Lady Maynard family. Thus, with Foljambe, and his Lady Maynard, and other tribes, Colling went on with his new course of breeding; but we do not find that Foljambe was directly used to any of the Colling-Duchess, or Stanwick family, as their pedigrees enter into the first volume of E. H. B. only in Mr. Bates' Duchess 1st, calved in 1810, got by Comet (155), and the fifth in descent from the Stanwick cow. Yet as Duchess 1st was descended through Comet and Favorite, who had the blood of Foljambe in them, the Duchess tribe had his blood also.

With the basis of the two tribes, Duchess, and Lady Maynard, in his hands, as well as with other cows which he had selected, Charles Colling began his remarkable in-and-in system of breeding, and pursued it with untiring pertinacity to the end of his Short-horn career in 1810. He bred comparatively few animals of his Duchess tribe, although equally in-and-in bred as the Lady Maynards. Foljambe, as an early sire, begat the bull Bolingbroke (86), in the cow

Young Strawberry, and also begat the cow Phœnix, in the dam of Young Strawberry (Lady Maynard), so that Bolingbroke was closely related to Phœnix in other ways than being her half brother. Then in Phœnix, his half sister and aunt, Bolingbroke begat Favorite (252), and Favorite in his own mother and sister (Phœnix) begat Young Phœnix, and in Young Phœnix (his own daughter as well as sister) he begat Comet (155), the famous 1000 guinea bull in the final sale of Colling's herd in 1810. In addition to this intensely close breeding, Favorite was used to his own heifers without stint in Colling's herd even to, in one instance (Robert Colling's Clarissa), the sixth generation, producing in every case sound, healthy offspring. No bull in Short-horn history has so many animals which trace back to him as Favorite. Not only to his own immediate family relations, but to the Duchesses and other tribes does his blood extend, so that running back to Favorite, in thousands of bulls and cows, from that day to this, his blood has been commingled in near and remote relationship.

Concurrent with Charles, his brother Robert had been equally vigilant. He had selected, probably, quite as good animals from the herds of Messrs. Milbank of Barningham, Hill of Blackwell, Best, Watson, Wright of Manfield, and Sir William St. Quintin of Scampston, all of whom were celebrated breeders of Short-horn or Teeswater cattle.*

Hubback had been used by Robert one year, and by Charles two years, as before stated, and sold by the latter at ten years of age, without a name, to go into the hands of Mr. Hubback, in Northumberland, who gave his own name to the bull, and in whose possession he died. After leaving Colling, little is known of Hubback's produce or to what classes of cows he was bred. The name of Mr. Hubback, the last owner of the bull, does not appear as a breeder in the early volumes of the Herd Book.

Let it be borne in mind that while the Collings were thus vigorously busy in working up their herds, the older breeders around them had not been idle. The selections of the Collings were made from among the cattle of those breeders, and it may well be supposed that they still retained in their hands animals probably equal in quality to any with which they had parted; but wanting the dash and enterprise of the later established Barmpton and Ketton breeders, they failed to bring their own herds into equally prominent notice.

---

* Thornton's Circular.

Succeeding Hubback, in Charles Colling's herd, we recall and notice Foljambe (263) [Hubback's grandson on the dam's side], by Richard Barker's bull (52), already mentioned. "Barker's bull was of good size and symmetry, but rather a hard handler, the winner of a premium, as a calf, in the year 1784, at Darlington, and generally known as 'Dicky Barker's black nose.'" Foljambe also had a dark nose, so said Mr. Bates. Foljambe's dam was Mr. Hall's cow Haughton (by Hubback), before named, and "Colling considered that Foljambe left him the best stock which he had.* He is described as a useful, thick beast, handle good, wide back, dark face, and was sold by Mr. Coates to Mr. Foljambe,† as a yearling for 50 guineas "‡ ($260).

Another description says that "he was a large, strong bull, a useful, big, bony beast, of great substance."

Thus the brothers Colling progressed. The prices of the Teeswaters at that day were low. The country, outside the counties where they were bred, knew little either of the cattle or their value. Waistell and Robert Colling had bought Hubback for ten guineas (about $52), and Charles paid them only eight guineas ($42) for him; and no wonder that they so bought him, when he had been serving cows indiscriminately at one shilling (or 22 cents) each! "Mrs. Charles Colling ridiculed her husband's niggardliness in giving Mr. Maynard only 30 guineas for the cow Favorite (Lady Maynard) and 10 guineas ($52) for her heifer, Young Strawberry, although he bid 50 guineas ($260) to Mr. Scott for 'Sockburn Sall,' the ancestress of the present Blanche tribe. The cows lay out in the fields, having a little hay taken out to them in bad weather, but always calved in a warm place. The calves had new milk till they were two or three weeks old, then for a month they got half and half (new and skim), afterwards skim milk with linseed bran, or other meal, or porridge; they were then turned out to grass, getting nothing else. Nurse cows were kept for the bull calves, going out on hire."‡

The Collings are the first mentioned Short-horn breeders who let bulls out on hire. Mr. John Hutchinson, in a letter dated in 1821, says: "Charles Colling, being an established breeder, exhibited in the spring of 1790, his first two yearling bulls for sale, and succeeded

---

* That Colling so said, we have no doubt. But from all collateral testimony we have as little doubt that it was the result of his chagrin at having so prematurely parted with Hubback, before he knew the intrinsic value of his blood and stock.—L. F. A.

† There appears to be some discrepancy as to the different transfers and ownerships, as well as to which—Hall or Colling—really bred Foljambe.—L. F. A.

‡ Thornton's Circular.

in selling them both. Mr. Coates, of Smeaton, was the purchaser of one for £26 ($130), and Mr. R. Thomas of the other, for £23 ($115)." Mr. Bailey, the Durham historian, writes in 1810, that "Messrs. Colling and Mason let bulls out by the year at fifty ($260) to one hundred guineas ($520) each, and these celebrated breeders cannot supply the demand for the pure blood, which they are cautious of preserving, and which takers of bulls are become so well acquainted with that the prices they give are in proportion to the good qualities of the individuals, and *merits of their progenitors, more regard being paid to their pedigree than to anything else.* Messrs. Colling have frequently sold cows and heifers for £100 ($500) each, and bull calves at the same. Charles Colling has refused £500 ($2,500) for a cow, and in the year 1807, Mr. Mason refused £700 ($3,500) for a cow."*

"The most noted breeders who hired Charles Colling's bulls, were John Charge, of Newton, who used Favorite (252); Mr. Mason, of Chilton; Mr. Jobling, of Styford; Mr. Gibson, of Corbridge; Sir George Strickland; Mr. Robertson, of Ladykirk; and Mr. Ostler, of Aylesby and Audley. Windsor (696) was used by Mr. Hustler in 1808-9; Mr. Parker, of Malton, had him five years, and George III. had him for three years, at £40 ($200) a year, for service on the royal farm at Windsor, whence he was named."†

The Mode of Charles Colling's Breeding.

To keep a run of Charles Colling's system of breeding: after Hubback (319) he used Foljambe (263), who got Bolingbroke (86), and Bolingbroke got Favorite (252), calved in 1793. He successively used Favorite, with occasional interims, for thirteen years, beginning his services at two years old. At ten years old Favorite begat Comet (155), calved in 1804; and the next year, at eleven years old he begat North Star (458), full brother to Comet, calved in 1805. These two bulls, celebrated in their day, were out of *Young* Phœnix, his daughter and sister (she out of Phœnix, mother to Favorite, the sire of Young Phœnix), as close interbreeding, perhaps, as could be made.

---

* Mr. Mason was contemporary with the Collings, a distinguished Short-horn breeder, and many animals of his herds were probably equal in excellence to those of the Collings, as he had early used the Colling bulls. His " Mason's white bull " (421), was got by either Bolingbroke or Favorite, out of Colling's Lady Maynard. Many descendants of his stock are found in the Herd Books.—L. F. A.

† Thornton's Circular.

COLLING'S MODE OF BREEDING.

That Colling bred his cattle with one persistent object in view there can be no question. It was to obtain the greatest *concentration* of *good* blood possible in his herd. His original cows he had selected from among the best at his command, and in order to cement that blood in its greatest strength, worked the blood of each into the descendants of others, as far as is possible, so that it should be common to all. His original animals were not alike, differing much in their various qualities, yet all having more or less good and sterling points of character. Those different points will be more fully noticed hereafter. In Favorite (252), Colling judged that the best blood could be transmitted more successfully than through the veins of any other bull. Nor was he mistaken. He used him for two, three, four, and in one recorded instance five successive crosses in his own heifers, with decided success and no deterioration of constitution or quality in the very last cross he made in their production. At the final sale of his herd in 1810, there were more of his animals running back into the blood of Favorite than in all the other bulls he had used, put together. The following analysis is so well expressed that I quote it from the Rev. J. Storer, in Mr. Carr's late History of the Booth Short-horns:

"Few people have any idea of the amazing extent to which in-and-in breeding was carried on by the Brothers Colling; and so great was the complication it involved, that few of those who know the outline of the circumstances, can adequately realize all their intricacies. It is almost impossible to describe even proximately in some of its stronger features the system they pursued. But the attempt ought to be made; for the Messrs. Colling's system of in-and-in breeding, is not only one of the most remarkable and authentic cases in the history of the reproduction of animals with which we are acquainted, but the earlier Booth bulls were amongst those most strongly subjected to its influence.

"Mr. C. Colling's bull Bolingbroke, and his cow Phœnix, were brother and sister on the sire's side, and nearly so on the dam's. They were of the same family; and the only difference in descent was, that Bolingbroke was a grandson of Dalton Duke, while Phœnix was not. But this apparent difference, slight as it is, was not all real; for Dalton Duke also contained some portion of their common blood. Arithmetically stated, the blood of the two being taken and divided into *thirty-two* parts, *twenty-nine* of those parts were of blood common to both, rather differently proportioned between them. Phœnix had *sixteen* of those parts, Bolingbroke *thirteen*; the latter having also *three* fresh parts derived from Dalton Duke, which made up the thirty-two.

"Being thus *very nearly* own brother and sister, they were the joint parents of the bull Favorite. That bull was next put to his own mother Phœnix, so nearly related to him on his sire's side also; and the produce was Young Phœnix. To this heifer Favorite was once more put, she being at once his daughter and *more than own sister too*. For their two sires, Bolingbroke and Favorite, were not only as nearly as possible consanguineous with each other, but also with the cow Phœnix, to which they were both put. The result was—Comet (155).

"Nor was this all. The system was carried much further. The celebrated Booth bull Albion (14) was not only a son of the in-and-in Favorite bred Comet, but his dam was a granddaughter of Favorite on both sides, and descended besides from both the sire and the dam of Favorite.

"It is not so possible to make an exact statement with regard to Pilot (496), for it is not known whether he was by Major (398), or Wellington (680). Nor does it much matter; for five-eighths of Major's and three-quarters of Wellington's blood were derived from Favorite, by repeated inter crossings; and Pilot's dam was not only by Favorite, but she was also the granddaughter of Foljambe, the sire of both the parents of Favorite.

"Marshal Beresford (415) was, like Albion, a son of Comet (155); and his dam was by a grandson of Favorite, out of a daughter of Favorite.

"Suworrow (636) was by a son of Favorite; and his dam was a daughter of Favorite; and Twin Brother to Ben (660) was from a cow by Foljambe, the double grandsire of Favorite.

"Even this does not exhaust the subject. Many of the above mentioned animals were otherwise related to each other by a common descent from Hubback, and from other progenitors.

"Albion has been called 'The Alloy Bull.' I think with very little reason. When it is remembered that he is the *seventh* in descent from that blood, and that therefore only *one* part of his blood came from 'The Alloy,'* against *one hundred and twenty-seven* parts which were not derived from it, the chances against either good or evil resulting therefrom were infinitesimally small; and so no doubt such an acute observer as Mr. Booth well knew."

---

* Through Washington (674). These bulls will be more particularly noticed hereafter in our remarks upon the Booth herds.—L. F. A.

COLLING'S MODE OF BREEDING.

To further illustrate Colling's in-and-in breeding, we give two diagrams of descent first published in Vol. 1, American Herd Book:

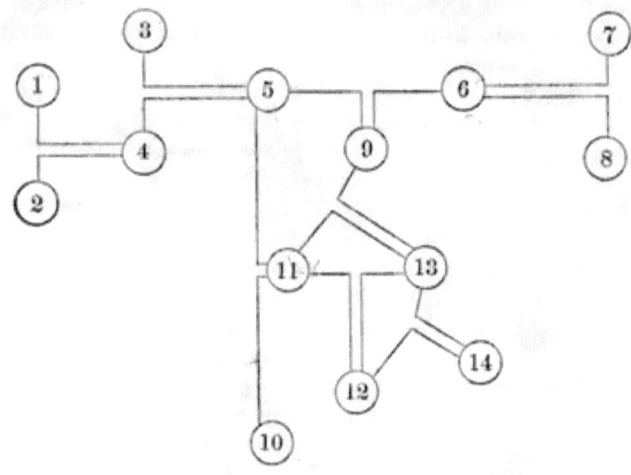

EXPLANATION OF FIGURES.

1. Bull, Hubback.
2. Dam of Haughton.
3. Richard Barker's bull.
4. Cow, Haughton.
5. Bull, Foljambe.
6. Cow, Young Strawberry.
7. Bull Dalton Duke.
8 and 10. Cow, Lady Maynard.
9. Bull, Bolingbroke.
11. Cow, Phœnix.
12. Cow, Young Phœnix.
13. Bull, Favorite.
14. Bull, Comet.

While on this subject we give a diagram of another animal, the cow Clarissa, which we find on record, bred by Robert Colling, to show the depth of a particular strain of blood which he acquired. This cow, it appears, has six consecutive crosses or 63-64ths parts of the blood of Favorite. Her pedigree (Vol. 1, E. H. B.) runs thus: "Clarissa, roan, calved in 1814, bred by Mr. R. Colling, got by Wellington (680), out of ——, by Favorite (252),—by Favorite,—by Favorite,—by Favorite,—by Favorite,—by Favorite,—by a son of Hubback." (See diagram on next page.)

In addition to the pedigree of Clarissa, we have run out that of Wellington, her sire, which also goes back to Favorite, showing that although Clarissa's dam had six crosses of Favorite's blood, Clarissa is met on the other side by a bull deeply impregnated with the blood of Favorite also. Clarissa proved a good breeder, and was the dam of several excellent animals.

After saying so much of the Collings, it may be asked, why they so rapidly achieved a reputation as Short-horn breeders, so young in the business, and outstripped their older neighbors to whom they were indebted for the *original* excellence in their herds, and had adopted a course of breeding opposed to the common opinions of the breeders around them, viz.: the in-and-in system of Bakewell.

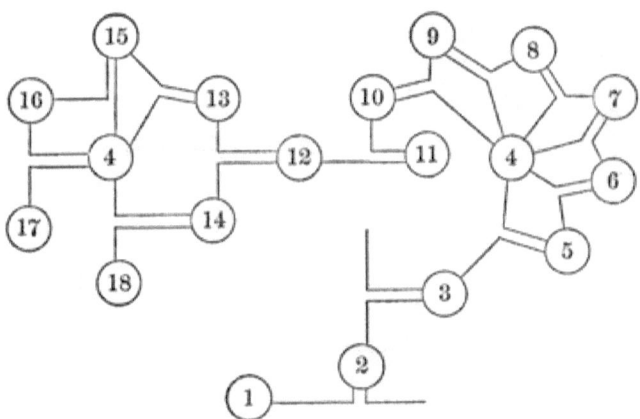

EXPLANATION OF FIGURES.

1. Bull, Hubback.
2. Son of Hubback.
3. Cow, by son of Hubback.
4. Bull, Favorite.
5. 1st Cow by Favorite.
6. 2d Cow by Favorite.
7. 3d Cow by Favorite.
8. 4th Cow by Favorite.
9. 5th Cow by Favorite.
10. 6th Cow by Favorite.
11. Cow, Clarissa.
12. Bull, Wellington, sire of Clarissa.
13. Bull, Comet.
14. Cow, Wildair.
15. Cow, Young Phœnix.
16. Cow, Phœnix.
4. Same bull Favorite on the side of Clarissa's sire, as on the sire of her dam.
17. Bull, Bolingbroke.
18. Granddaughter of Hubback.

They bred their stock intensely and pertinaciously in-and-in, as has been seen by the crosses and diagrams we have given, to the closest relationship. They had selected from the herds of other breeders not only as good blood as they could obtain, but as good animals, and by their course of close breeding had *concentrated* that blood into its utmost compactness in their stock, thus enabling their bulls to transmit it with nearly absolute certainty into the thoroughbred animals of their get. Of course their herds had acquired a character and type of their own, measurably distinct from those of other breeders, who, in following the old idea that near relations should not be crossed in stock breeding, possessed herds of miscellaneous character, although, perhaps, in many points of excellence quite equal to the Collings. We do not aver that the Collings' stock was better than that of some of the other careful, painstaking breeders around them, other than in their fixed and undeviating characteristics, and their thus acquired power of transmitting those characteristics into their progeny, when put upon cows of blood not related to them. This the deeply in-and-in bred Colling bulls did, beyond a question, and hence their rapidly acquired popularity.

Still, the Short-horns were a local breed of cattle, confined chiefly to the counties of ancient Northumbria, and the best of them were to be found in and about the valley of the Tees. The Collings, in the exercise of their usual foresight and sagacity, determined to give their cattle a wide reputation through the kingdom, and for that purpose Charles prepared the

Durham Ox

for public exhibition. As this ox achieved a wide reputation and successfully drew the merits of the Short-horns to the attention of the cattle breeding public, although it has been frequently published, a full account of him will be repeated. He was among the earliest calves got by Favorite (252), "bred in the year 1796, and out of a common black and white cow, bought for Charles Colling by John Simpson, at Durham Fair, for £14 ($70)."* Although the dam of the Durham Ox was said to have been "a common cow," from the price which Colling paid for her, and the marvellous excellence and beauty of the ox descended from her, it is altogether probable she possessed much of the "common" *Short-horn* blood of the vicinity.† Yet, from the "black" in her she may not have been highly bred, but of remarkably good quality. This calf, made a steer, Colling fed up to his greatest flesh-taking capacity until nearly five years old, when he had attained a weight of 3024 pounds. He was then purchased to be exhibited, by Mr. Bulmer of Harmby, in February, 1801, for £140 ($700). Bulmer had a traveling carriage made to carry him through the country, and after traveling and exhibiting him five weeks, sold the carriage and ox at Rotherham to John Day, for £250 ($1,250). On the 14th of May ensuing, Mr. Day could have sold him for £525 ($2,625); on the 13th of June, for £1,000 ($5,000), and on the 8th of July, for £2,000 ($10,000), but he refused all these offers, which were strong proofs of the excellence of the ox, as well as his exhibiting

---

* Thornton's Circular.

† The ox, like his sire, Favorite, was light roan in color. Did not that color, like the wonderful excellence he otherwise possessed, demonstrate the *certainty* with which the highly concentrated blood of Favorite was capable of being thrown into his produce?

value. Mr. Day traveled with him nearly six years, through the principal parts of England and Scotland, till at Oxford, on the 19th of February, the ox dislocated his hip bone, and continued in that state till the 15th of April, when he was killed, and notwithstanding he must have lost considerable flesh during these eight weeks of illness, yet his dead weight was:

Four quarters,	2322 pounds.
Tallow,	156 "
Hide,	142 "
	2620 pounds.

This was at the age of eleven years, under all the disadvantages of six years traveling in a jolting carriage, and eight weeks of painful lameness. At ten years old Mr. Day stated his live weight to have been nearly 3400 pounds.

About the year 1806, Robert Colling reared a thoroughbred heifer, afterwards called the "White Heifer that Traveled," which he sent out through the principal agricultural counties for exhibition; the date of her birth is not given in the first volume E. H. B., where her pedigree is recorded. She was also got by Favorite (252), her dam called "Favorite Cow," also bred by R. Colling; the name of "Favorite Cow's" sire is not given. Her gr. dam, "Yellow Cow," was by Punch (531), and her g. gr. dam was by Anthony Reed's bull (538), and bred by Mr. Best, of Manfield. The "White Heifer" being twinned with a bull, and herself not breeding, she was no doubt fed up to her greatest flesh-taking capacity during her life. Her age, when slaughtered, is not given, but the account states that her live weight could not have been less than 2300 pounds, and her dead (profitable) weight was estimated at 1820 pounds.

There were other extraordinary large and heavy cattle bred and fed by the Short-horn breeders contemporary with the Collings, whose recorded weights we might give, but as they all run in about the same scale, it is not important to record them here. It is sufficient to say that the great reputation which the Collings and their animals acquired was through the wider knowledge which the public abroad obtained of them by these public exhibitions. Thus the Collings became conspicuously known, and were considered by those not intimately acquainted with the other breeders around them, as, if not the founders, at least the great improvers of that newly advertised and meritorious race.

Robert Colling and his Short-horn Breeding.

Although he has been frequently mentioned in the account of his brother Charles, as they often bred their stock through an interchange of bulls, yet Robert had a herd in blood distinctly his own, and bred many cattle as highly distinguished in their merits as were those of Charles.

Previous to his taking the farm at Barmpton in the year 1783, he lived at Hurworth, a short distance away. When a youth he had been apprenticed to a grocer, but his health declining, he embraced farming. He had often visited Mr. Culley, a noted farmer, stock breeder, and agricultural writer, and took lessons from him in farming, turnip growing, and stock feeding. He had obtained Leicester sheep from Bakewell, and for many years bred and sold them with great success, simultaneous with his pursuit of Short-horn cattle breeding. His annual ram-lettings were extensive and profitable.

Some of his earliest stock he obtained from Mr. Milbank, of Barningham. They were considered as among the best of the Teeswater cattle, and noted for their excellent grazing properties. He also selected the best cows to be obtained from other breeders, and having the bull Hubback (319), as previously stated, in the year 1783, by which he had seventeen cows served, it may well be supposed that he made a ready and sure start through the best blood and the best animals he could obtain in the foundation of his herd. He bred with skill and judgment, and founded several different families, or tribes of females, as the Wildair, the Red Rose, the Princess, the Bright Eyes, and others, which became in future hands, as well as his own, widely noted as the bases of superior herds. He also bred many noted bulls. Among the earliest of them were "Broken-horn" (95), by Hubback (319), etc.; "Punch" (513) by Broken-horn; Ben (70), and "Twin Brother to Ben" (660), by Punch; "Colling's (Robert) white bull" (151), by Favorite (252); "Marske" (418), by Favorite [his dam and grand dam also by Favorite; great grand dam by Hubback (319),—by Snowdon's bull (612),—by Masterman's bull (422),—by Harrison's bull (292),—by Studley bull (626); Marske was a noted bull, useful thirteen years, and died at fifteen years old]; "North Star" (459), by Favorite [and full brother to the "White Heifer that Traveled"]; "Phenomenon" (491), by Favorite; "Styford" (629), by Favorite; besides many later bulls which were sold, or occasionally used by him, or let for service to other breeders.

Among the cows bred by Robert Colling was one which has obtained celebrity through her descendants as "The American Cow;" and it has been a subject of inquiry during late years, both in England and America, why a cow so ancient in lineage should have been called by a name so foreign to her birth-place, and after a country where the Short-horns at that time were almost unknown. We first find her name in the pedigree of Red Rose, in first edition of Vol. 1, p. 457, E. H. B., as follows: "Red, calved in 1811, bred by Mr. Hustler, property of Mr. T. Bates, got by Yarborough (705), dam (bred by R. Colling, and called The American Cow), by Favorite (252), gr. d. by Punch (531), g. gr. d. by Foljambe (263), g. g. gr. d. by Hubback (319)."

In the above pedigree The American Cow is originally identified. In Vol. 2, p. 497, first edition E. H. B., the same Red Rose is again recorded as Red Rose 1st, her dam being "The American Cow," as before. In a conversation with Mr. John Thornton, of London, when in this country in the winter of 1870–71, (who is as well versed in English Short-horn pedigrees, perhaps, as any other,) he remarked that he had never learned why the *American Cow* was so called, although he had made diligent inquiries in England for the reason.

The *American* history of the cow, as we have been informed on authority which we deem good, is this: In some year, not long after 1801, a son of Mr. Hustler, who was a Short-horn cattle breeder in Yorkshire, emigrated to New York, and brought with him some Short-horn cattle, among which was this nameless cow, or then heifer, afterwards dam of the Red Rose 1st, which his father bought of Robert Colling. The younger Hustler went into business in New York City, and put his cattle into the adjoining county of Westchester. After a few years stay in America, he returned to England, and not finding his Short-horns appreciated on this side the ocean, (as we find no record of them or their produce in this country,) Mr. Hustler took this cow back with him, as she was a remarkably good beast, and put her into his father's herd. Then, on being put to Yarborough, she became the dam of Red Rose, afterwards purchased by Mr. Bates, he calling her Red Rose 1st, which, in his hands, was the original of the tribe of Red Rose, from whom many excellent animals have descended. The only *English* account we have of The American Cow, aside from her pedigree, which we have quoted, is, that "she was sent to America, and taken back to England."

It is hardly necessary to follow Robert Colling through the various particulars of his breeding, as we have done more closely with

Charles, for, as has been previously remarked, they bred much in concert, followed the same system of intercrossing their blood, and in fact were almost identical in their practice. To sum up the results of their joint action, it may be said that they, in the midst of older and more experienced breeders, combatted the ancient prejudices of the day, and through their in-and-in system, established a *new school* in breeding.

CHAPTER III.

Were the Collings the Earliest and Chief Improvers of the Short-horns?

In the discussion of this question a wider range of observation may be necessary than has usually been taken from hearsay, tradition, or even what in some cases has been written by men claiming a personal knowledge of the subject. *Assertion* is one thing; *proof* is another thing; and sometimes widely different, in the settlement of *facts*. It has long been so commonly reported among those who have never gone into an investigation of the matter, that to the Collings—especially Charles—was due the great merit of transforming the ancient, coarse, ungainly race of Short-horns, which had long existed anterior to their coming upon the stage, into the stately and more highly perfected condition in which they left them, that it may seem, if not an act of audacity, at least a bootless task to combat a belief which has heretofore been so commonly entertained. We shall, however, carefully examine all the facts at command and strive to place the subject in as true a light as possible.

To the first question: "Were the Collings the *earliest* improvers" of the Short-horn race? our previous narrative has clearly shown they were not. At the outset of their career as breeders they found the Short-horns, or Teeswaters, a valuable, profitable, and highly approved, as well as established breed, in three or four different counties of England, where, time immemorial, they had lived and flourished; and in whatever state of improvement over that of their ancient progenitors they then existed, their improvement was *not* made by the Collings. Therefore their claims to the *early* improvement may be dismissed without further discussion.

The next question: "Were they the *chief* improvers" of the Short-horns of their own day? If improved at all during their career is now the question to be examined. We have seen that when the Collings commenced business various breeders in their vicinity had excellent cattle. All, or nearly all, the bulls anterior to their time which the English Herd Book has recorded have been mentioned, and many of the chief points and excellencies, as well as defects of their animals, have been noticed, and every bull and every cow to which the Collings traced their best or choicest blood in animals of their own breeding were bred by others, and not by themselves. That it was a master stroke of sagacity, as well as policy, in their collecting some of the best cattle to be found on which to base their herds will be conceded; for having the tools in their hands the value of their workmanship in the use of them could best be judged.

Let us follow (although it may be repeating a portion of what we have already stated) the course of the Collings somewhat in detail, for it is only in details that accurate results can be gathered. In the year 1784 Charles bought the Stanwick, or original Duchess cow, from the estate of the Duke of Northumberland in Yorkshire. The cow Haughton (by Hubback) he soon afterwards bought from Mr. Hall; and in 1786 or '87, he bought "Favorite, or Lady Maynard," and her daughter, "Young Strawberry," from Mr. Maynard. Here were four prime cows to start with, and from which most of his animals on which his chief reputation was acquired descended. In 1784 he bought the bull Hubback from his brother Robert and Mr. Waistell, neither of whom *bred* him. In the pages of Vol. 1, E. H. B., are found some animals bred by Colling having a double cross of Hubback; but as he did not keep the bull more than two years, not giving time enough to put him to his own daughters, except as the latter were yearlings, it is not probable that he had that double cross in his own breeding. Aside from this we have the authority of the late Thomas Bates, who was familiar with Colling's whole course of breeding, that he made no such second cross in any heifer bred by himself. Of course, if he had cows with a double cross of Hubback in their blood he must have obtained them from other parties, of which we may suppose there may have been several in the neighborhood, as the bull had been freely used in getting calves, as before stated, at a shilling each. Thus he had an early infusion of Hubback blood. Next to Hubback he used Foljambe,* out of the cow Haughton, and she by Hubback, thus combining the Hubback blood through Foljambe more closely in his herd. Colling bred a heifer, by Hubback, out of the Duchess (Stanwick) cow, but we have no record of a female by Hubback out of either Lady Maynard or her daughter, Young Strawberry; but out of Lady Maynard he bred the cow

---

* Got by Barker's (Richard) bull (52), "Dickey Barker's black nose," previously mentioned.

Phœnix, by Foljambe, and out of Young Strawberry (daughter to Lady Maynard, and half sister to Phœnix) he bred the bull Bolingbroke (88), also by Foljambe. Then Bolingbroke was bred to his more than half sister, and aunt, Phœnix, producing Favorite (252), and then this Favorite put to Phœnix (his own mother, and more closely related, if possible), produced the cow Young Phœnix, and she in turn being bred to Favorite, her own sire (brother and all other sorts of close relationship), produced Comet (155), a bull individually more admired than any other one of his day.

This system of interbreeding Charles Colling pursued, or as closely to it as possible, with all the best families in his herd. He had selected his original animals with an eye to particular models of excellence. He could not find a finished model in any one animal of his original selections. They had various points of excellence, as well as some defects, and his object was to get rid of their defects and combine their excellencies into the younger stock so as to create a uniformity of character as near his own standard of perfection as possible. He had in the bull Favorite, got as much of the blood of his cow Lady Maynard, and through Foljambe of Hubback's, as was probably possible to obtain, and he bred from Favorite more or less for thirteen years, as long as he was useful.

Let it be borne in mind that Colling acted on the axiom that blood, in order to be most useful in perpetuating its good qualities in breeding, must be *concentrated* as closely as possible in the veins of the breeding animals, as only through such concentration of blood could its individual properties and character be transmitted with absolute certainty to their progeny. Thus the choicest of the Colling cattle had a *uniformity of type* which so far, provided their qualities were good, was a decided improvement in them, beyond those animals which had been miscellaneously bred from different bulls having no blood relations with each other, or with the cows to which they were bred, thus striking out into various incongruities of character, and transmitting their own qualities, even if of the best kind, with no certainty to their offspring. Robert bred under the same system as did Charles; but it is unnecessary to follow his herd with the same particularity of detail, as several of his best have already been noticed. Many pages of Vol. 1, E. H. B., would have to be quoted to illustrate their breeding.

As both the Collings were considerable breeders, it is not to be supposed that *all* their cattle were so closely interbred. They frequently bought good cows from other breeders, even after their own choice tribes were established; these cows they bred to their best bulls, and sold their produce to different breeders, so that the Herd Book, not originating until 1822, some years after they had both given up cattle breeding, does not represent all the animals of their herds. Their stock, outside of the choicest families, were not uniform in either their several qualities, or individual merits. But having prime animals of their best families, those gave them their reputation as leading breeders, or improvers of the Short-horn race.

Comparing the various characteristics of the most noted cattle in the Colling herds let us see what was said of them by their contemporaries:

Lady Maynard, red roan, is described as a beautiful cow, and her daughter, Young Strawberry, color not given, as having much of her character.

Hubback was yellow red with little white, a smooth, small bull, and the quality of his flesh, hide and hair, seldom equaled; head good; horns small and fine; breast forward; handling firm; shoulders rather upright; girth good; loins, body and sides fair; rumps and hips extraordinary; flank and twist wonderful. His dam a beautiful little cow, and became so fat by running in the lanes of Darlington that she would not afterwards breed and was slaughtered. She—the dam of Hubback—was got by Banks' bull, of Hurworth (not in the Herd Books), and he, Banks' bull, had a great belly. The grand dam of Hubback, on the dam's side, was bred by Mr. Stephenson, of Ketton. Snowdon's bull (626), sire of Hubback, was out of a daughter of a cow bought from the same Mr. Stephenson.

The cow Haughton (dam of Foljambe), yellow red and white (got by Hubback), her dam by John Bamlet's bull (not in Herd Book), gr. d. by Waistell's bull (669), g. gr. d. Tripes, bred by C. Pickering. We find no description of her. Charles Colling afterwards bought Bamlet's bull, from which fact we presume he was possessed of excellent qualities.

Foljambe, "white, with a few red spots, and a *dark* nose; handle good; wide back; dark face; a large, strong bull; a useful, big, bony, thick beast of great substance."

Duchess (the Stanwick cow), "Charles Colling bought 14th June, 1784, for £13 ($65), a massive, short-legged cow; breast near the ground; a great grower, with wide back, and of a beautiful yellowish flaked red color."* Colling himself said that "she was better than

---

* Mr. Bates, in Bell's History.

any he ever produced from her, though put to his best bulls, which improved all other cattle." She was bred to Hubback. The produce was a heifer, and from her the present tribe of (Bates') Duchesses, on the female side, are descended.

Cherry, a fine cow, bought at Yarm Fair, by his father, also came into Charles Colling's possession, and from her he bred his "Cherry" tribe. We have no description of her.

It was conceded by a company of old breeders in 1812, in discussing the question of the improvement of Short-horns, that no stock of Mr. Colling's breeding ever equaled Lady Maynard,* the dam of Phœnix, and grand dam of Favorite (252). Robert Colling told Mr. Wiley that his brother's and his own cattle were never better than anybody else's until his brother Charles got Maynard's two cows.

From the above descriptions and opinions of breeders at the time, it will be seen that there was little uniformity in the character of the Collings' *original* stock, and if they afterwards acquired a *uniform* excellence in their several herds—which, no doubt, to a considerable extent they did—it was by persistence in their course of in-and-in breeding, which has been described.

So much has been said of the bull Favorite (252), into whose blood more good Short-horns of the present time trace a portion of their lineage than any other bull of his day, that we give his description. His color was light roan. "Mr. Coates thought him a large beast, with a fine, bold eye, body down, low back, and other parts very good. Mr. Waistell said Favorite was a grand beast, very large and open, had a fine brisket, with a good coat, and as good a handler as ever was felt."

"His (Favorite's) dam Phœnix was a large, open-boned cow, and coarser than her dam—'the beautiful Lady Maynard'—partaking more of her sire's (Foljambe) character. Favorite, the son, partook more of his dam's (Phœnix) character, and possessed remarkably good loins, long and level hind quarters; his shoulder points stood wide, and were somewhat too coarse, and too forward in the neck, and his horns, in comparison with Hubback's, were long and strong. His sire, Bolingbroke (86), was by Foljambe, out of Young Strawberry (daughter of Lady Maynard). In color he was red, with a little white, and the best bull George Coates ever saw. Favorite

---

* The judgments of men are sometimes fallible. We think there must be some error in this statement, for it is evident that the stock produced from her would not have held so high a reputation had they not exhibited some particular qualities above those which their ancestry possessed.—L. F. A.

(252), born in 1793, died in 1809, was used indiscriminately upon his own offspring, even in the third generation." Yes, even to the fifth and sixth generations in some one or two prominent instances.

As Phœnix, the dam of Favorite, has been partially described in connection with her son, her measurement is here given:

Height,	4 feet 8 inches.	Length of quarter,	1 foot 9 inches.
Width of hip,	2 " 2¾ "	Length of back,	5 " 1½ "
Width of loin,	1 " 7¼ "	Girth at chime,	7 " 1 "
Girth of shank,	7½ "	Girth at neck,	3 " 2½ "

THE GALLOWAY CROSS—REV. HENRY BERRY'S YOUATT HISTORY.

We now arrive at an episode in Short-shorn annals—no less than the introduction of the notorious "Alloy" admixture, through the blood of a Scotch Galloway cow, into the herd of Charles Colling. As this incident in its partial detail at the hands of Mr. Berry has given rise to an altogether erroneous idea of the *origin* of the "*improved*" Short-horns, and created a belief, or supposition, that the present type of Short-horn excellence is of recent date, or about the year 1800, through an admixture of "Galloway" blood with the ancient race, a full history of the matter will be given.

In the first volume E. H. B., Rev. Henry Berry, of Acton Rectory, Worcestershire, Eng., is recorded as in the years 1821 and '22, the breeder of two animals, the bull Pirate (500), and a heifer, called Rebecca. The dam of the bull was bred by Mr. Hustler, and traces back into the stock of Robert Colling; the dam of the heifer was bred by Mr. Wright, of Cleasby. To these he afterwards added other animals, and became, to a moderate extent, a Short-horn breeder. In addition to his clerical and cattle breeding duties he appears to have been somewhat addicted to controversy, and engaged in discussing the relative merits between the Short-horn and Hereford breeds of cattle as feeding or flesh producing animals, in which he advocated the Short-horns. To substantiate their claims he wrote a pamphlet entitled

"IMPROVED SHORT-HORNS, AND THEIR PRETENTIONS STATED, BEING AN ACCOUNT OF THIS CELEBRATED BREED OF CATTLE, DERIVED FROM AUTHENTIC SOURCES." The first edition was issued in the year 1824.

From the rather ambitious title of his pamphlet one would suppose that an elaborate history would be given. Instead of any such, he gave less than eleven pages in large, open type, slightly alluding to the Short-horns and their characteristics, as an ancient race, with the names of a few noted early bulls owned and used by Charles Colling; about eighteen pages, enumerating the weights of various bullocks, cows and heifers, fed for slaughter; a list of eleven extraordinary milk cows owned by Jonas Whitaker, of Otley, in Yorkshire (the cows derived mainly from the stocks of Robert and Charles Colling), and closing with extracts from the lists of the great herd sales of the two Collings in 1810 and 1818. These, with three or four additional pages of miscellaneous matter, fill the history. The remainder of the pamphlet is devoted to the Hereford controversy, which is now of little consequence.

This pamphlet was reprinted in 1830, being a copy of the other, with no particular alteration beyond an additional preface. We might quote at large from Berry's pamphlet, but as his historical matter is nothing more than a condensation of previous history which we have already related in much more extended remark, it is unnecessary here to repeat it. The weights of cattle, also, which he gives, although proving their great size, ripe points, good feeding qualities and early maturity, are not extraordinary, compared with those of a later period. The main drift of his account aims to establish Charles Colling as the master-spirit of his day in "improving" the Short-horn race of cattle, and to publish the fact of such improvement to the world, and also distinguish Mr. Whitaker, from whose herd he (Berry) had become a considerable purchaser, as Colling's principal successor in Short-horn breeding and excellence.

In 1834, ten years after Berry's first pamphlet (in 1824), an elaborate work entitled "CATTLE, THEIR BREEDS, MANAGEMENT AND DISEASES," purporting to give a history of the various races and breeds of neat cattle belonging to the British Islands, was published in London. This was edited under the superintendence of "The Society for the Diffusion of Useful Knowledge," of which the late Lord Brougham was the head. The work was compiled by William Youatt, a veterinary surgeon, of Middlesex Hospital, London, a man of ability, and in his profession, of extended repute. The historical matter of his book was drawn from various sources through individual correspondents in different parts of the kingdom. In addition to that were added several hundred pages on "Management and Diseases," rendering it a work, with some exceptions, of standard *English* authority on the subjects of which it treated—particularly those parts which Youatt had closely studied, and with which he was personally familiar.

In the "Short-horn" history of his book Youatt, himself, seems to have taken but little part. He jobbed that portion of it out to Mr. Berry, who, in its compilation made it quite a different narrative from that which his previous pamphlet contained. Much that was *in* his pamphlet history is omitted, and much that was *not* in the pamphlet is added in the Youatt history. In the latter Charles Colling still holds the chief place as a breeder and *improver*—a few other names are slightly mentioned; but Whitaker, with whom it is said he had had a difference since the pamphlet was published, is not mentioned at all. Berry at that time was also possessed of some of the "Alloy" blood, or Galloway cross, originally introduced by Charles Colling, of which he makes prominent mention, and that cross he asserted was the grand feature of "improvement" in the Short-horn race which he now claimed that Colling had established.

As this pretended *improvement* to which so much importance is ascribed by Berry, was the sheerest fallacy, we shall lay it before the reader. In the year 1791, after Charles Colling had been ten years a Short-horn breeder, and got his choicest Short-horn families well established, one of his neighbors, Colonel O'Callaghan, purchased two Scotch Galloway, hornless heifers, and brought to his farm. He agreed with Colling to have the heifers served to his bull Bolingbroke (86), with the understanding that if the calves were bulls, Colling was to have them; if heifers, O'Callaghan was to retain them. One of these heifers, red in color, dropped a red and white roan bull calf, in the year 1792, which immediately became the property of Colling. The other calf was a heifer, which was kept by O'Callaghan. Colling had an aged Short-horn cow, "Old Johanna," bred by himself, of moderate quality, got by "Lame bull" (358), bred by Robert Colling. That is all which is given of her pedigree, no dam being mentioned. Yet Lame bull had two crosses of Hubback (319) in him, and his great grand dam was by James Brown's red bull (97), so far giving *him* an excellent pedigree. Old Johanna not having bred a calf for two years, was put to this Son of Bolingbroke (from the Galloway heifer), when a yearling, and he got her in calf. The produce was another bull calf, in 1794, Grandson of Bolingbroke (280), red and white in color, which Colling also kept, being three-fourths Short-horn and one-fourth Galloway blood. Colling's cow Phœnix, the dam of Favorite (252), had become somewhat aged, and not having had a calf since the birth of Favorite in 1793 or '94 (for both those dates are given with his pedigree in the English Herd Book; but Mr. Bates states it was in October, 1793, that he was born), although put to good bulls and not breeding, as a last resort she was coupled to this Grandson of Bolingbroke, when a yearling, in 1795, and by him she had a red and white heifer calf in the year 1796. This calf Colling called "Lady." She had one-eighth part Galloway blood. Proving a very good one, Colling reared this heifer, and at maturity bred her successively to his bulls Favorite (252), her half brother; Cupid (177), otherwise closely related to her; and to Comet (155), still more closely related. She produced the heifers Countess, one-sixteenth Galloway, by Cupid; and Laura, also one-sixteenth Galloway, by Favorite, both of which proved fine cows. Her bull calves were Washington (674), one-sixteenth Galloway, by Favorite; also Major (397), one-sixteenth; George (276), one-sixteenth; and Sir Charles (592), one-sixteenth Galloway, the three last ones by Comet (155).

The two "Alloy" bulls, "O'Callaghan's Son of Bolingbroke" (469), and "Grandson of Bolingbroke" (280), as well as the cows Lady, and her daughters Countess and Laura, and some of their descendants, many years after Colling had sold them, were recorded in Vol. 1, E. H. B., with their Galloway crosses distinctly given.

Such, through a single cross only in a Galloway cow, is the origin of Berry's celebrated "Alloy" *improvement*, on the female side of which the cow "Lady," only one-eighth of that blood (never breeding back, either by herself or her descendants, to the Galloway again, but on Short-horn blood continuously thereafter), was the sole founder.

In review of this whole matter which Mr. Berry has worked up, through the Galloway cross in the cow Lady and her progeny, as a deliberate plan for *improvement* by Colling on the blood and quality of the Short-horns, we think it simply an *accident*. "Old Johanna" had apparently ceased breeding—not having dropped a calf for two years; and Son of Bolingbroke, in the failure of Colling's better bulls to effect it, was used to restore her to fertility. It was under like circumstances with the cow Phœnix. Although she had brought several calves, and then ceased to breed from his best bulls, Colling required further use of her, and as a last resort, put her to the Grandson of Bolingbroke. This connection producing a calf (Lady), he then put her to her own son, Favorite, and Young Phœnix, the future dam of Comet (155), was the produce. If Colling *really intended the improvement*, why did he not, after she had produced Lady, again put her to the bastard to continue his improvement?

We think he would surely have done so, if he had any faith in such a process.

Again: as to the real "improvement" claimed by Mr. Berry in the *best* of the Colling blood. The year 1796 was the earliest date in which Grandson of Bolingbroke had any produce (that being the year in which Lady was born), and none of his blood could have gone into any stock previous to that time, as the "Grandson" was discarded after his service to Phœnix. We hear no more of his produce afterwards. There was no *public* Herd Book then; nothing but Colling's own *private* record to show Lady's lineage; nor, as we shall soon show, did the *public* then, or even at the sale in 1810, fourteen years afterwards, *positively* know the fact. These things all put together fully prove, as we think, that Mr. Berry got up the story of the Galloway bastard's pretended improvement to answer a purpose of his own.

Colling's best bulls were used in each cross on "Lady," and her female produce, Countess and Laura, and their female progeny, so that Youatt, in a foot note to Berry's exalted estimate of the good quality of "Lady," remarks: "The dam of Lady was also the dam of the bull Favorite; and as the Grandson of Bolingbroke is not known to have been the sire of any other remarkably good animal, it is most probable that the unquestionable merit of Lady and her descendants is to be attributed more to her dam than to her sire."

In the year 1810 Charles Colling made a public sale of his herd and retired from breeding, having realized a fortune sufficiently ample for the residue of his days. A more extended account of this sale will be given in subsequent pages, as we wish now to follow the "Alloy" blood until it passed out of his hands. The account is taken from the (English) *Times*, of Friday, October 19, 1810. The prices and purchasers' names of the "Alloy," as reported at the sale, are here quoted:

Lady [by Grandson of Bolingbroke, one-eighth Galloway], 14 years old, to C. Wright, Cleasby, Yorkshire, 206 guineas ($1,071).

Countess [daughter of Lady, one-sixteenth Galloway], by Cupid, to Major B. Rudd, 400 guineas ($2,080).

Laura [daughter of Lady, one-sixteenth Galloway], by Favorite, 4 years old, to Mr. Grant, Lincolnshire, 210 guineas ($1,092).

Selina [daughter of Countess above, and one-thirty-second part Galloway], by Favorite, 5 years old, to Sir H. C. Ibbotson, Denton Park, Yorkshire, 200 guineas ($1,040).

Cora [daughter of Countess above, and one-thirty-second part Galloway], by Favorite, 4 years old, to G. Johnson, Yorkshire, 70 guineas ($364).

Major (397) [son of Lady, above, and one-sixteenth part Galloway], by Comet (155), to Mr. Grant, Lincolnshire, 200 guineas ($1,040).

Alexander (22) [son of Cora, above, and one-sixty-fourth part Galloway], by Comet (155), 1 year old, to W. C. Fenton, 63 guineas ($328).

Young Favorite (254) [a calf, and son of Countess, above, and one-thirty-second part Galloway], by Comet, to P. Skipworth, Lincolnshire, 140 guineas ($728).

George (276) [before mentioned, a calf, and a son of Lady, by Comet, and one-sixteenth part Galloway], to Mr. Walker, Yorkshire, 130 guineas ($676).

Young Laura [daughter of Laura, by Comet, and one-thirty-second part Galloway], 2 years old, to Earl of Lonsdale, 101 guineas ($525).

Young Countess [daughter of Countess, by Comet, and one-thirty-second part Galloway], 2 years old, to Sir H. C. Ibbotson, 206 guineas ($1,071).

Lucilla [calf, daughter of Laura, by Comet, and one-thirty-second part Galloway], to Mr. Grant, 106 guineas ($551).

Calista [calf, daughter of Cora, by Comet, and one-sixty-fourth part Galloway], to Sir Henry Vane Tempest, Durham, 50 guineas ($250).

These thirteen animals are all we find of the "Alloy" blood in that celebrated sale, and the prices which they brought, are most of them extraordinary in comparison to those for the other thirty-four *pure* Short-horns sold at the same time. The entire lot of thirteen females, sold for $10,816, or an average of $832 each. But, when it is recollected that these Alloys had only a small fraction of Galloway blood in them, and were got by Colling's best bulls, and far above the others in *flesh* (the "Alloys" being very moderate milkers), and most of them sold to the newer breeders who were taken by the good looks of the animals, the high prices will be readily accounted for.

Let us now see what was afterwards said of the Galloway or "Alloy" cross. "Mr. Mason (a noted Short-horn breeder) stated that he did not recollect any *experienced* breeder who made an offer for the mixed breed, and he was sure that if Charles Colling had not made that mistake, his stock at Ketton would have sold for some thousand pounds more. This was read by Col. Mellish at the King's Head (tavern), Darlington, and caused great consternation in the neighborhood, as the catalogue did not mention any particulars of the breeding of Grandson of Bolingbroke." [It will be remembered that the first volume E. H. B., containing the pedigrees of Short-horn cattle was not published until 1822, twelve years after the sale.] "Many were disappointed, and others said if they had known of the transaction they would not have purchased. Mr. Robert Colling also told Mr. Wiley that he had no doubt it was quite a thousand pounds ($5,000) loss to his brother having the Alloy blood in his herd."

So much, therefore, for Mr. Berry's pretended "improvement" of the Short-horns by Charles Colling in his breeding, rearing and selling thirteen animals only of this Galloway cross at the final sale of his herd. He might, possibly, previous to the sale have bred other animals of that cross, but as it appears that the "Alloy" blood was little known out of his own neighborhood, if he did breed others, they might have been sold by him, and neither their names nor the names of their produce ever got into the Herd Books.

To show even Colling's estimate of the value of the "Alloys," he never put Grandson of Bolingbroke to any superior cow, except Phœnix, the dam of Lady (and probably would not have used him with *her*, if she would have bred to his other bulls, which she would not). Nor did he use any Alloy bull, except Lady's first calf, Washington (694). He only put him one season, to three or four cows, and they produced nothing of any prominent value. "The Alloy blood was confined to Lady, her daughters, and the produce of her daughters; nor did he suffer it to run into any other of his choice tribes. The Alloys were deficient in milk, which always kept them in good condition, and being round and plump in form, with fine hair, those qualities, in spite of their slight fraction of Galloway blood, while their Short-horn blood being of the very best, sold them so well. Nor were the prices the Alloy family brought equal to some other families. The Alloys averaged about 160 guineas; the Phœnix family, including Comet, 491 guineas (without Comet, 237 guineas); and the Daisy family 175 guineas." The best breeders did not touch the Alloys.

Berry winds up his account with a triumphant flourish over this final sale of Charles Colling, in which the Alloys sold at such good prices, and as a consequence, claimed that the Galloway cross was an actual improvement in the original Short-horn blood. But it must be remembered that Berry was a partisan, was breeding the Alloy blood in his own herd, and so states the fact, besides illustrating one of his Alloy cows by a portrait in the Youatt history. No new revelations had been made to him of the merits of that blood since first publishing his pamphlet (ten years previous to his Youatt story), in which the Galloway is not mentioned. In view of the whole matter, we are forced to conclude that Berry's claim of the Alloy *improvement* on the Short-horn blood and quality, was simply a fancy of his own. Had Youatt understood the truth of that pretended history and its unfounded assumptions, he would never have given it a place in his book.

Yet there being no other Short-horn history before the public than his, and so many years had elapsed since the transaction, it was widely copied by almost every subsequent writer on Short-horn cattle, both in England and America, and has been so often repeated in agricultural periodicals, and other papers, that the great majority of cattle breeders, on both sides the Atlantic, have, until a recent period, believed it. There are few well-bred Short-horns now living which have more than a remote dash of the "Alloy" blood in their veins; and what they possess is so minute in quantity as not to be discoverable to their detriment.

We have given more space to this pretended "improvement" than it deserves, and but for the belief, so generally prevalent, of its truth, should hardly have mentioned it. Yet, honest history should be vindicated. It is but candid, however, to say, that in the remote earlier breeding of the Short-horns, *stealthy* crosses with other breeds are known to have been made; but they are now so distant in time, and as no "improvement" upon the original Short-horn blood has been *claimed* for any such possible crosses, they need not be made a subject of remark. Alien crosses, in ages back, have been traced in the blood, or turf horse of England, either on the "cold" blooded native mares of the country, or with selected foreign ones of the neighboring continent; but so many pure bred crosses of English, Arabian, or Barb stallions have since intervened, that the well-authenticated pedigrees of modern date are acknowledged by record in the English Stud Books. And so with all our modern Short-horn cattle which can trace their pedigrees into the records of the earlier volumes of the English, and from them into the American Herd Books. All are "Herd Book" animals; but those who prefer to run pedigrees back to their remotest sources, will make their selections of those strains of blood which best suit their genealogical preferences.

Animal physiology is so critical, and so subtle a science, and the laws of descent are so various in their operation, sometimes striking back into the characteristics of a distant ancestor deficient in good quality, and reproducing an almost exact likeness, that those who aim at the highest style of perfection in their animals will scrutinize closely the strains of blood through which they have descended. We cannot but consider that Mr. Berry, in his exaltation of the Galloway cross, has done a decided injury to the Short-horn interest by striving to inculcate the belief that this noble race may be improved by crosses outside of their own blood, thus misleading inexperienced breeders, who, if they practiced on his teaching, would adopt a wretched system of bastardy to stain the finest breed of cattle which the world has produced.

Charles Colling's Final Sale of His Herd.

Tracing the brothers Colling through their breeding career from the year 1780 to 1810 with Charles, and to 1818 and 1820 with Robert, a period of thirty years with one, and forty years with the other, we have witnessed their sagacity in selecting the best stock obtainable from the herds of the earlier breeders in their vicinity, as the foundation of their own. They bred and reared them in the best manner, adopting a system begun by Bakewell, whom they appear to have taken as a model for their own future practice. Finding it successful they then had the enterprise to make the Short-horn race, previously confined to their own secluded locality, known throughout the richest agricultural portions of the kingdom; and through animals of their own breeding, made themselves supposed the leading or master-spirits in their production. Each had been successful in his vocation, working in concert, and interchanging, to more or less extent, their bulls in the service of each other's herds. They originated the system of letting bulls for the season to other breeders at roundly paying prices, and as a consequence sold many of them, as well as females, at values hitherto unparalleled in amount.

Enjoying the prestige of success and reputation, in the month of October, 1810, Charles Colling made a public sale of his herd at Ketton, and retired from breeding. It was then the heyday of agricultural prosperity in the British Islands. England had engaged in the continental wars of Europe against the first Napoleon; specie payments had been many years suspended by her banks, and at the national treasury; prices of agricultural produce were highly inflated, and so far as pounds, shillings and pence then rated—probably quite double to what they were ten years afterwards—the sums which were bid for his cattle were both unprecedented and enormous.

The approaching sale was well advertised, and its results marked an era in Short-horn history. An account of it was given in "The Times" of Friday, October 19, 1810, as previously stated. It is of such historical interest, and so many of our modern Short-horns run their genealogies back into some of the cattle of that sale that the entire list is quoted. The numbers to the bulls, subsequently inserted in Vol. 1, E. H. B., are here added. The Alloys are repeated in the list, and marked thus *:

COWS.

Lot.		Guineas.
1.	CHERRY, out of Old Cherry, by Favorite (252), 11 years old, dam of Peeress (Lot 3), Mayduke (22), and Ketton (30). Bought by J. D. Nesham, Haughton-le-Spring, Durham. Bulled by Comet.	83
2.	KATE, 4 years old, by Comet. J. Hunt, Morton, Durham. Bulled by Mayduke.	35
3.	PEERESS, 5 years old, out of Cherry, by Favorite; dam of Cecil (36). Major B. Rudd, Marton Lodge, Yorkshire. Bulled by Comet.	170
4.	COUNTESS,* 9 years old, out of Lady, by Cupid; dam of Selina (5), Cora (12), Young Favorite (31), Young Countess (40). Major B. Rudd. Bulled by Comet.	400
5.	SELINA,* out of Countess, by Favorite, 5 years old. Sir H. C. Ibbotson, Bart., Denton Park, Yorkshire. Bulled by Petrarch.	200
6.	JOHANNA, out of Johanna, by Favorite, 4 years old. H. Witham, Cliff Hall, Yorkshire. Bulled by Petrarch.	130
7.	LADY,* out of Old Phœnix, by Grandson of Bolingbroke (280), 14 years old; dam of Countess (4), Laura (8), Major (21), and George (32). C. Wright, Cleasby, Yorkshire. Bulled by Comet.	206
8.	LAURA,* out of Lady, by Favorite, 4 years old; dam of Young Laura (39), and Lucilla (44). Grant, Wyham, Lincolnshire. Bulled by Comet.	210
9.	CATHALENE, out of a daughter of the dam of Phœnix, by Washington (674), 8 years old; dam of Charlotte (42). G. Coates for G. Parker, Sutton House, Malton, Yorkshire. Bulled by Comet.	150
10.	LILY, out of Daisy, by Comet, 3 years old; dam of White Rose (46). Major B. Rudd. Bulled by Mayduke.	410
11.	DAISY, out of Old Daisy, by a grandson of Favorite, out of Venus; 6 years old; dam of Lily (10), and Sir Dimple (33). Major R. Bower, Welham, Malton, Yorkshire. Bulled by Comet.	140
12.	CORA,* out of Countess, by Favorite, 4 years old; dam of Alexander (27), and Calista (45). G. Johnston, Hackness, near Scarborough, Yorkshire. Bulled by Petrarch.	70
13.	BEAUTY, out of Miss Washington, by Marske (417), (a son of Favorite) 4 years old; dam of Albion (35). C. Wright. Bulled by Comet.	120

Lot.		Guineas.
14.	RED ROSE, out of Eliza, by Comet, 4 years old; dam of Harold (29). W. C. Fenton, Lovison, near Doncaster. Bulled by Mayduke.	45
15.	FLORA, 3 years old, by Comet; dam of Narcissus (34). R. Mowbray for the Earl of Lonsdale. Bulled by Mayduke.	70
16.	MISS PEGGY, 3 years old, by a son of Favorite (253). Hill for Oliver Gascoigne, Parlington, Yorkshire. Bulled by Comet.	60
17.	MAGDALENE, 3 years old, by Comet, out of a heifer, by Washington; dam of Ossian (28). C. Champion, Blyth, near Doncaster. Bulled by Comet.	170

BULLS.

18.	COMET (155), 6 years old, out of Phœnix. Wetherell, Trotter, Wright, and Charge, near Darlington. Got by Favorite.	1000
19.	YARBOROUGH (705), 9 years old, out of a daughter of Favorite. Gregson, Low Linn, Northumberland. Got by Cupid.	55
20.	CUPID (177), 11 years old, out of Venus, by a son of Favorite. Being rather lame was not offered for sale.	
21.	MAJOR* (397), 3 years old, out of Lady. Grant. Got by Comet.	200
22.	MAYDUKE (424), 3 years old, out of Cherry. Smithson. Got by Comet.	145
23.	PETRARCH (488), 2 years old, out of Venus, Major B. Rudd. Got by Comet.	365
24.	NORTHUMBERLAND (464), 2 years old, out of a daughter of Favorite. Buston, Cotham Stob, Durham. Got by Comet.	80
25.	ALFRED (23), 1 year old, out of Venus. Thomas Robinson, Acklam, Yorkshire. Got by Comet.	110
26.	DUKE (226), 1 year old, out of Duchess. Anthony Compton, Carham Hall, Northumberland. Got by Comet.	105
27.	ALEXANDER* (22), 1 year old, out of Cora. W. C. Fenton. Got by Comet.	63
28.	OSSIAN (476), 1 year old, out of Magdalene. R. Mowbray for the Earl of Lonsdale. Got by Windsor (698).	76
29.	HAROLD (290), 1 year old, out of Red Rose. Sir Lambton Loraine, Bart., Kirk Harle, Northumberland. Got by Windsor.	50

BULL CALVES, NOT ONE YEAR OLD.

30.	KETTON (346), out of Cherry. Major R. Bower. Got by Comet.	50
31.	YOUNG FAVORITE* (254), out of Countess. P. Skipworth, Aylesby, Lincolnshire. Got by Comet.	40
32.	GEORGE (276),* out of Lady. Walker, Rotherham, Yorkshire. Got by Comet.	130
33.	SIR DIMPLE (594), out of Daisy. T. Lax, Ravensworth, Yorkshire. Got by Comet.	90
34.	NARCISSUS (447), out of Flora. C. Wright, Cleasby. Got by Comet.	15
35.	ALBION (14), out of Beauty. T. Booth, Killerby, Durham. Got by Comet.	60
36.	CECIL (120), out of Peeress. H. Strickland, Boynton, Yorkshire. Got by Comet.	170

HEIFERS.

Lot.		Guineas.
37.	PHŒBE, 3 years old, by Comet, dam by Favorite. Sir H. C. Ibbotson, Bart. Bulled by a son of Comet.	105
38.	YOUNG DUCHESS, 2 years old, by Comet, dam by Favorite. T. Bates, Halton Castle, Northumberland. Bulled by a son of Comet.	183
39.	YOUNG LAURA,* 2 years old, by Comet, out of Laura. R. Mowbray for the Earl of Lonsdale. Bulled by Comet.	101
40.	YOUNG COUNTESS,* 2 years old, by Comet, out of Countess. Sir H. C. Ibbotson, Bart. Bulled by Comet.	206
41.	LUCY, 2 years old, by Comet, dam by Washington. C. Wright. Bulled by Comet.	132
42.	CHARLOTTE, 1 year old, by Comet, out of Cathalene. T. Sale for R. Colling, Barmpton, Durham. Bulled by Petrarch.	136
43.	JOHANNA, 1 year old, by Comet, out of Johanna. George Johnston. Bulled by Petrarch.	35

HEIFER CALVES.

44.	LUCILLA,* out of Laura. Grant. Got by Comet.	106
45.	CALISTA,* out of Cora. Sir H. V. Tempest, Wynyard, Durham. Got by Comet.	50
46.	WHITE ROSE, out of Lily. H. Strickland, Boynton. Got by Yarbro'.	75
47.	RUBY, out of Red Rose. Major R. Bower. Got by Yarbro'.	50
48.	COWSLIP. R. Mowbray for the Earl of Lonsdale. Got by Comet.	25

SUMMARY.

29 Cows and Heifers, average,	£140 4s. 7d.	£4066 13s.
18 Bulls and Calves, "	169 8 0	3049 4
47 averaged £151 8s. ¾d.	Total,	£7115 17

The guinea is 21 shillings sterling; and by calculating the pound sterling (20s.) at $5, the sum in dollars which each animal sold for can be easily ascertained.

It will here be seen that three-fourths of the 48 cattle enumerated were got by the bulls Favorite (252), and Comet (155) his son; and the other fourth by bulls of their get, and a large majority of the cows were in calf to Comet, which fact, undoubtedly—so high was the reputation of the bull—added much to their prices, notwithstanding any prejudices existing against their intense in-and-in breeding.

We quote still further remarks relative to the sale from Thornton's Circular, of April, 1869:

"The sale was on a fine October day, and early in the morning people rode and drove to Ketton, leaving their horses and gigs at the adjoining farms; all the strawyards were full, and the throng at the sale immense; everything was eaten up, so that bread had to be sent for into Darlington. Mr. Kingston, the auctioneer, sold the cattle by the sand-glass, and in accordance with the custom of the time received about five guineas for the business, the work of the sale falling more on the owner than the auctioneer. The cattle were not fed up for the sale, but kept naturally, and sold when they were in great condition from natural keep.

"The Ketton stock at this time is described by Mr. Wright as of great size and substance, with fine, long hind quarters; the space from the hip to the rib was long and counteracted by a broad back and high, round ribs. The shoulders of the males were upright, and the knuckles, or shoulder points, large and coarse—a defect not so apparent in the females. The general contour, or side view, was stately and imposing, but their great superiority consisted in their extraordinary inclination to fatten. On handling, the skin was loose and pliant, and the feel under it remarkably mellow and kind. The color was greatly varied; red, red and white, roan, and also white being found in the same kindred; while in all cases of close affinity there was a tendency to white, with red ears and spots.

"Many of the cows were excellent milkers, giving twelve full quarts at a meal. Cherry, the first lot, was one of them, a plain cow in color, red and a little white, whose descendants are now in existence in the neighborhood of Stockton-on-Tees and Malton, Yorks. Countess [Alloy] was undoubtedly the finest cow in the sale, but she wanted hair and milk; in character she came nearest to Mason's style, and her back and belly formed parallel lines. She produced three heifers and the bull Constellation (163), in Major Rudd's possession, and died in 1816. Selina [Alloy] had the style of her dam Countess, but not her magnificent appearance; she bred ten calves at Denton Park, and her descendants in the ninth and tenth generations are still in existence at Siddington, Gloucestershire. Lady lacked elegance, but had great substance and good hair; in color she was red and white.

"Lily, pure bred, sold to Major Rudd for 400 guineas ($2,152), a splendid white cow, was the highest priced female, but did nothing in Major Rudd's possession. Daisy, a small roan cow, but a grand milker, was most fruitful with Major Bower; her dam, Old Daisy, who gave thirty-two quarts of milk a day, had been sold to Mr. Hustler, who bred Fairy from her, the ancestress of Rev. J. D. Jefferson's Lady Abbesses. This Fairy was afterwards bought by Mr. Bates, who reckoned her to be the finest specimen of quality imaginable;

she had a long, thick, downy coat, with a superb flesh underneath, which, to a superficial observer, appeared hard, the cow being in a rapidly advancing condition. Cora [Alloy], out of the 400 gs. ($2,000) Countess, had a pretty red frame, but ugly cock horns, and was re-sold to Major Bower, who bred ten calves from her. Magdalene was a little red cow, with a large bag and belly and short quarters; although the dam of the celebrated red and white bull, Blyth Comet (85), her only produce besides Ossian (476); she was not first rate and wanted hair, yet when dry had a great propensity to feed.

"The only cow that Charles Colling reserved was Magdalena [by Comet, dam by Cupid], a great favorite and an extraordinary milker, giving sixteen quarts *twice* a day. Mr. Whitaker prevailed upon Charles Colling to let him have her; the numerous and well known 'Chaff' tribe is descended from this cow.

"Comet (155) was the great attraction of the sale, and his close breeding [by Favorite (252), dam by Favorite (252), out of Favorite's (252) dam], did not detract from his value or appearance. Charles Colling declared him to be the best bull he ever bred or saw. He was a beautiful light roan, dark [red] neck, with a fine masculine head, broad and deep breast, shoulders well laid back, crops and loins good, hind quarters long, straight, and well packed, thighs thick, twist full and well let down, with nice straight hocks and hind legs. He had fair sized horns, ears large and hairy, and a grandeur of style and carriage that was indescribable.* It was admitted that no bull so good had ever before been seen, and eminent breeders have since said that they never again saw his equal. In one point, however, opinions differed. Some few objected to his shoulders as not being good, or a little too strong in the knuckles; others asserted that he was there, as in every other point, faultless. The near shoulder was slightly shrunk in, apparently diseased, which may have arisen from a violent sprain that he received when a calf. When brought into the ring, he was put up at 600 guineas. Thomas Newton, a small dairyman at Bishop Auckland, bid 850 guineas, and Mr. John Wright, standing beside him, asked why he bid? 'To take in cows at a good profit,' said he, and whilst talking the glass† run out at 1000 guineas ($5,000). Mr. John Hutton, of Marske, who was unable to get to the sale, bid 1600

---

* Comet's portrait is represented in frontispiece of 3d volume American Herd Book.—L. F. A.

† In those days it was a rule with the English stock auctioneers to sell by the hour or minute glass—an article now little known. A given number of minutes was allowed for the bidding, and when the sand run out the article on sale was struck off.—L. F. A.

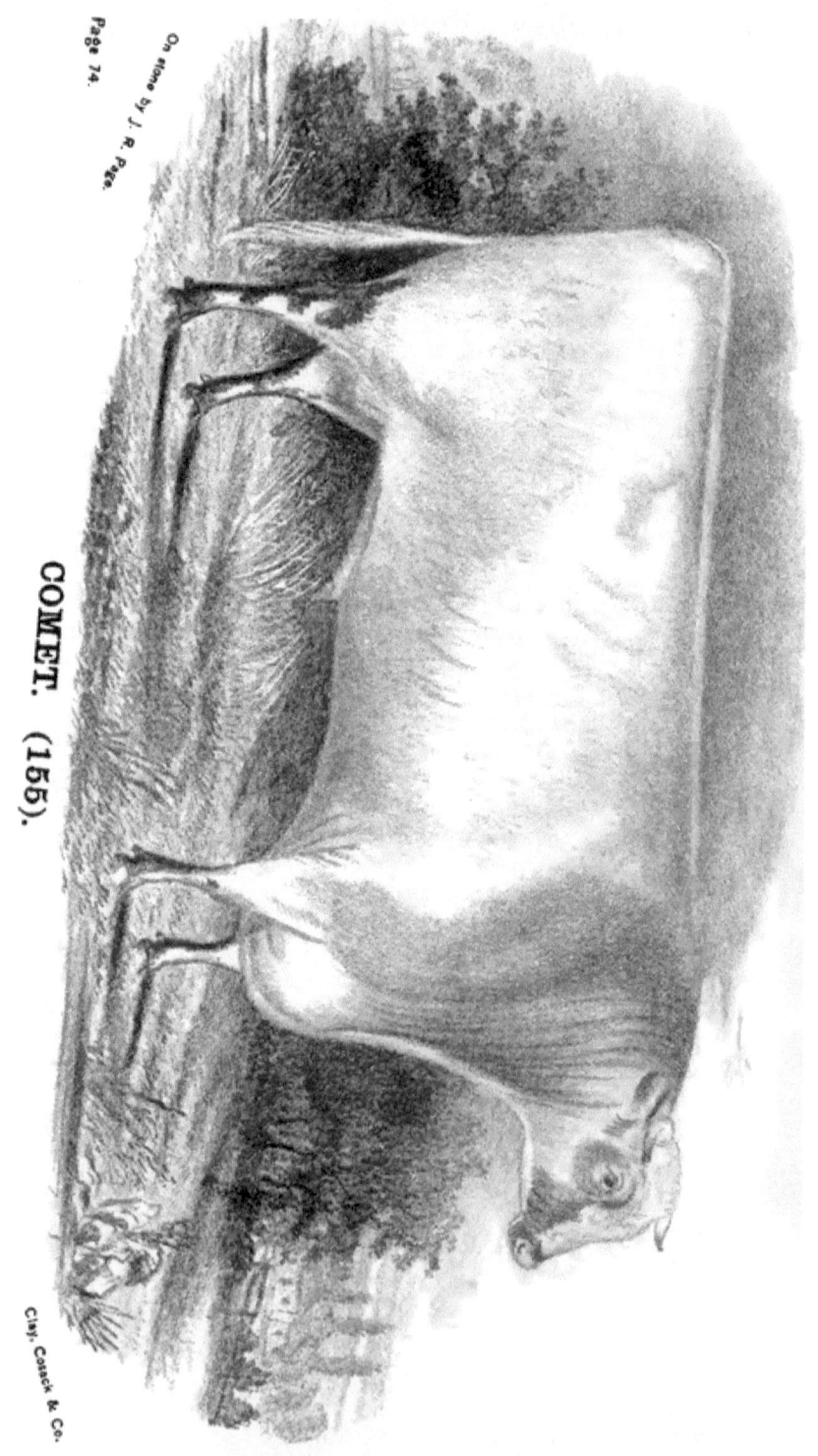

On stone by J. R. Page.
Page 74.
COMET. (155).
Clay, Cosack & Co.

guineas for him, as well as Sir H. Vane Tempest, who was delayed, and drove up just as the sale was finishing. Comet was located at Cleasby, three miles from Darlington, and was kept in a small paddock, with a loose box in the corner. The condition of purchase was that the four buyers should send twelve cows each annually to him, and Mr. Wright was to have one extra for his keep. Mr. Wright died in the meantime, and Comet gradually sank, his body breaking out into sores. Remus (550) is supposed to have been his last calf. Miss Wright kept a man expressly to attend to Comet, and when the bull died he was buried in the center of the paddock, and a chestnut tree planted on his grave. The paddock is known as 'Comet's garth' [enclosure] to this day. Mr. Thornton, of Stapleton, purchased this field, and the tree having grown to an enormous size, was grubbed up on the 3d of February, 1865, and Comet's skeleton laid bare; his rib bone measured 2 feet 1 inch, and the leg bone, knee to ankle joint, 9 inches to 5 inches circumference. Many of the other bones were quite perfect, and the whole are preserved in a glass case as a curiosity at Stapleton, near Darlington.

"North Star (458), own brother to Comet, and a year younger, was used and died at General Simpson's in Fifeshire; he was a little lighter in color, but fully as fine in quality, or perhaps rather thicker, though not such a perfectly elegant animal as Comet. Young Phœnix, their dam, only produced one other calf, a heifer, that died young.

"Major (397), a nice bull, but not particularly handsome, and of a red and white color, begot much good stock in Lincolnshire for many years. He was hired by Mr. John Charge, who bred Western Comet (689) by him, out of Gentle Kitty. Western Comet was acknowledged to be the best bull and finest stock getter ever brought into Cumberland. He was used to his daughters and granddaughters, and from this close alliance came the Wharfdale tribe, recently so successful in Ireland. Petrarch (488) was a splendid looking bull, but wanted hair, whilst Northumberland (464), who had big knuckles, was used, like Ossian (476) in Westmoreland, for several seasons, both becoming celebrated sires. Ketton (346) also showed strong knuckles, and eventually went into Nottinghamshire. Albion (14) is said to have done more good than any other bull used at Killerby [Thomas Booth's]. Young Duchess, known afterwards as Duchess 1st [bought by Thomas Bates], was a fine red heifer, and developed into a large, handsome cow, with a good deal of the elegance and style of her sire Comet. She was never quite so splendid an animal as her granddam the Duchess,* by the Daisy Bull (186). Young Countess, a thick, stylish, red heifer, was re-sold to Mr. Earnshaw, and produced three calves, twin bulls, one of which was the celebrated bull Count (170), and a red and white heifer. She died from a broken blood vessel in 1814."

In regard to floating rumors that Charles Colling had made use of Kyloe blood in his herd, Colling himself, in a private letter to the Rev. Henry Berry stated, "'that Hutchinson was egregiously wrong in charging the Collings with an indiscriminate use of Kyloe blood.' George Coates declared unequivocally that he never observed anything in that stock designated pure Short-horns, that could induce him for a moment to entertain a suspicion that the animals were nearly or remotely allied to the Kyloe. Mr. Charge, as well as Mr. Coates and C. Colling, always deemed Hubback (319) a pure Shorthorn; and neither he nor his descendants, when put on cows of the pure blood, begot any calves which denoted, in their features or color, any other breed than the pure Short-horn. His stock had capacious chests, prominent bosoms, thick mossy coats, mellow skins, with a great deal of fine flesh spread equally over the whole carcass, and were either red and white, yellow roans, or white. The produce of the Alloy blood † increased in size, rotundity, and heavy flesh, but afterwards seemed to lose their fine hair and milking properties. The highest priced cows at the sale were those in the highest condition, and they were mostly of the Alloy blood."

That sale finished the vocation of Charles Colling as a Short-horn breeder. He lived in retirement twenty-six years afterwards, and died in the year 1836, at the patriarchal age of 85 years, leaving no children.

Robert Colling's Sale of 1818.

Eight years after the sale of Charles' herd, Robert Colling, in the year 1818, made a partial sale of his herd, and in 1820 the closing sale, which finished his career as a breeder. At the time of his first sale in 1818, he had been before the public as a leading and prominent breeder thirty-eight years, and at his final sale in 1820, forty years. During all that time, like his brother Charles, he had been a large seller of stock as well as considerable purchaser. He sold his surplus animals to other breeders, through which the blood of many

---

* Frontispiece to Cows, Vol. 3, American Herd Book.—L. F. A.

† These were all by thorough-bred bulls.—L. F. A.

of his best animals were imparted to their herds, since become famous. Like his brother Charles, wherever he had found a *well-bred* female whose superior good qualities pleased him, if it were possible, he also availed himself, by purchase, of her merits.

As with the sale of Charles in 1810, the widely advertised first sale of Robert in 1818, with a greater number of animals, brought a large attendance of the most spirited breeders of England. It took place on the 29th and 30th days of September. The following account of the sale is given:

COWS.

Lot.		Guineas.
1.	RED ROSE, 17 years old, by Favorite (252), dam by Ben (70), gr. d. by Foljambe, g. gr. d. by Hubback. Having a complaint upon her, was not offered for sale.	
2.	MOSS ROSE, 11 years old, by Favorite, dam lot 1. Being not likely to breed again, was not offered for sale.	
3.	JUNO, 11 years old, by Favorite, dam Wildair by Favorite, gr. d. by Ben, g. gr. d. by Hubback, g. g. gr. d. by sire of Hubback, g. g. g. gr. d. by Sir James Pennyman's bull, descended from the stock of the late Sir W. St. Quintin, of Scampston. Bought by the Hon. J. B. Simpson, Babworth, Nottinghamshire. Bulled by Lancaster (360).	78
4.	DIANA, own sister to lot 3. Lord Althorp, Wiseton, Nottinghamshire, afterwards Earl Spencer. Bulled by Lancaster.	73
5.	SALLY, 11 years old, by Favorite, dam by Favorite, gr. d. by Favorite. W. Smith, Dishley, Leicestershire.	34
6.	CHARLOTTE, 9 years old, by Comet (155), dam (Cathalene). Bought at the Ketton sale. F. Brown, Welbourn, Grantham, Lincolnshire. Bulled by Midas (435).	50
7.	WILDAIR, 6 years old, by George (275), dam Wildair by Favorite. Sister to lot 3. C. Duncombe, Duncombe Park, Yorks, afterwards Lord Feversham. Bulled by Lancaster.	176
8.	LILY, 6 years old, by North Star (459), dam by Favorite, gr. d. by Favorite, g. gr. d. by Favorite. P. Skipworth, Aylesby, Lincolnshire. Bulled by Lancaster.	66
9.	GOLDEN PIPPIN, 6 years old, by North Star, dam by Favorite, gr. d. by Favorite, g. gr. d. by Favorite, from the cow that obtained the first premium given at Darlington. W. Cattle (re-sold to Whitaker, Greenholme, Otley). Bulled by Lancaster.	141
10.	BLACKWELL, 6 years old, by Wellington (680), descended from the stock of the late Mr. Hill. T. Hopper, Sherburn, Durham. Bulled by Lancaster.	31
11.	TULIP, 6 years old, by George, dam by Favorite, gr. d. by Favorite, g. gr. d. by Favorite. C. Tibbets. Barton Seagrave, Northamptonshire. Bulled by Barmpton (54).	70

Lot.		Guineas.
12.	TRINKET, 6 years old, by Barmpton, dam by Favorite, g. gr. d. by Favorite. W. Smith. Bulled by Lancaster.....	143
13.	MARY ANNE, 6 years old, by George, dam by Favorite, gr. d. by Punch. W. Smith. Bulled by Midas.	62
14.	LOUISA, 5 years old, by Wellington, dam by Favorite, gr. d. by Favorite. W. Smith. Bulled by Lancaster.	37
15.	EMPRESS, 5 years old, by Barmpton, dam Lady Grace, by Favorite. C. Champion, Blyth, Nottinghamshire. Bulled by Lancaster.	210
16.	CAROLINE, 5 years old, by Minor (441), dam (Wildair) by Favorite. H. Witham, Lartington, Yorks. Bulled by Lancaster.	160
17.	CLARISSA, 4 years old, by Wellington, dam by Favorite, gr. d. by Favorite, g. gr. d. by Favorite. T. Robson, Holtby (re-sold to Right Hon. C. Arbuthnot, Woodford Lodge, Northamptonshire). Bulled by Lancaster.	151
18.	YOUNG MOSS ROSE, 5 years old, by Wellington, dam (2). C. Duncombe. Bulled by Lancaster.	190
19.	VENUS, 5 years old, by Wellington, dam by George, gr. d. by Favorite, g. gr. d. by Punch (531), from a sister to the dam of the White Heifer that Traveled. Hon. J. B. Simpson. Bulled by Lancaster.	195
20.	ROSETTE, 4 years old, by Wellington, dam (1). Lord Althorp. Bulled by Lancaster.	300
21.	YOUNG CHARLOTTE, 3 years old, by Wellington, dam (6). R. Thomas, Eryholme, Durham. Bulled by Lancaster.	72
22.	VESPER, 3 years old, by Wellington, dam by Favorite, gr. d. by Favorite. Dam sister to Trinket's dam. J. White, Coates, Leicestershire. Bulled by Lancaster.	111
23.	NONPAREIL, 5 years old, by Wellington, dam (3). Lord Althorp. Bulled by Lancaster.	370
24.	DAISY, 3 years old, by Wellington, dam by Favorite. Hon. J. B. Simpson. Bulled by Lancaster.	32
25.	KATE, 3 years old, by Wellington, dam by Phenomenon (491), gr. d. by Favorite. H. Witham, Cliff Hall, Yorkshire. Bulled by Lancaster.	50
26.	AMELIA, 2 years old, by Lancaster, dam by North Star, gr. d. by Favorite, g. gr. d. by Punch. J. C. Maynard, Harsley Hall, Yorkshire. Bulled by Barmpton.	76
27.	AURORA, twin sister to 26. W. Smith. Bulled by Barmpton.	78
28.	PRINCESS, 2 years old, by Lancaster, dam (9). P. Skipworth. Bulled by Barmpton.	156
29.	CLARA, 2 years old, by Lancaster, dam (19). R. Thomas. Bulled by Barmpton.	190
30.	FANNY, 2 years old, by Wellington, dam (5). C. Tibbets. Bulled by Barmpton.	160
31.	WHITE ROSE, 2 years old, by Wellington, dam by Wellington, gr. d. by Favorite. W. Smith. Bulled by Barmpton.	51
32.	RUBY, 2 years old, by Wellington, dam (1). T. Robson. Bulled by Lancaster.	331

ROBERT COLLING'S SALE.

Lot.		Guineas.
33.	LAVINIA, 2 years, by Lancaster, dam (18). T. Robson. Bulled by Barmpton........	105
34.	HEBE, 2 years old, by Jupiter (345), dam (8). J. Thompson, Scremerston, Berwick-on-Tweed. Bulled by Barmpton.	90
35.	JESSY, 2 years old, by Wellington, dam from the stock of the late Mr. Hill. J. Hutchinson, Stockton-on-Tees. Bulled by Barmpton......	43
36.	JEWEL, 2 years old, twin sister to 35. F. Brown. Bulled by Lancaster.	50

HEIFERS AND HEIFER CALVES.

37.	VIOLET, by North Star, dam by Midas, gr. d. by Punch. P. Skipworth.	48
38.	SWEETBRIER, by North Star, dam (23). J. C. Maynard.	145
39.	SNOWDROP, by Wellington, dam (11). Thompson, Stockton, Durham...	71
40.	COWSLIP, by Wellington, dam by Favorite, gr. d. by Punch. Leighton, North Willingham, Lincolnshire.	54
41.	LADY ANN, by Wellington, dam by George, gr. d. (3). W. Wetherell, Holme House, Darlington........	100
42.	FLORA, by Lancaster, dam (5). J. Thompson........	47
43.	CLEOPATRA, by Lancaster, dam by George, gr. d. by Favorite, g. gr. d. by Punch. W. Wetherell........	133
44.	RESTLESS, by Lancaster, dam (17); calved Sept. 26, 1817. T. Robson.	52
45.	A HEIFER, by Lancaster, dam (12); calved 28th October. S. Wiley, Brandsby, Yorkshire........	56
46.	MISS COLLING, by Wellington, dam by Wellington; calved October 20. W. Smith........	28
47.	A ROAN HEIFER, by Lancaster, dam (13); calved November 16. W. Cattle (G. Alderson, Ferrybridge)........	42
48.	LOUISA, by Lancaster, dam (14); calved November 20th. Hon. J. B. Simpson........	38
49.	A RED AND WHITE HEIFER, by Barmpton, dam (15). C. Champion. ...	100
50.	ROSINA, by Barmpton, dam (20). T. Robson for C. Arbuthnot........	123
51.	LAURA, by Barmpton, dam (6). Major B. Rudd, Marton Lodge, Yorkshire........	55
52.	BARMPTON TRINKET, by Barmpton, dam (12). Hon. J. B. Simpson. ...	110
53.	AMELIA, by Barmpton, dam by Cleveland (144), gr. d. by Comet, g. gr. d. by Favorite. J. White........	80

BULLS.

54.	MARSKE (418), 12 years old, by Favorite, dam by Favorite, gr. d. by Favorite, g. gr. d. by Punch, g. g. gr. d. by Hubback, g. g. g. gr. d. by the sire of Hubback, g. g. g. g. gr. d. by Sir James Pennyman's bull, descended from the stock of the late Sir W. St. Quintin, of Scampston. J. C. Maynard........	50
55.	NORTH STAR (459), 11 years old, by Favorite, dam Yellow Cow, by Punch. T. Lax, Ravensworth, Yorkshire........	72
56.	MIDAS (435), 10 years old, by Phenomenon, dam (1). S. Wiley........	270

Lot.		Guineas.
57.	BARMPTON (54), 8 years old, by George, dam (2). Being lame was not sold.	
58.	MAJOR (398), 5 years old, by Wellington, dam by Phenomenon, gr. d. by Favorite, g. gr. d. by Favorite. W. Brooks, Laceby, Lincolnshire. ...	185
59.	LANCASTER (360), 4 years old, by Wellington, dam (2). Hon. J. B Simpson and W. Smith, ...	621
60.	BARONET (62), 3 years old, by Wellington, dam (1). Being engaged, was not put up.	
61.	REGENT (544), 3 years old, by Wellington, dam Rosebud, by Windsor, gr. d. (1). Lord Althorp.	145

BULL CALVES.

62.	DIAMOND (206), 1 year old, by Lancaster, dam (19). Donaldson, Harburn House, Durham................	102
63.	ALBION (17), rising 1 year old, by Lancaster, dam by Wellington, gr. d. by Favorite, g. gr. d. by a son of Favorite. Russell, Brancepeth Castle, Durham..	140
64.	HAROLD (291), rising 1 year old, by Wellington, dam (7). J. Whitaker, Greenholme, Otley, Yorks..............................	201
65.	PILOT (496), rising 1 year old, by either Major or Wellington (being bulled by both), dam (1). J. Booth, Killerby, Yorkshire.	270

SUMMARY.

51 Cows and Heifers, average,............	£111 13s. 0d.	£5694	3s.
10 Bulls and Bull Calves, "	215 17 7	2158	16
61 averaged £128 14s. 9d.	Total,	£7852	19

ROBERT COLLING'S CLOSING SALE IN 1820.

The final closing sale of Robert Colling was made on October 3d, 1820, and like that of 1818, attracted wide attention. The account of it is thus given:

COWS.

Lot.		Guineas.
1.	SNOWDROP, 3 years old, by Wellington, dam by Favorite. G. Alderson, Ferrybridge. Bulled by Barmpton.................................	20
2.	OLD DINSDALE, 10 years old, by Phenomenon, dam by Favorite. J. Hepworth, Rogerthorpe, Pontefract, Yorks. Bulled by Barmpton....	27
3.	YOUNG DINSDALE, 6 years old, by Wellington, dam lot 2. W. Asheton, Brandon House, Coventry, Warwickshire. Bulled by Adonis (8).	54
4.	CRYSTAL, 5 years old, by Cleveland, dam by Comet, gr. d. by Favorite. R. Dobson, Bishop Auckland, Durham. Bulled by Young Lancaster (361)..	42
5.	LADY, 4 years old, by Wellington. S. Wiley, Brandsby, York. Bulled by Barmpton.......................................	26

Lot.		Guineas.
6. POMONA, 6 years old, by Wellington, dam by Favorite. J. G. Dixon, Holton-le-Moor, Lincolnshire. Bulled by Barmpton...............		27
7. CICELY, 12 years old, by Favorite, dam by Punch. W. Smith, Dishley, Leicestershire. Bulled by Barmpton............................		22
8. CHERRY, 5 years old, bought of G. Coates, near Darlington. R. Fletcher, Burdon, Yorkshire. Bulled by Barmpton........................		22
9. KATE, 3 years old, by Wellington. Major Rudd, Marton, Cleveland. Bulled by Barmpton..		28
10. WHITE ROSE, 5 years old, by Wellington. W. Jobson, Newtown, near Chillingham. Bulled by Barmpton..................................		51
11. STRAWBERRY, 5 years old, by Wellington, dam by Favorite. J. G. Dixon, Holton-le-Moor, Lincolnshire. Bulled by Barmpton...............		30

Lots 12 to 18, inclusive, were Horses.

TWO-YEAR-OLD HEIFERS.

19. IRIS, by Barmpton, dam Backwell, lot 10 in the sale catalogue for 1818. J. Hepworth. Bulled by Barmpton............................		19
20. WILDAIR, by Barmpton, dam Wildair, lot 7 in the sale, 1818. J. Graham, Netherby, Cumberland. Bulled by Barmpton......................		35
21. DIANA, by Young Barmpton (55), dam lot 3. P. Skipworth, Aylesby, Lincolnshire. Bulled by Barmpton.................................		51
22. DAISY, by Barmpton, dam Daisy, lot 24 in the sale, 1818. W. Donkin, Sandhoe, near Hexham. Bulled by Barmpton.......................		101
23. LILY, by Barmpton, dam Lily, lot 8 in the sale, 1818. G. Alderson, Ferrybridge. Bulled by Barmpton..................................		102
24. CAROLINE, calved in 1817, by Young Barmpton, dam Wildair, lot 7 in the sale, 1818. Dinning, Newlands, near Belford. Bulled by Barmpton.		53
25. DAMSEL, by Barmpton, dam lot 2. R. Jobson, Turvelaws, near Wooler, Northumberland. Bulled by Barmpton............................		58
26. COUNTESS, by Barmpton, dam Young Charlotte, lot 21 in the sale, 1818. W. Jobson. Bulled by Barmpton................................		68
27. YOUNG NONPAREIL, by Barmpton, dam Nonpareil, lot 23 in the sale, 1818. W. Smith. Bulled by Barmpton.............................		151
28. SALLY, by Alexander. W. Robinson, St. Helens Auckland, Durham. Bulled by Barmpton...		33
29. BELL, by Major. Henderson, Belford, Northumberland. Bulled by Barmpton..		16
30. ARABELLA, by Lancaster. Henderson. Bulled by Adonis.............		32

ONE-YEAR-OLD HEIFERS.

31. FLORA, a roan, by Lancaster. R. Ferguson, Harker Lodge, Carlisle....		15
32. LUCY, a roan, by Lancaster, dam by Favorite. Hon. J. B. Simpson. ...		30
33. BETSY, a mottled, by Lancaster. G. Alderson........................		14
34. MARY, a white, by Lancaster. G. Alderson.........................		10½
35. SPRIGHTLY, a light roan, by Lancaster. Dinning.....................		25

HEIFER CALVES, IN 1820.

Lot.		Guineas.
36.	Miss Colling, a roan, by Barmpton, dam lot 6. J. Claridge, Jerveaux Abbey, Yorkshire.	19
37.	A Light Roan, by Barmpton. Major Rudd.	11½
38.	Barmpton Strawberry, a red fleck, calved April 1, by Barmpton, dam lot 11. Hon. J. B. Simpson.	30
39.	A Roan, by Barmpton. W. Harrison, Neasham Lane, near Darlington.	6
40.	A Roan, by Barmpton. Major Rudd.	4½
41.	A Light Roan, by Barmpton. Major Rudd.	4
42.	Dinsdale, fleck red and white, by Barmpton, dam lot 2. W. Smith, Dishley.	22
43.	Miss Colling, a light roan, by Barmpton, dam lot 5. S. Wiley.	20
44.	A Red Roan, by Barmpton, dam lot 9. Major Rudd.	25
45.	A Fleck, by Barmpton, dam lot 3. S. Wiley.	17

BULLS.

46.	Barmpton (54), 10 years old, by George, dam Moss Rose, lot 2 in the sale, 1818. R. Thomas, Airy Holme, near Darlington.	115
47.	Baronet (62), 5 years old, by Wellington, dam Red Rose, lot 1 in the sale, 1818. Sir C. Loraine, Bart., Kirk Harle, Northumberland.	350
48.	Young Barmpton (55), 3 years old, by Wellington, dam a daughter of Juno, lot 3 in the sale, 1818. J. Graham.	130

BULLS ONE YEAR OLD.

49.	Young Lancaster (361), by Lancaster, dam lot 3. J. Pearson, Acklam, Cleveland.	73
50.	Adonis (8), by Lancaster. H. Vansittart, Kirkleatham, Yorkshire.	50

BULL CALVES.

51.	A Light Roan, by Barmpton, dam lot 4. M. Culley, Fowberry, Northumberland.	16
52.	Eclipse (238), a light roan, calved in July, 1820, by Barmpton, dam lot 27. T. Charge, Newton, Yorkshire.	100
53.	A Light Roan, by Barmpton, dam lot 1. Clayton, Halnaby, Yorkshire.	10

SUMMARY.

38 Cows and Heifers, average,	£ 36 10s. 4d.	£1387 11s. 6d.	
8 Bulls and Calves, "	110 15 6	886 4 0	
46 averaged £49 8s. 7d.	Total,	£2273 15 6	

Total of the two sales, £10,126 14s. 6d. Average of 107 head, £94 12s. 10d.

Following this last sale we find a running summary of Robert Colling's herd and breeding in Thornton's Circular. Although in some parts it has been already given in previous pages, it is so full of connected interest that we insert it entire:

"Robert Colling, the elder of the two brothers, was born at Skerningham, and when a youth was apprenticed to a large grocer; his health being delicate he returned home and joined his brother Charles in partnership, until Charles went to Ketton, and Robert took the Barmpton farm in the spring of 1783, having previously resided at Hurworth; he often visited Mr. Culley, and imitated many of his principles of farming, more especially turnip growing, and in later years his own farming at Barmpton became high and excellent in every degree. For many years his Leicester sheep, which were obained from Bakewell, were more successful than his Short-horns, and his Ram shows or lettings were continued for many years. Mr. Wiley, of Brandsby, took sheep of him for fourteen years in succession, and upon one particular occasion asked him what a good Short-horn should be like. Pointing to one of his finest tups, called Shoulders (from the excellence of that point), Mr. Colling advised him to breed his cattle like that. A favorite expression of his was to liken his cattle to a barrel; he did not approve of the breast being very prominent, preferring it rather short but very thick and wide, especially between the fore legs, as he generally considered beasts with very prominent breasts had thin shoulders and chine, and lacked width and substance in their fore quarters.

"Improved Short-horns, however, did not at first attract his attention. Sheep were the profit of the farm, and no doubt in later days the ram lettings led to bull hirings, as they do at Aylesby, at Givendale, at Brandsby, and elsewhere, even to this day. Bailey wrote in 1810, after an experience of Durham county for forty years, that 'Robert Colling has frequently crossed with the improved Short-horned bulls and the best Kyloe cows he could procure; the produce made very fat and much earlier than the pure Kyloe; but he has now given it up, finding that the pure improved Short-horns are more profitable.'

"Although Mr. Robert Colling had several tribes, and went to different breeders for his original cattle, yet the majority of those animals which were sold in the 1818 sale, were descended from four families, of which some account will now be given.

"It appears that some of his earliest stock came from Mr. Milbank of Barningham, about 1780. These were supposed to be the best Teeswater cattle, and noted for their excellent grazing properties. The original of the Yellow Cow, by Punch (531), came from this stock; and her descendants were Venus, lot 19; Clara, lot 29; and Diamond (206), lot 62, got by Lancaster (360), out of Venus, all sold for high prices in the 1818 sale. Of Diamond, Mr. Dickson in an essay on judging, said that he was small, of beautiful symmetry, and a perfect model, with a thick, fine coat. The Yellow Cow, by Punch, bred a heifer,* by Favorite (252), which heifer was the dam of the 'White Heifer that Traveled.' No record gives the date of this white heifer's birth (supposed 1806), but the fashion at that time of feeding to an enormous weight, and the success of John Day in his wanderings with the Durham Ox, induced two butchers to purchase her for exhibition. Unlike John Day, they left no pamphlet of the 'pure genuine breed,' nor of their travels throughout the country. A small handbill alone tells of the merits of the White Heifer; it runs as follows:

"'To be seen at the stables of the Three Kings, Piccadilly, near the Glo'ster Coffee House, the greatest wonder in the world of the kind, the wonderful Durham fat heifer, of the improved Short-horned breed, which weighs 306 stone (8 lbs.) [2,448 lbs.], bred and fed by Robert Colling, of Barmpton, near Darlington, in the county of Durham. She is sister *(half sister by the sire)* to the Durham Ox and bull Comet (155), which was sold for 1000 guineas at the sale of Charles Colling, Esq., at Ketton, for which 1500 guineas has since been offered. This heifer is now the property of Messrs. Robinson and Spark. It is particularly worthy of notice that this justly-celebrated heifer was a twin.† A correct portrait of this beautiful heifer has been taken by Mr. Weaver, of Shrewsbury, from which an engraving (by Mr. Ward, an eminent artist in London) and prints taken from it are published at one guinea each.‡ Printed by Mr. Glendon, Rupert street, Haymarket.'

"Mr. Bailey said also, that 'Mr. Robert Colling has a white heifer, four years old, a perfect counterpart of his brother Charles' ox, being, like him, completely covered over her whole carcass with fat; she is estimated to weigh 130 stone (14 lbs.), [1820 lbs.] Mr. Robert Colling also sold at Darlington Market, April 18, 1808, a two-year-old steer for £22, supposed to weigh 63 stone (14 lbs.), the price of the fat stock being 7s. per stone. The Yellow Cow put to Favorite (252), produced lot 55, North Star (459). At the time of the sale he was eleven years old, a grand old bull, with fine hair and handling. Mr. Wetherell used him at Holme House two years, Mr. Wiley had

---

* Called "Favorite Cow," recorded p. 310, Vol. 1, English Herd Book.—L. F. A.

† She was twinned with a bull—a free marten, and of course, barren.—L. F. A.

‡ White Heifer's portrait is frontispiece to Vol. 5, American Herd Book.—L. F. A.

Page 84.

On stone by J. R. Page.

THE WHITE HEIFER THAT TRAVELLED

Compton, Cosack & Co., Buffalo.

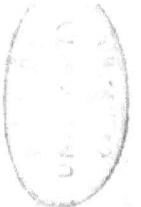

him also for a period at 120 guineas, and Mr. Hustler also. He was sire of the highest priced heifer, Sweetbrier, lot 60, and of Golden Pippin, lot 9. Venus appears to have bred a bull, Adonis (7), and a heifer with the Hon. J. B. Simpson, and Clara two bulls—one of them Eryholme (1018), and a heifer with Mr. Thomas. Sir H. Vane Tempest bought Tragedy of this tribe privately from Mr. Robert Colling, and through Sir Charles Knightley's herd we believe descendants of this line may still be traced.

"Another tribe (Wildair or Hubback tribe) came originally from the stock of Sir William St. Quintin, of Scampston. This was a favorite family with Mr. Robert Colling, who considered (Major Rudd stated) that this tribe came from the same source as Hubback (319). Juno, lot 3, and Diana, lot 4, sisters, were of it, also Wildair, lot 7, and Nonpareil, lot 23, the highest priced cow, a fine roan, considered the best animal in the sale, and one of the finest cows ever seen. Her heifer, Sweetbrier, lot 38, bought by Mr. Maynard, was a red and white, and made the greatest price among the heifers. Marske (418) was of this family, and although in his twelfth year made 50 guineas. He had previously been hired by Mr. Hutton, of Marske, whence his name; by Mr. Bates, and Lord Strathmore. Earl Spencer was not fortunate with those he purchased, as most of their produce died or brought bull calves. Nor was the Hon. J. B. Simpson lucky with his. At Mr. Maynard's sale in 1839, descendants of Sweetbrier, made the highest prices. One of them, May Rose (103 guineas), was bought by Mr. Wetherell for Mr. Fox, Ireland, with whom she bred four calves, and was purchased in 1841 by Mr. Parkinson, of Ley Fields. Formosa (38 guineas), out of May Rose's dam, was bought as a heifer by Mr. Houldsworth, of Farnsfield, and at his sale in 1841, Mr. Torr bought her heifer, Flora of Farnsfield, as a yearling, for 41 guineas. It is from this heifer that the Flower tribe, the finest animals at Aylesby, are bred, and which trace directly back to this favorite family of Mr. Robert Colling. Lord Feversham's Wildair bred one heifer, Phœnix, and four bulls, amongst them Emperor (1013). At Barmpton she first produced Caroline, lot 16, and the celebrated bull Harold (291), lot 64. This bull, a white, was used by Mr. Wiley, and went to Messrs. Whitaker, Alderson, and Earnshaw. In the 1820 sale the highest priced female is also of this tribe, viz.: Young Nonpareil, lot 27, sold for 151 guineas to Mr. W. Smith. She bred three bulls, and was sold in 1827 to the Earl of Chesterfield. Her son, lot 52, Eclipse (238), was used by Messrs. Craddock & Charge.

"Golden Pippin, lot 9, and Clarissa, lot 17, were evidently from one tribe (Beauty or Punch tribe); Mr. Colling got it from Mr. G. Best, of Manfield, and it traces further back than is stated in the catalogue. Beauty, who was from the cow that bred Punch (531), took a first premium at Darlington; her excellence brought Punch (531), a yellow red bull, into notice. Punch was the sire of the dam of Charles Colling's Old Daisy, whose granddaughter, Lily, was the highest priced cow at the Ketton sale. Also of Ben (70), and Twin Brother to Ben (660), both used by Mr. Booth. Mr. Robert Colling said that Ben had the best blood, and he begot the dam of Red Rose, lot 1, and Old Wildair, own sister to the celebrated bull Phenomenon (491), used by Sir H. Vane Tempest, and whom Mr. Parrington considered a finer bull than Comet (155). This line of blood is happily yet preserved. Mr. Whitaker bred Nonsuch and others from Golden Pippin; the family then went to Mr. Maynard, from whom it has passed by various changes, under the name of Nonsuch, to the present possessor, Mr. Adkins, of Milcote.

"There is no record from whence the Red Rose* tribe, lot 1, came. She was own sister to the American Cow, the first female named in the now fashionable Cambridge Rose line. It is said that the American Cow got her name from going out to America early in the century.† She was bred by R. Colling, and sold by him when a yearling to go to America. When the stock of Red Rose and Moss Rose became of such note she was brought back by Mr. Hustler to England, and produced at Acklam in 1811, Red Rose, by Yarborough (705), for which Mr. Hustler refused 400 guineas, and which Mr. Bates bought in 1819. At the time of the sale Red Rose, then seventeen years old, had been a magnificent cow, but was very patchy; she had large cushions of fat on her rumps, whilst her fore quarters were light. Moss Rose, lot 2, her daughter by her own sire, was a very good cow, a handsome roan, very even, wide and massive, of fine symmetry and quality, but by some thought to be rather small. Red Rose had been a regular and excellent breeder, more especially of bulls, among which were Miner (441), used by Lord Strathmore and Mr. Jobling, with whom he got Wellington (683), Midas (435), lot 56, a great, fine bull, with hind quarters super-excellent, Baronet (62), lot 60, and Pilot (496), lot 65, also the granddam of Lord Althorpe's Regent (544), lot 61. Of these bulls, Midas (435), had been let to Mr. Robertson, Ladykirk, for three years at 300 gs., to Mr. Arbuthnot for

---

* Calved in 1801, English Herd Book, Vol. 1, p. 456.—L. F. A.
† See page 54, *ante*.—L. F. A.

two years, at 300 gs., and into Yorkshire, making altogether, in lettings and sale, 1100 guineas. Sir W. Cooke bid for him, but Mr. Wiley bought him for 270 guineas. He died suddenly at Brandsby, having got only two calves. Mr. Wiley returned to Mr. Colling greatly disappointed, and asked for the use of Barmpton (54), but Mr. Colling would not part with him then to anybody, as he considered him one of the best bulls he ever had. The two calves, however, turned out to Mr. Wiley a great profit; one was Midas (1230), and the other the famous Grazier (1085). This bull became a great celebrity; he was used three years by Sir John Johnstone, who christened him Grazier on account of his good qualities. Mr. W. Smith, West Rasen, had him two years, Mr. Slater one year, and Lord Feversham and the Earl of Carlisle for some time. He then went home and was used by Mr. Wiley, and afterwards, in his old age, by Sir John Ramsden, with whom he died in his fourteenth year, and was buried in his skin. He was a fine, massive bull, a dark red, and a little white in his fore quarters. Baronet (62), also a good bull, was hired by Sir Charles Loraine, who bought him in 1820, and took in five cows of Mr. Wetherell's at 10 guineas ($52) each. Pilot (496) has been described in Mr. Carr's History of the Booth Cattle; he was a red and white, rather a small bull, but of good quality and a good stock getter. At the time of the sale, Mr. J. G. Dixon and Major Brown joined purses in order to buy a good bull, and Mr. Dixon bid from 100 to 250 guineas, at 10 guineas biddings, opposed by Mr. Thomas Booth, who bought him for 270 guineas ($1,404).

"Red Rose's daughter, Rosette, lot 20, made 300 guineas, and bred four heifers, of which there is now no trace. At eleven years old she was sold at Lord Althorp's sale in 1825, for 25 guineas. Ruby, lot 32, made the second highest female price, 331 guineas, and went into Mr. Robson's large herd, which is said to have contained more grand cows than any other herd in Lincolnshire. Moss Rose bred four calves, three bulls—Barmpton (54), Lancaster (360), and one that died young—and one heifer, lot 18, Young Moss Rose, which went to Lord Feversham for 190 guineas. She produced one heifer, lot 33, at Barmpton, which went, with Ruby, lot 32, into Lincolnshire, and two heifers at Duncombe, from one of which, Beauty, by Baron (38), we have descendants even now at Stockeld Park. Barmpton (54) was a small-sized, beautiful roan bull, as neat as his dam, and got splendid stock; he had a very broad back, fine quarters, but rather upright shoulders, and most of the heifer calves at both sales were by him. Mr. John Wright used him two years, first at 60, and then 70 guineas, and he was also let to Mr. Brooks and Mr. Codd in Lincolnshire; his stock were considered to be better than North Star's (459). His sire, George (275), was a very magnificent bull, and an excellent getter; he fell by accident and broke his neck, not before, however, Mr. Colling had sold privately five out of his six heifers at 200 guineas each. He was out of Lady Grace, the dam of Empress, lot 15, a grand animal, and a high priced one; Mr. Champion bought her and her daughter, lot 49, but there is none of the tribe left now. Lancaster (360) was a white bull, of fine quality, but narrow, thin, lanky, and small; he was let as a yearling, to Major Rudd, who, at the time of the sale, had fourteen extraordinary two-year-old heifers, got by him, in one pasture, which were the talk of the country. This, perhaps, with the fact of his being from so grand a cow, and having served all the stock, made him sell so high. Mr. Whitaker was the chief opponent, and at 620 guineas claimed the bull; the auctioneer, however, ruled against him, having had another guinea bid by Messrs. Simpson & Smith. Mr. Whitaker then had Mr. Charge's bull, Frederick (1060). A rumor was current that Lancaster was delicate and unhealthy, but he got stock at Dishley till 1827 [then 14 years old], and at the Hon. H. B. Simpson's sale in 1838, Mr. White, the auctioneer, alluded to this rumor, and said there were animals ten years of age before the bull left the farm. Besides the Cambridge Roses and those at Stockeld Park, we believe there are a very few animals remaining that can now be traced to this magnificent family.

"The two high priced heifers, lots 41 and 43, bought by Mr. Wetherell, were unfortunate; when of age they were sent for service to Mr. Mason's, at 15 guineas each. Lady Ann died in calf with twins, and Cleopatra had a heifer calf that never bred; they were two magnificent heifers. Lot 40, Cowslip, bred a heifer by Ratify (2481), called Young Cowslip. This heifer was sold to Mr. Dudding, of Panton, and produced a large family, from which came Mr. Rich's Ursula tribe, and many others from the Panton sales.

"Of the other sources whence Mr. Robert Colling derived his stock, little is known, except that, like Charles, he selected the best county stock from his neighbors, and occasionally bought at Yarm fair. Mr. Watson, of Stapleton, Mr. Alexander Hall, of Haughton, Mr. Wright, and Mr. Best, of Manfield, supplied females, and some came from Mr. Hill, of Blackwell (see lot 10). It was from this stock of Mr. Hill's that Captain Turnell, of Reasby, Lincolnshire, got his first cattle, which were the originals of the well known and still favorite red Turnell blood in South Lincolnshire. The following letter from Mr. Hutchinson relates to lots 35 and 36:

"'In October, 1818, when Mr. Robert Colling's sale catalogue came out, I was glad to perceive two heifers, Jessy and Jewel (twins); their dam from the stock of the late Mr. Hill, of Blackwell, were there advertised, got by Wellington (680), and the former in calf to Barmpton (54), both bulls highly esteemed, and Jessy herself what I thought an excellent heifer, and the better of the two. My idea was that this heifer from the Blackwell herd, with only two crosses by the leading bull of Mr. R. Colling's, would be a better speculation and more likely to breed better stock than any cow or heifer of what was then considered pure blood, all of which had been bred through thick and thin for countless generations. On Jessy's coming to the hammer, I became her purchaser at 43 guineas, the very lowest priced cow that day, excepting a six-year-old cow of the same breed, Old Blackwell; and Mr. Brown, of Welbourn, Lincolnshire, immediately after bought Jewel, her twin sister, at 50 guineas. I was well satisfied with my bargain, and Mr. Brown expressed himself so with his. In the April following Jessy produced me a heifer calf, very small and very delicate, which, however, with great care was reared, and is now the heifer I invite connoisseurs to inspect. She is a wonderful and beautiful sight, and may safely challenge a comparison for excellence with the highest priced cows of that day. Jessy has since produced me two heifers to my own bulls, which promise to make very large, fine cows, and she is now giving twelve quarts of milk at a meal, six months after calving.'

"The sale in 1820 contained those Short-horns which were not in condition for sale in 1818. At this sale, Mr. J. G. Dixon of Caistor was the purchaser of two lots. Mrs. Charles Colling was present and told him that Barmpton's blood should always be kept sight of, as he was one of their best tribes. Strawberry was intended for the first sale, but she calved and did not do well, and so was reserved till 1820. On the long walk home she slipped calf, but bred well afterwards. Young Strawberry, her daughter, took a prize at sixteen years old, and lived till she was twenty-seven.* Descendants of these cows are still in Mr. Dixon's possession, and their bull produce has been disseminated among the farmers in Lincolnshire to the great improvement of the stock in the district.

---

* Who will say that the Short-horns, as a race, lack either constitution, vitality, fertility in breeding, or longevity?—L. F. A.

"Hubback was one of the first bulls Mr. Robert Colling used, of which an account is given in the Ketton Short-horns. He had seventeen cows served by him in the season, and in November, as the bull was bought at Easter, Mr. Charles Colling said if the bull was done with for the season he would give 8 guineas for him; he was sold, the original cost, 10 guineas, being divided by Mr. Robert Colling and Mr. Waistell. The bull took offense at a gray pony Mr. Robert Colling used to ride, and was a little troublesome. Manfield (404) was used at a very early period. Broken Horn (95), appears to have succeeded Hubback, and was followed by Punch (531), Favorite (252), Comet (155), Wellington (680), a very fine bull, used four seasons, and others as in the catalogue. He also had the use of his brother's bulls at Ketton.

"Northumberland, Durham, Yorkshire and Lincolnshire, supplied most of the bull hirers, and the buyers at the sales came from those counties as well as Nottingham, Leicester, and Northampton. Culley, in his general view of the Agriculture of Northumberland, says, 'hiring bulls for the season is practiced in this county; as high as 50 guineas have been paid for a bull of the Short-horn breed for one season, and from 3 to 5 guineas given for serving a cow, but the more common rate is a guinea.' The principal hirers were Lord Strathmore, Sir H. Vane Tempest, Sir G. Strickland, Mr. Robertson, Mr. Jobling, Mr. Jobson, Mr. Gibson, Colonel Trotter, Major Rudd, Mr. Baker, Mr. Barker, Mr. Booth, Mr. Buston, Mr. Hustler, Mr. Wetherell, and Mr. Wiley. Mr. Jobson also stated that prior to 1773 his father got bulls from Durham, and the last cross of the well known Sonsie tribe is a Son of Ben (70), or Punch (531).

"At the sale in 1818 Mr. Robert Colling was asked, 'Who has your best blood?' 'Well, I think,' said he, 'Lincolnshire has got most of my best blood.' The breeders from Lincolnshire, who hired, were Mr. R. Ostler and Mr. Skipworth at Aylesby; Mr. W. Brooks and Mr. R. Cropper at Laceby; Mr. J. Grant, Wyham; and Mr. J. Codd, Holton, all living in the district between Grimsby and Caistor. The bulls were slightly shod and walked down about eight or nine miles a day, and age had little consideration. The most noted bulls were Own Brother to the White Heifer [that Traveled], Colling's (Robert) White Bull (151), Aylesby (44), Barmpton (54), and Major (398). C. Colling's Major (397), bought at the Ketton sale, was thought the handsomer and better of the two.

"There is no mention made in this paper of Sir H. Vane Tempest's celebrated cow Princess, nor of Col. Trotter's stock, both of whom, as well as Mr. Robertson, Mr. Champion, and others, bought privately from Mr. R. Colling. The Princess tribe may possibly be noticed in a future paper, when Sir H. Vane Tempest's catalogue is reprinted, but the name of the Sylphs (Sweethearts and Charmers) and the Mantalinis, the former tracing from 'Russell,' the latter from 'Alpine,' both cows by Robert Colling's Son of Favorite (252) [the Son being out of a Punch cow] and from Col. Trotter's herd, are high evidence, even in the present day, of the excellence of the original Barmpton stock.

"It has been said that Robert Colling's stock were delicate; there is little foundation for this, and it may have arisen from the delicacy of Mr. Champion's cattle; Mr. Paley said that the rottenness of the Warrior (673) family came from Diana, lot 3, and Mr. Champion's son attributed it to Mason's Charles (127); Mr. Bates also attributed delicacy to Mason's St. John (572). Land and atmosphere may have had something to do with this. Those who saw the herd in its best days, before and at the sales, say that the cattle were always seen in good condition and shewed vigorous constitutions; it is, however, a singular fact that we have now scarcely any stock remaining from those animals that went into the Retford (Notts) district, whilst there are numbers tracing from that blood which went into Yorkshire, Lincolnshire, and the Lake district, where the yellow roan and red were looked upon as the pure breed, the dark red being held in no favor.*

"Although the average of the Barmpton sale, 1818, was under that of Ketton, 1810,† there is every reason to believe that it was a better sale. In 1810 things were at war price and everything high, whilst in 1818 there was peace, and a general depression upon agriculture. The Alloy blood, too, in the Ketton stock tended to promote competition for the purer strains at Barmpton. The bulls are said by Mr. Wetherell to have been the finest lot he ever saw at one sale. They doubled the average of the cows, and, taking the highest priced family at Ketton against the highest priced one at Barmpton, we have the following result in favor of the Barmpton stock: At Ketton, the Phœnix tribe, sixteen (including Comet 1000 guineas) averaged £221 3s.; at Barmpton, the Red Rose tribe, eleven (including Lancaster 621 guineas) averaged £269 3s. 6d.; and the thirteen favorite Wildairs averaged £142 17s. 6d.

---

* The strong partiality to a *deep* red color in Short-horns, which now prevails among a large majority of the American breeders, and which we think a mistaken partiality, had then no existence among the English breeders.—L. F. A.

† Charles Colling's sale.—L. F. A.

"Mr. Robert Colling always opposed his brother using [the Alloy] Grandson of Bolingbroke (280), and told Mr. Wiley that he did not consider his brother's herd nor his own better than other good herds, except the Phœnix tribe. In 1815 he stated that 'whatever I know of the art of breeding cattle I owe to the late Mr. George Culley.'* He [Robert Colling] was a stately, reserved man, the opposite to his brother Charles, kind in his manner and straightforward in all his dealings, keeping a good house and high company, and was liked by all who knew him. Robert was one of the earliest disciples and most intimate friends of the great Bakewell, and there is little doubt that Bakewell's great principle of in-and-in breeding was carried out most successfully by the Collings. Father to daughter and mother to son, were the principal direct alliances, and the system was continued so long as robustness and form were upheld."†

Comparing the two herds of Robert and Charles, somewhat different opinions were entertained by their contemporaries of the superiority of one over the other. Both of them bred animals of marked excellence and fame in their own time, and that excellence and fame have been perpetuated through their blood down to the present day. Robert, in his personal character, was more quiet and reticent; Charles, the more active, self-confident, and prominent before the public. Robert was equally sound in judgment, dabbling in no experiments, while Charles was more or less versatile in both opinion and practice. In a striking and no doubt accurate portrait of the two brothers in our possession, that of Robert is remarkably good-looking and portly, the features of the face expressive of an honest, upright man. That of Charles, although still portly in look, is less handsome than his brother; the face has not an equal frankness, and a little cunning, withal, seems lurking in the expression.

---

* Culley was an advocate of Bakewell's system of breeding.—L. F. A.

† We have no account that the "robustness and form" ever died out while the in-and-in breeding stock remained in the hands of the Collings.—L. F. A.

DID THE COLLINGS IMPROVE THE QUALITY OF THE SHORT-HORNS ABOVE THEIR EXISTING CONDITION WHEN THEY COMMENCED BREEDING? WERE THE COLLINGS' HERDS SUPERIOR TO THOSE OF THEIR CONTEMPORARY BREEDERS AT THE TIMES OF THEIR FINAL SALES?

After discussing at such length as we have already done the practice in breeding by the Collings, it may seem superfluous to add another word. We have seen that they were men of sagacity and enterprise; that they found, in the outset of their breeding life, the Short-horns a *local*, although ancient breed, existing in but a few counties of the north-eastern quarter of England; that although these cattle possessed admirable qualities in themselves, and of great value, through the crosses of their blood, as instruments to improve the general herds then existing in other sections of the Short-horn region, they were still little known beyond their own immediate localities. In view of these facts, when establishing their own herds they selected the best animals within their reach, bred them with success, and determined to make them known, and give them a currency throughout those parts of the kingdom where they hitherto had been, and measurably were still strangers. In this they succeeded. Not only did they so succeed, but by adopting a course of breeding at that time, and in their own immediate section, almost if not altogether unpracticed, they reared superior cattle to many of the herds around them, and drew public attention conspicuously to their own herds and to their modes of breeding.

It is possible that some of their contemporaries may have charged them with a species of *pretension* in their practice, but as their course of breeding was open and well known to those around them, and they relied on public favor to sustain their efforts by purchases of their stock, it is to be presumed their persistence in the course which they had adopted was on the conviction that it was the correct one, leading to the largest success, not only in a pecuniary result, but in the improvement of their stock to the highest perfection of their day. Such, it appears, was the conclusion of those who closely studied their practice, and to the Collings should be awarded the credit of success.

Not but that there were other breeders—unnamed, or but slightly alluded to in these pages—who, by a different course of breeding, had produced animals equally good as those of the Collings', but by their less active enterprise they failed to achieve that notoriety and high position which the Collings attained and held until they retired from the pursuit. The blood of their stocks, from their frequent bull sales and lettings became widely disseminated through other herds, far and near. Many of their cows were distributed by sales into neighboring as well as distant herds, and the agricultural public at large were benefited, so far as it chose to be, by their labors.

One thing is certain, more good Short-horns for eighty years past, trace their pedigrees into the blood of the Colling bulls, through the Herd Books, than into the bulls of any twenty other English breeders put together, which may be deemed circumstantial if not positive testimony of the successful results of their breeding. "All," to be sure, "is not gold that glitters," as we have seen too much of assumption in our own day to believe that all men are benefactors who receive the laudations of the public for acts in which, were the truth wholly known, other less pretentious parties would have the credit; yet it is but justice that we record a testimonial of his old friends and neighbors, awarded to Charles on his retirement from breeding, soon after the public sale of his stock. It was the offering of a valuable piece of plate with the following inscription:

<blockquote>
PRESENTED TO
MR. CHARLES COLLING,
THE GREAT IMPROVER OF THE SHORT-HORNED BREED OF CATTLE,
BY THE BREEDERS
(Upwards of fifty),
WHOSE NAMES ARE ANNEXED,
AS A TOKEN OF GRATITUDE DUE FOR THE BENEFIT THEY HAVE DERIVED FROM HIS JUDGMENT,
AND ALSO AS A TESTIMONY OF THEIR ESTEEM FOR HIM AS A MAN.
1810.
</blockquote>

The address and adroitness of Charles may possibly have had something to do with this exclusive testimonial, to a share in which we think his brother Robert was equally entitled. Uncharitable minds might liken it to the defrauding of Esau of his birthright by his more cunning brother Jacob, but as the more generous Robert did not complain, we may suppose the offering to be an honest one, so far as Charles was concerned. In summing up the labors of the brothers Colling, from all the evidence we have been enabled to glean—not forgetting the meritorious efforts of many of their contemporary breeders—they may be said, Robert equally with Charles, to have improved the many admirable qualities of the Short-horns, and in such result merited the appellation of benefactors.

CHAPTER IV.

THE BOOTH FAMILY AND THEIR SHORT-HORNS.

IN chronological order, next to the Collings, among the prominent earlier breeders come the Booths. As our account must of necessity be an intermixture of their several names in the notices of their herds, an explanation of their personalities will, as we proceed, become necessary.

Thomas Booth, the elder and first of the family connected with Short-horn breeding, was contemporary with the Collings. His grandson, the present Thomas C. Booth, related to the late Richard L. Allen, of New York, who met him at the great Yorkshire Agricultural Show, in August, 1869, that "his grandfather began breeding Short-horns in 1777, at or near Studley Park, and was a neighbor and rival of Robert and Charles Colling." Yet we have no particular account of the earlier animals of his breeding, or what was their particular character. We find no record of animals of their herd earlier than such as are recorded in Vol. 1, E. H. B., where all their animals trace their genealogy into bulls bred by the Collings, from which it is presumed that they derived their stock on the sires' side chiefly, or altogether, from them some years after they began breeding; so that the elder Booth in the production of the stock which gave him his chief celebrity bred them from the Colling bulls. The legitimate foundation of his herds may be dated at Killerby, in Yorkshire, about the year 1790. Previous to this he had become the owner of the estates of Killerby and Warlaby, not far apart, and at no great distance from Darlington, and within easy access to the places then occupied by the brothers Colling. Thomas Booth had two sons, Richard and John, both of whom afterwards became Short-horn breeders, conjointly with, and succeeding their father. Of the brothers, Richard was probably the most skillful, and being through life a bachelor, with no family cares to divert his attention, his sympathies and affections were chiefly absorbed in the propagation and improvement of his stock; John was also a good Short-horn breeder. Like the brothers Colling, they interchanged, and bred mainly from the same sources of blood.

Passing from the stage, a valuable portion of the herds of the brothers fell into possession of the present Thomas C. Booth, of Warlaby, son of John, and nephew to Richard. He is *the* Booth of the present day, although his brother John and *his* son J. C. Booth, of Killerby, are also Short-horn breeders to some extent, and chiefly in the stocks of the family tribe.

With these preliminaries, necessary to the future narration of their herds, we are fortunately favored with "The History of the Rise and Progress of the Killerby, Studley, and Warlaby herds of Short-horns, by William Carr," published in London in 1867. This work, although highly laudatory, and written apparently with a view of giving a special prominence to the "Booth blood," is valuable in the many facts it contains touching the career of the earlier Booths, and their course of breeding, as also for its many hints and suggestions profitable to breeders of the present day, and the information it conveys of the dissemination of their animals. The book itself is scholarly in style, graphic in narration, and if a poetic or imaginative tint is now and then detected in its pages, they may be imputed only to the enthusiasm of the author, and not to a disposition to mislead the reader into a false estimate of the noble animals he so partially exalts.

We can do no better, perhaps, than to quote literally from the work in question, with occasional explanatory notes of our own, in order to give the reader a true history, so far as may be necessary for our purpose, of the Booth Short-horns:

"Mr. Thomas Booth was no servile imitator. He was a contemporary of the Collings, and began his career quite independently of them, as an improver of the cattle of the same district, and he commenced it nearly at the same time. Mr. Booth had been a breeder of Short-horns many years when the celebrated Durham Ox, bred by Mr. Charles Colling, was first exhibited throughout the kingdom, and drew universal attention to the Short-horns. He afterwards did what wisdom dictated, availed himself of the Collings' best blood, and incorporated it with his own; while his sons and grandsons at Killerby, at Studley, and at Warlaby, have continued the same herd down to the present time, and given it a world-wide fame.

"Previously to the year 1790 Mr. Thomas Booth, who was then the owner of the Warlaby and Killerby estates, and farmed them both, commenced at Killerby the breeding of Short-horns. * * * He obtained his rudimentary stock from some of the best specimens of these Teeswater Short-horns. He appears to have proceeded on the principle that whilst the general similitude and mingled qualities of both parents descend to the offspring, the external conformation—subject, of course, to some modification by the other parent—is *mainly* imparted by the male, and the vital and nutritive organs by the female. Acting on this hypothesis, he was careful to select such well-framed cows only as evinced, by an ample capacity of chest, a robust constitution and a predisposition to fatten, and such moderate sized males as possessed in the highest degree then attainable the particular external points and proportions he deemed desirable to impress upon his herd. A dairy farmer under Lord Harewood, a Mr. Broader,* of Fairholme, in the parish of Ainderby, appears to have possessed some cows having the qualifications required. Tradition speaks of them as unusually fine cattle for that period; good dairy cows, and great grazers when dry; somewhat incompact in frame, and steerish in appearance,† but of very robust constitution. Previously to the year 1790, Mr. Thomas Booth had bought some calves from these cows. Strawberry Fairholme, Hazel (*i. e.* flecked roan) Fairholme, and Eight-and-twenty-shilling Fairholme, purchased from Mr. Broader's farm, have the honor of being the ancestresses of several illustrious families of Short-horns.

"I have said that Mr. Thomas Booth selected *moderate-sized* males. His observant eye had recognized, as indispensable to any improvement in the symmetry of these Teeswater animals, the necessity of reducing in size and stature their large, loosely-knit frames. With this view he decided on selecting his bulls from the stock of his contemporaries, Messrs. Robert and Charles Colling, who had themselves, to some extent, effected this reduction of size,‡ and improvement of form and fattening capacity in their stock, chiefly through the use of Hubback, a small, short-legged bull. Twin Brother to Ben (660), bred by the Collings, and Booth's Son of Twin Brother to Ben (88), were the first bulls used by Mr. Thomas Booth to these Fairholme heifers. These bulls had the short legs, the long and level hind quarters, the firm backs and good twists, to which Mr. Thomas

---

* Mr. Broader's cattle do not appear among the early records of the English Herd Book. He probably kept nothing but notes of his herd, if he kept pedigrees at all.—L. F. A.

† That "steerish" appearance, in the *heads*, particularly, still appertains to many of the *purely* bred Booth cows of the present day.—L. F. A.

‡ It might be a *reduction in size*, but it was an actual *increase of weight* which the Collings effected by breeding smaller boned, more compact and massive animals, than their progenitors.—L. F. A.

Booth attached so much importance, and their offspring amply testified to his discrimination. It is recorded that one cow by the former, and her daughter by the latter bull, produced six calves in one year, the dam having twice produced twins, and the daughter once. Four of these calves were heifers. Some of the offspring were very superior cows. In proof of the excellent foundation they afforded for the formation of a herd, it is affirmed on high authority that one of the Twin Brother to Ben cows produced, to Son of Twin Brother to Ben, a cow quite equal to Faith, by Raspberry, the dam of the famous Hope. Many of the cows were deep milkers, but running dry sooner than was then usual, when they gained flesh very rapidly. The late Mr. Ewbank, of Sober Hill, questioning the milking capacity of some of them in this condition, Mr. Thomas Booth pointed to their broad backs, and exclaimed, 'Look there! that is worth a few pints of milk!' These cows were further open to Mr. Ewbanks criticism as having *raw* noses, as he contemptuously termed that feature when flesh-colored; alleging that in *his* early days the farm stock was nearly all *black-nosed*, and that he never knew a raw-nosed cow that was not delicate—a prejudice which has long since passed away.

"Having thus judiciously selected the best animals procurable of both sexes, Mr. T. Booth was careful to pair such, and such only, of the produce of these unions as presented in a satisfactory degree the desired characteristics, with animals possessing them in equal or greater measure, and unsparingly to reject—especially from his male stock—all such as were not up to the required standard. Having by these means succeeded in developing and establishing in his herd a definite and uniform character, he sought to ensure its perpetuation by breeding from rather close affinities, as in his opinion the only security for the unfailing transmission, and transmission in an increased ratio, of these acquired distinctions to the offspring. In tracing the pedigrees of these herds, it will be seen that from the earliest period the same system of breeding from close relations which was pursued by the Collings was followed by the Booths. An examination of the pedigree of Lady Maynard (*alias* the cow Favorite) will show to what a length the system was carried by the earlier breeders, and how closely the first families of the Colling strain were allied to the Booth tribes. Further proof of this may be found in the pedigrees of the earliest bulls used by Mr. Thomas Booth, namely, Twin Brother to Ben (660), Suworrow (636), Albion (14), Pilot (496), and Marshal Beresford (415). Take, for example, the three last named. Albion—purchased at Mr. Charles Colling's sale in 1810, by Mr. T. Booth, Sr., for 60 guineas, when a calf—was by a bull which was both a son and grandson of Favorite (252); his dam was by a son of Favorite, and his granddam by a bull who was not only a son of Favorite, but also of Favorite's half-sister. Pilot, bred by Mr. Robert Colling, was by Major (398) or Wellington (680). Major was by a son and grandson of Favorite, his dam by a son of Favorite, his granddam by Favorite, and his great granddam by Favorite. Wellington was by a son and grandson of Favorite, and his dam was by Favorite. Marshal Beresford was by a son and grandson of Favorite, his dam by a grandson of Favorite, and his granddam by Favorite. Marshal Beresford came into the herd in an exchange for some cows with Major Bower, Mr. Thomas Booth's brother-in-law, a Short-horn breeder, then living at Welham. On returning home one day, Mr. R. Booth found, to his great annoyance, that his father had re-sold the Marshal to Major Bower. He thought that if either had been parted with it should have been Albion. It proved fortunate, however, for the Booth herd that Albion was retained; for though not so stylish as the Marshal in appearance, he proved far superior to him as a sire. Albion is said to have done more good in the herd than any other of the earlier bulls, notwithstanding that he had, through Washington (674), one-sixty-fourth part of the Alloy, which was the term of reproach cast upon Lady, by Grandson of Bolingbroke, and her descendants in the early days of Short-horn breeding.* The offspring of Albion were, in general, very round, compact, and near the ground.

"I must here, however, revert to the Fairholme calves. A slight survey of the tribes which have sprung from these early mothers of the herd may not be without interest to some of my readers. From them proceeded the Fairholme or Blossom tribe, the old Red Rose tribe, and the Ariadne or Bright Eyes tribe.

"Of the Fairholme or Blossom tribe, one branch terminated in the bull Easby (232). Another, which Mr. R. Booth took with him to Studley, produced Moss Rose, by Suworrow, Madame, by Marshal Beresford, Fair Maid, by Pilot, Miss Foote, by Agamemnon (9), and Young Sir Alexander (513). A third division, which, in the cow Eve passed into the hands of Major Bower, has representatives in the herd of Lord Feversham—Skyrocket, the first prize bull at the Royal show at Leeds in 1861, being one of them. Of a fourth branch—the descendants of Beauty by Albion—one portion remained in the hands of Mr. John Booth, and produced Modish, sold to Mr.

---

* See page 71 *ante*, in notice of Charles Colling's breeding.—L. F. A.

R. Holmes (who bred from her Belzoni (783); the other passed into the hands of Sir Charles Knightly, who had at one time several representatives of it. From a fifth branch, retained by Mr. Thomas Booth, sprang Twin Cow, by Albion, her son Navigator (1260), whose spirited portrait adorns the dining-room at Warlaby, and a long array of prize animals, amongst which may be mentioned Bloom, Plum Blossom, Nectarine Blossom, Venus Victrix, Baron Warlaby, and Windsor.

"The old Red Rose* tribe is extinct, except in the progeny of Julius Cæsar (1143) and Belshazzar (1703).

"From the Bright Eyes tribe, in the possession of R. Booth, at Studley, came Ariadne, the prize cow Anna, by Pilot, and many other fine animals dispersed at the Studley sale.

"Besides these Fairholme tribes, there was the Halnaby or Strawberry tribe, which also dates from this period. The first of them was of that *yellow red and white hue*, which, though out of favor at the present day, *was then the prevailing color* of the Short-horn.† She was bought in Darlington market, and one of the earliest recollections of Mr. R. Booth was of that cow coming home. The type of old Halnaby of 1797, who is said to have been a very finely made cow, has often been reproduced in her descendants in the herd. Mr. Thomas Booth considered this as one of his finest families, quite equal to the Blossom and the Ariadne tribes. Young Albion (15) is the first bull of note in the Halnaby family. He was much used in the herd, and was one of the first that was let out on hire. He went to Mr. Scroope's, of Danby Hall, near Middleham, who had a fine, large, robust herd of cattle, related, through some of the bulls used, to the Colling blood. In 1812, the Squire of Danby challenged Mr. Thomas Booth to show, 'for rump and dozen' (the usual stakes at that day being rump stakes and a dozen of wine), the best lot of heifers he had, against the same number of his own, the match to be decided at Bedale. Although a good lot, the Danby had to give place to the Killerby and Warlaby contingent. Of the Halnaby tribe came also the bull Rockingham (2551), and Priam (2452), the latter, sire of Necklace and Bracelet. The only female representatives of the family are in the hands of the present Mr. Booth, of Warlaby. From Strawberry 3d came the Bianca and Bride Elect branch; whilst the famous cow White Strawberry, the dam of Leonard (4210), was the ancestress of Monk, Medora, Red Rose, and

---

* Not the Red Rose tribe of Robert Colling.—L. F. A.

† Roans, and whites, are still the prevailing colors of the Booth Short-horns.—L. F. A.

her daughters, the queenly quartette. Young Matchem (4422) is descended from White Rose, own sister of Young Albion, and therefore, on the dam's side, of the Halnaby family, and the same branch of it gives the dam, Young Rachel, of Mr. Ambler's Grand Turk.

"The Bracelet tribe sprung from a cow by Suworrow, of whose origin there is no record. She was the ancestress of a very superior cow, calved in 1812, Countess, by Albion (14), the Alloy bull; also of Toy, and her twin daughters Necklace and Bracelet, and of Col. Towneley's Pearly, and Mr. Torr's Young Bracelet tribe.

"The early representatives of the above mentioned tribes formed the herd of Mr. Thomas Booth down to the year 1814, when (his son) Mr. Richard Booth, taking the Studley farm, near Ripon, left Killerby. Mr. Thomas Booth was at that time the most enterprising and skillful improver of cattle in his district, if not of his day.* It is said there were some cows in Mr. Thomas Booth's herd of that period as good as any herd of the present time can boast; though, being bred for use rather than show, the generality of them were wanting in the refinement of the modern Short-horn. At that period there were, happily, no shows to demand the sacrifice of the best cattle in the kingdom, or the few that were held could be reached by the majority of cattle attending them only by such long journeys on foot as would be impracticable by animals in such a state of obesity as is now a *sine qua non* with the judicial triumvirate. *High feeding at that time meant no more than good pasture for cows early dried of their milk;* and the term 'training' was never heard except in relation to horses. The first breeder who introduced the system, which has since run into such ruinous excess, of house-feeding cows and heifers in summer on artificial food, was Mr. Crofton; and in that year he, of course, took all before him in the show yards. The general treatment of the females of a herd at that day was a simple hay diet during the winter months. They were put early to breeding, and generally calved at two years old. A few were taken from the lot to milk. The remainder suckled their calves until winter. They were then taken up, dried, and fed off by the time they were three years old; the same course being pursued, in their turn, with their progeny.

"Mr. Thomas Booth was as liberal as his successors in allowing the free use of his bulls to his poor neighbors; and, like most public benefactors, was occasionally imposed upon. A ludicrous instance

---

* Rather too laudatory, we think.—L. F. A.

of this is still remembered. An old fellow at Ainderby, not contented with the bull set apart for this purpose, and being anxious to have a calf by another, that Mr. Booth especially prized and kept exclusively for his own herd, took his cow into the lane adjoining the field where the prohibited animal was grazing. The bull broke through the fence; and—the old Yorkshireman's object was achieved. The latter, knowing how indignant Mr. Booth would be, thought it safest to act on the principle of taking the bull by the horns; and, assuming an injured air, at once repaired to him, exclaiming, 'O maister, maister! sic an a thing has happened! Your gurt ugly beast has broken through t'hedge, and I doubt he'll hae gitten my cow wi' cauf. It's a sad bad job; for I were boun' to feed her off.'

"Mr. Richard Booth's removal to Studley forms a new era in the history of these herds. From 1814 down to its dispersion in 1834, the Studley colony took precedence of the parent stock. We may now, therefore, before proceeding with the history of the Killerby Herd, turn our attention to that of Studley.

The Studley Herd.

"Mr. Richard Booth inherited with his father's name his full share of his father's skill as a breeder, with an equal fondness for the pursuit; and his new farm, which he held under the wealthy and well-known Mrs. Lawrence,* was speedily stocked with superior Shorthorns. He began with his father's cattle, and carried on to even greater perfection his father's work. Among the first importations which were made from Killerby to Studley, when Mr. Richard Booth went there in 1814, the following may be mentioned: He purchased from his father Bright Eyes, by Lame bull (359), and her daughters Ariadne, then a two-year-old, and Agnes, a yearling, both by Albion. Ariadne was own sister to Agamemnon, the grandsire of Isabella, by Pilot. She was the dam of the famous Anna, by Pilot (496), who won numerous prizes at the best shows of the day; and who, in 1824, performed the feat of walking from Studley to Manchester, taking the first prize there, walking back, and producing within a fortnight Young Anna. Anna is said, by those who well remember her, to have borne a very strong resemblance in color and character to Queen of the Ocean. She was the dam of Adelaide, who, through her sire Albert, was also granddaughter of Isabella. Adelaide was the highest

---

* Previously alluded to in a letter to the writer, by R. L. Allen.—L. F. A.

priced female sold at Mr. R. Booth's Studley sale in 1834, and was the granddam of Mr. Storer's cow Princess Julia. From Anna, more remotely through her daughter, Young Anna, are descended two of Mr. Torr's families; and from Agnes, daughter of Bright Eyes, came Mr. Fawkes' Verbena and her descendants. Agamemnon, the own brother of Ariadne, was a bull of extraordinary substance, with good hind quarters, heavy flanks, deep twist, and well covered hips. He was eventually sold, with two heifers, to Mr. White, of Woodlands, near Dublin. Even in these early days Mr. Booth had bulls out on hire. Alonzo (27), a son of Ariadne, by Rockingham (559), was let to Mr. Hutton, of Marske, who, to promote the improvement of the breed of cattle in his district, had at that time yearly shows on his estate. Protector (1347), another bull of the Bright Eyes family, was hired by Mr. Powlett, of Bolton Hall. He was a large, red bull, and a capital sire.

"In the first year of his residence at Studley, Mr. R. Booth bought in Darlington market* the first of what was afterwards known as the Isabella tribe. She was a roan cow, by Mr. Burrell's bull of Burdon (1768), and, for a market cow, had a remarkably ample development of the fore quarters. She was put to Agamemnon. The offspring was 'White Cow,' which, crossed by Pilot, produced the matchless Isabella, so long remembered in show-field annals, and to this day quoted as a perfect specimen of her race. Pedestrians crossing the fields to the ruins of Fountains Abbey might generally see her and Anna, perhaps the two best cows of their day, with a blooming bevy of fair heifers, attended by Young Albion (15); and many a traveler lingered on his way to admire their buxom forms, picturing to himself perhaps how the monks of the old abbey would have gloried in such beeves."

It was from this estate that the name of "Studley bull" was given to the noble animal, calved in 1737, through whose loins a larger number of the noted older Short-horns trace their lineage than to any other. His Herd Book pedigree only states that he was "red and white, bred by Mr. Sharter, of Chilton." In a note to that pedigree,

---

* It is a pregnant fact, as the fashion of the day then was, before a Herd Book, recording the pedigrees of Short-horns was established, or perhaps even thought of, and even to a much later time, that the breeders and farmers of the Short-horn counties sent many of their valuable surplus animals to the local fairs for sale. They had no *written* pedigrees, yet their breeders had access to and used in their herds the pure bred bulls of leading breeders for some cattle generations back. They were *Short-horns*, to all intents and purposes, and probably as pure in blood as any to be found. Not only the Booths, but other discriminating breeders purchased them, and in their produce many noted animals have risen to well-merited distinction.—L. F. A.

written by the late Mr. Thomas Bates, he remarks that "he was of the Barningham breed, which came from Studley, where they were bred for many generations." So that the ancient domain of Studley, as with Alnwick Castle, "home of the Percy's high-born race" of men, was equally a home of the high-born race of Short-horn cattle.

"Isabella and her descendants brought the massive yet exquisitely moulded fore quarters into the herd, and also that straight under-line of the belly, for which the Warlaby animals are remarkable. That such a cow should have had but three crosses of blood is striking evidence of the impressive efficacy of these early bulls, and confirms Mr. R. Booth's opinion that four crosses of really first-rate bulls of *sterling blood upon a good market cow, of the ordinary Short-horn breed*, should suffice for the production of an animal with all the characteristics of the high-caste Short-horn."*

"'White Cow,' by Agamemnon, produced, besides the famous Isabella, 'Own Sister to Isabella,' and Lady Sarah, and was then sold to Mr. Paley, of Gledhow. Her dam, the Darlington cow, had previously been disposed of to the master of a boarding-school at Ripon, one of whose pupils, Mr. Bruere, of Braithwaite Hall—a highly esteemed friend of the late Mr. Booth's—well remembers the brimming pails of milk she gave. 'Own Sister to Isabella' was the dam of Blossom, by Memnon (2295) (a son of Julius Cæsar and Strawberry, by Pilot), and Blossom was the dam of Medora, by Ambo (1636), one of the neatest cows Mr. Booth ever bred. Medora was sold to Mr. Fawkes, in whose hands she was the progenitress of his Gulnare, Haidee, Zuleika, and others. Mr. Fawkes' Lord Marquis, the first prize three-year-old bull at the Royal Show at Lewes, in 1852, and the Yorkshire Show at Sheffield, in the same year, was also a descendant of Medora's.

"'A gentleman,' says the writer of 'Short-horn Intelligence,' 'who has been intimately conversant with the herds of Great Britain for at least a quarter of a century, declares that one of the most interesting sights he ever saw at an agricultural exhibition was on the show ground at Otley, some years ago, when, after the judging, the famous Booth cow Medora, by Ambo, was led round the ring, followed by her six daughters, all of them, as well as the mother, decorated with prize favors. The daughters were Gulnare, Haidee, and Zuleika (by Norfolk) (2377); Victoria, and Fair Maid of Athens (by Sir Thomas

---

* The American breeder must understand that "the ordinary *Short-horn breed*," named above, were true Short-horns, but without Herd Book pedigrees, and not the *common* cattle of the country, like ours.—L. F. A.

Fairfax) (5196); and a heifer named Myrrha, not in the Herd Book, under that name at least, by Rockingham (2550).'

"Blossom was bought by the Earl of Lonsdale, at the Studley sale in 1834, and, after breeding four calves, was slaughtered in 1840. Own Sister to Isabella, also had Imogen, by Argus (750), which was sold at the Studley sale to the Earl of Carlisle, and became the dam of Isabel, by Belshazzar (1703). This Belshazzar (1703),* who was contemporary with Mr. Booth's Belshazzar of the old Red Rose tribe, was from Lady Sarah, the third sister of Isabella, by Pilot. Lady Sarah became the property of the Earl of Carlisle, and produced at Castle Howard three bulls and four heifers, one of which was the dam of Lord Stanley (4269), purchased by Messrs. Booth and Maynard.

"Isabella, by Pilot, now the best known to fame of the three sisters, produced, at Studley, Isaac (1129), by Young Albion (15), Albert (727) by the same bull, Isabella, sold to Mr. Bolden, Young Isabella to Mr. Paley, and Belinda to the Earl of Carlisle, and four others; and on the sale of the Studley herd she alone was retained, and transferred to Warlaby, where she gave birth, in her eighteenth year, to Isabella Matchem, afterwards the dam, as will be seen, of a numerous progeny. The demand for bulls was then only commencing. Isaac had been let for a year to Miss Strickland, of Apperley Court, and on his return, Mr. Booth not requiring him, he was unfortunately fed to make room for younger ones, before his eminent merits as a sire had been discovered. The Isabellas had all great capacity for rapidly acquiring ripe condition on pasture. As an illustration of the fallaciousness of the usual mode of judging cattle by the softness of their flesh, it may be worthy of mention that at one of the Yorkshire agricultural meetings held at Northallerton, a grass-fed heifer, a daughter of Isabella, by Ambo, was shown, and rejected as being too hard-fleshed. Not breeding, she was slaughtered at York for Christmas beef. Her two successful rivals also failing to breed were slaughtered, and the palm for the best carcass of beef was awarded to Mr. Booth's heifer over her Northallerton rivals. Nor is this case without many a parallel in the history of Royal Shows. Numerous as have been the prizes which the Booth cattle have received, their number would have been greatly increased if judges had always carefully distinguished between flesh and fat. When their decisions have

---

* This must be a mistake of Mr. Carr's. The English Herd Book, Vol. 3, records Belshazzar (1704) as the Son of Lady Sarah. Mr. Booth bred (1703), and the Earl of Carlisle bred (1704).—L. F. A.

been on this ground—as they often have been—adverse to the Booth cattle, many an experienced butcher has proclaimed a very different opinion; and could the appeal *ad crumenam* have been adopted by an immediate sale of the rival animals to the shambles, how useless would it have been in most instances to contest the supremacy of the Booths!

"Another cow which Mr. Booth took with him to Studley was Madame, by Marshal Beresford, also of the Fairholme Blossom tribe. From her came Fancy and Fair Maid, both by Agamemnon. The former was the dam of Fatima, a very neat, middle-sized cow, which, put to Mr. Maynard's Sir Alexander (591), produced the famous bull Young Sir Alexander (5139). This bull was the sire of Strawberry, whose daughter, White Strawberry, by Rockingham (559), held, perhaps, equal rank in Mr. Booth's estimation with Anna, Isabella, and her own contemporary rivals, Necklace and Bracelet. Fair Maid, the other daughter of Madame, by Marshal Beresford, was the dam of Miss Foote, whose descendants were very numerous, and were all disposed of at, or previously to, the Studley sale. They united in a remarkable degree the two properties of good milking and rapid fattening. Fair Maid herself was sold to Mr. Ellison, of Sizergh, where she bred many calves, and proved herself an excellent dairy cow. Miss Foote was sold to Captain Shawe, and Fair Helen, her daughter, who was the dam of the noted bull Cossack (1880), to Sir Charles Tempest, with whom she bred four heifers. I remember, in 1853, a stray waif of this famous tribe in the hands of an inn-keeper, at Clapham, in Yorkshire. It was, in fact, the broad, level back, and symmetrical proportions of this cow, that induced me to purchase my first Short-horn, her bull calf. The cow was a granddaughter of Miss Foote, being a daughter of Lady Helen, then the property of Mr. Foster, of Clapham. She was sacrificed whilst still in her prime, her owner being tempted by the offer of a high price for her from a butcher.

"Some mention of the bulls bred and used by Mr. Booth during his residence at Studley seems here to be required.

"One of the first bulls of superior mark bred by Mr. Richard Booth, after his removal to Studley, was Julius Cæsar (1143), a bull of very symmetrical proportions, which he had the merit of impressing in a surprising degree upon his offspring. No matter how dissimilar and opposite in form and breed the cows to which he was put might be, the produce all bore the unmistakable stamp of their sire. The offspring, by him, of the shabbiest lane-side cow, had, it is said, all the character of the pure-bred Short-horn. It may be worth while to inquire how far the remarkable property which distinguished this bull may be traced to the preponderating influence of any particular progenitor or progenitors in his pedigrees, an investigation of which, it may be here sufficient to say, will show him to be descended half a dozen times, and some of them very nearly, from Twin Brother to Ben.

"This circumstance lends weight to the opinion of many experienced breeders, that, in general, the capability of a bull to transmit to his offspring his own peculiar mould and properties depends upon his having inherited them from a succession of ancestors endowed with similar characteristics. It is doubtless to the concentration of hereditary force thus derived that the extraordinary transmissive power of such bulls as Comet, Favorite and Julius Cæsar, is to be attributed. At the same time it is a curious circumstance, and one that should not be forgotten—as often modifying to some extent the principle above enunciated—*that amongst animals similarly bred there are some bulls, and some cows too, that possess an immeasurably greater transmissive influence than pertains to others.*

"Pilot (496), another of the bulls of this period, was bred by Mr. R. Colling, and purchased by Mr. T. Booth at the Barmpton sale in 1818, for 270 guineas. He was used in all the three herds, and there was no bull to which they were more largely indebted. The close in-and-in breeding of this animal has already been shown. He was let to Mr. Rennie for a short time; but his stock at home proved so good, that he was recalled at the expiration of his first season. Pilot was a small, compact bull, somewhat undersized, but possessed of great thriving propensity. He was a capital sire, and may be appropriately cited as a striking example of the preceding remarks. I am indebted for this account of Pilot to one who remembers him well—that old friend of the Booths, the much respected Nestor of the Short-horns, Mr. Wetherell, who, like his friend Mr. Wiley, of Brandsby, is still hale and strong, a living record of early Short-horn times, from whom younger men learn the lessons of the past.* Isaac, another bull of note, bred by Mr. Richard Booth, has already been referred to. Burley (1766) and Ambo (1636), both containing a large amount of the Favorite blood, were partially used in the herd during the last three years before the sale.

"In the year 1834 Mr. Richard Booth, finding that some of his best pastures were required by their owner for other purposes, gave up the

---

* Mr. Wetherell died in February, 1871.—L. F. A.

farm at Studley, and selling off the whole of his herd, with the exception of Isabella, by Pilot, retired to Sharrow, near Ripon. After residing there for a year, which, from being bereft of his favorites, he used to describe as the least happy period of his life, Mr. R. Booth, in consequence of his father's death, succeeded to the estate and Short-horn herd of Warlaby. The sale of the Studley herd was a step which Mr. Booth always regretted, for many of the animals it contained were, in his opinion, every whit as good as any he afterwards bred. They were dispersed into many hands, and though Old Cuddy's* assertion, that they have 'a' swealed away,' is certainly too sweeping, it may be doubted whether, even in the hands of very celebrated breeders, like Mr. Fawkes and others, the descendants of these famous cattle have ever quite equaled their cousins at Warlaby.

"It is now necessary to go back a quarter of a century to resume the history of

The Killerby Herd.

"We have seen that in the year 1814, Mr. Richard Booth took with him to Studley some of the animals then forming the Killerby herd. Mr. Thomas Booth shortly afterwards supplied the place of these with other cows, which became the foundresses of three famous tribes—the Farewell tribe, from which sprang Faith, Hope, and Charity; the Broughton tribe, from whence came Bliss, Blithe, and Bonnet; and the Dairymaid, or Moss Rose tribe, from which are descended Vivandiere, Camp Follower, and Soldier's Bride. The first of the Farewell tribe came from Darlington; the first of the Broughton tribe from a dairy farmer in a village of that name, who had some good cattle, but, pedigrees being slightly valued in those days by the tenant-farmer class, nothing further is known about them. † The first of the Dairymaid tribe came from an equally good stock in the village of Scorton.

"In the year 1819, on the occasion of Mr. J. Booth's marriage, Mr. T. Booth removed to Warlaby, giving up to his son, Mr. J. Booth, the Killerby estate and a part of the Short-horn herd, and taking the remainder with him. A portion of the Fairholme or Blossom tribe, and of the Old Red Rose tribe, were removed to Warlaby, the

---

* Mr. Booth's herdsman.—L. F. A.

† A fact like this may explain the want of pedigrees to the Kentucky importation of Shorphorns to America in the year 1817, only three years later than 1814.—L. F. A.

remainder being left with Mr. John Booth. The Halnaby family was also divided, but the famous Bracelet tribe was all left at Killerby. From this period down to the year 1835, when Mr. R. Booth succeeded to his father's herd at Warlaby, there is comparatively little known of the two herds. The times were unpropitious for the Shorthorn. The spirit of improvement which the example of the Collings had evoked only partially survived. There was a general depression in all agricultural produce, and consequently but little demand for animals, the purchase of which appeared at that time to partake so much of the nature of a speculation. Not yet did

'Generous Britons venerate the plow,'

or regard with respect bucolic occupations. A man gained more *eclat* by a display of science and judgment in going across country than in the breeding of cattle. In some districts, a gentleman almost lost caste by devoting himself to such ignoble pursuits, and was sarcastically dubbed, by his companions in the pink, 'cow-scratcher.'*

"But though 'fallen on evil days,' the stock at Killerby was of high character, and was frequently resorted to by the few good breeders of that period for the purchase of animals. It is a house where all comers were, and still are, regaled with the welcome of the olden times. Killerby is one of the pleasantest of the pleasant homes of England. It is a substantial, square, manor-house, picturesquely situated on a gentle eminence to the south of the river Swale, and two miles from Catterick, the site of the once important Roman camp and city of Cataractonium. The house occupies the site of the ancient castle of Killerby, once a stronghold of great magnitude, founded in the reign of Edward the First by Sir Brian Fitzalan, Earl of Arundel. It is approached by a road winding through verdant pastures thrown together into the form of a park, adorned here and there with noble elm and walnut trees. The estate consists of about 500 acres of arable and pasture land. The soil, which is very mixed—gravel, strong clay, marl, and peat being sometimes found in the same field—is more adapted for sheep than heavy cattle, though there are two or three excellent pastures. Several of the inferior grass fields have been plowed up of late, and heavy crops of oats and turnips grown in their place, which has allowed the number of sheep kept to be greatly increased. Although half-bred sheep are occasionally seen

---

* It will be seen that there were ebbs and flows in the demand for Short-horns in those days,—most mistakenly for the interests of the stock breeding public,—as there have been since.—L. F. A.

on the farm for summer grazing, the staple stock are pure Leicesters, for the wool of which Mr. J. B. Booth, the present owner, has gained several prizes at the Yorkshire shows.

"The late Mr. John Booth, of Killerby, was known and beloved throughout the county as a strikingly genial example of the worthy and hospitable northern agriculturist, ever devoting himself to the service of his friends (and he had many) to the advancement of agricultural improvement. The humblest, equally with the most important, agricultural societies might always rely on his good offices, whether as patron or judge, in which latter capacity being confessedly unrivaled, he was in great request, and would most good naturedly consent to officiate, though his doing so involved the exclusion of his own cattle from competition. As might have been expected, from his fine and manly character, he was also a keen sportsman; like Chaucer's squire,

> 'Well could he sitte a horse and faire y-ride;'

and Yorkshire, that modern Thessaly of horsemen, knew no more thorough judge of hack or hunter. His skill in this respect still survives in his sons; many a field and many a showyard testify that in this regard, as in others, Killerby has not degenerated from its ancient fame. He had, too, a natural taste for the fine arts, and when from illness he could not go far from home, he had his horses led out, and would sit on the lawn, or in the hall, to paint them. Here, too, his taste survives, and if I touch lightly on the subject it is because more delicate fingers now hold the brush, and I would not trespass unbidden upon the elegant recreations of Killerby's fair Mistress.

"When, on the establishment of the national shows in 1839, the superiority of the Killerby Short-horns had been proved in contest with the best animals of the day, the herd attracted many visitors, and its inspection was as free to all classes as were the fruits of its owner's experience in breeding, which he was ever ready to communicate to the neophyte. It may not be uninteresting to the present fair enthusiasts in Short-horn matters to learn, that in the absence of her husband, the late Mrs. Booth—a lady who will long be remembered in that neighborhood for her benevolent disposition and engaging manners—would herself most affably do the honors of the herd, leading the way to her especial favorites, and expatiating on their pedigrees, points, and perfections, sometimes with a dash of arch humor, and always with the grace and delicacy of the thorough-

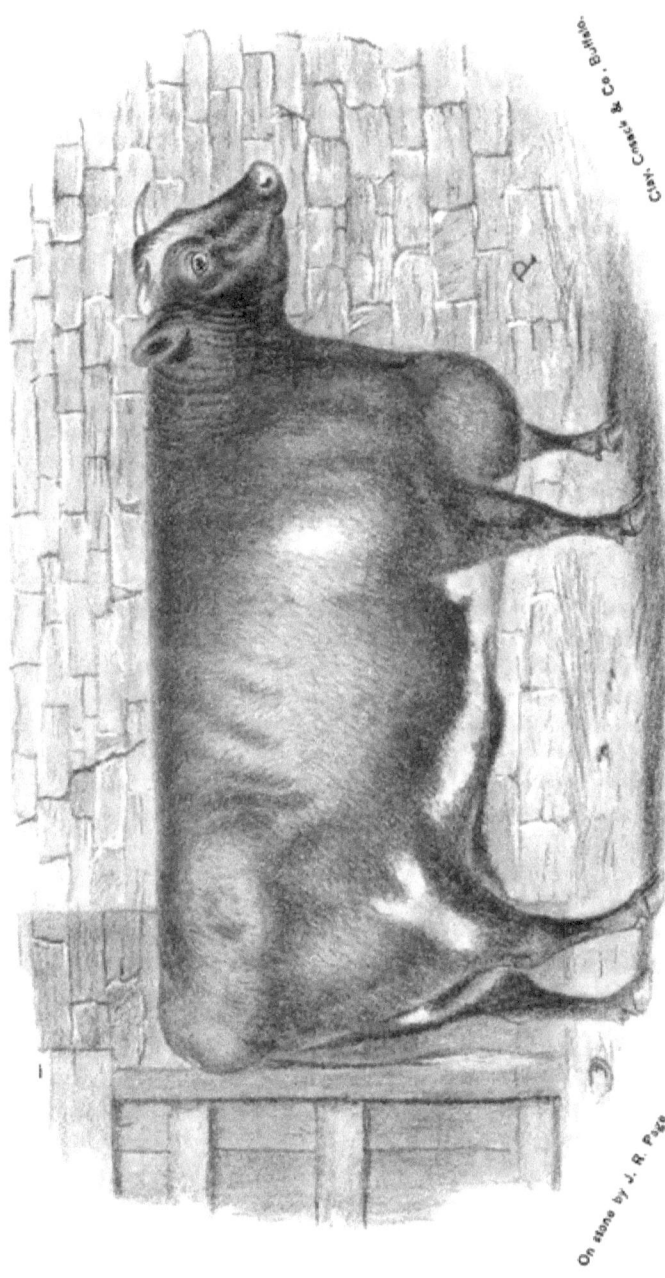

NECKLACE. BY PRIAM. (2452).
AT 6 YEARS ("TWINNED WITH BRACELET").

bred lady that she was. Mrs. Booth's sister, Miss Wright, had an equally keen appreciation of the merits of a good Short-horn, and would stop any one of kindred tastes, who happened to be passing through Cleasby, to have a chat on her favorite topic, or to lead them to the Garth (since known by his name), where in the fullness of his days and honors repose the remains of Comet (155)."*

At Killerby the herd was carefully bred, and many fine animals reared, which are duly mentioned and exalted as prize-takers at the shows, truly, no doubt, by Mr. Carr, but which we have not space to record—all being represented in the volumes of the English Herd Books of the times. Among the cows, very deep milkers are occasionally named. Mr. Carr remarks:

"It does not appear that Mr. John Booth was a very frequent competitor in the show-fields until the establishment of the Royal and Yorkshire Shows in 1839. Before this time Short-horn cattle were kept chiefly for dairy and grazing purposes; the majority of the male stock were steered, and many a fine heifer that took the butcher's eye was converted into Christmas beef. Necklace and Bracelet [twin heifer calves of Toy, before named] shared the pasture and the straw-yard with the ordinary stock of the farm until nearly two years old. As calves they never had more milk than their dam, who suckled them both, supplied; and, throughout the whole of their victorious career, they derived their chief support from the pasture, with a daily feed of corn meal and [oil] cake. Yet Bracelet won seventeen prizes at the various meetings of the Royal Agricultural Society of England, the Highland Society of Scotland, the Yorkshire Society, and other local shows; and at the Yorkshire Show in 1841, where she won the first prize for extra stock, the sweepstakes for the best lot of cattle not less than four in number, was awarded to Bracelet, Necklace, Mantalini, and Ladythorn. Necklace won sixteen prizes and one gold and three silver medals at the various meetings above mentioned, as well as at the Smithfield Club,† where she finished her career as a prize-taker in 1846, by winning the first prize of her class and the gold medal (for which there were thirty-seven competitors) as the best animal exhibited in any of the cow or heifer classes."

After relating at some length the practice of Mr. Booth's close breeding, (for the brothers seldom bred any bulls of strange blood into their herds after they had become permanently established, unless

---

* Vide page 75, *ante.*—L. F. A.
† The Smithfield Show at London, is for *fat*, and not breeding animals.—L. F. A.

to take a single cross, and then at once to return to the blood of their own stock,) and the names of sundry prize animals of the herd, Mr. Carr remarks:

"It has been asserted by *over*-zealous advocates of the system of close interbreeding, that the crosses of Mussulman, Lord Lieutenant, Matchem, and others, introduced scarcely any fresh blood into the Booth herds; for inasmuch as no alien bulls were used but those whose veins were surcharged with the blood of Favorite, the recourse to them was nothing more than a recurrence to, or renewal of, the old family strain; but this is really only what is true of every wellbred Short-horn of the period, and therefore proves nothing. Take any one of them, and trace back the pedigree of each of its progenitors (whose numbers of course increase each generation back in a geometrical progression), and this bull Favorite will be found to recur directly and indirectly a surprising number of times. The following elaborate calculations, for which I am indebted to the Rev. J. Storer, of Hellidon, may be quoted in illustration of this: Mussulman is 64 times descended from Favorite; namely, through Magnum Bonum 30, through Pirate 22, through Houghton 9, through Marshal Blucher 3; total, 64 times. Lord Lieutenant was 106 times descended from Favorite, and Matchem 52 times. Crown Prince is 1,055 times descended from Favorite, and Red Rose by Harbinger 1,344 times. So the produce of the two are descended from him 2,399 times. But work out the Duchesses or any Short-horns of good blood, and the result will be found very much the same. It will not do, therefore, to claim bulls as of kindred blood on this ground only. Moreover, it must in candor be admitted by the advocates of in-and-in breeding that a careful consideration of the above facts leads to one unavoidable conclusion. Very strong in-and-in breeding is a totally different thing in our case from what it was in the case of the earlier breeders, the Collings and Mr. Thomas Booth—so different that there can be but little analogy between the two cases. They bred in-and-in from animals which had little or no previous affinity. We breed in-and-in from animals full of the same blood to begin with. In our case the *via media*, and therefore the *via salutis*, would seem to lie in the adoption of two apparently opposite principles—*in-and-in breeding*, and *fresh blood*. It is manifest, however, that this latter principle should be acted upon with extreme caution, or to a very limited extent, when it is desirable to preserve and perpetuate the distinctive type of any particular tribe, especially when, as in the Warlaby herd, there is no visible deterioration in symmetry, substance, or stamina, or any want of fertility traceable to in-and-in breeding. Yet even in such cases it is doubtless advisable to have occasional recourse to remote alliances, taking care to have as many removes as possible between members of the same family; or, where using bulls nearly related to the cows, giving preference to such as have been subjected to different conditions of life, it being a well-known physiological fact that a change of soil and climate effects perhaps almost as great a change in the constitution as would result from an infusion of other blood."*

These remarks would, perhaps, be more in place when on the subject of breeding, but finding them here in connection with the Booth system, now under discussion, they will be duly considered by the reader.

In July, 1852, the Killerby herd was sold at auction. The sale was largely attended by breeders from all parts of the kingdom. At that time there was an unusual depression in all agricultural values; the prices at which the cattle sold were comparatively low, and did not realize at all what their several merits and celebrity demanded. Some of them afterwards changed hands and sold for thrice the prices they brought at the Booth sale.

Mr. J. Booth retained a few choice cows from the general sale, which Mr. Carr says were of "distinguished lineage, and if more recent in their origin, have given rise to other families proved to trace that origin to the herds of the Booths, and the quiet meadows of Killerby." Mr. J. Booth continued at Killerby until his death, in 1857, when his sons, Thomas C. and John, came into possession of his herd.

The Warlaby Herd.

"It is now necessary to take a retrospect of the herd at Warlaby, commencing with the year 1835, when Mr. Richard Booth, inheriting the estate, went to reside there. Mr. Booth's residence at Warlaby is a modest, unassuming, country house. It stands environed by well-timbered paddocks, in a rich meadowy tract of country, bounded by distant hills, and known as the Vale of the Wiske. It is one mile from the village of Ainderby, of which it is a hamlet, and about three from Northallerton, the central town of the North-Riding, in Yorkshire. The farm, as occupied by Mr. Booth, consisted of 310 acres, about half in pasture; other farms then let off, have since his

---

* Sound physiological principle that should be heeded by all careful breeders.—L. F. A.

death been added to it. The land is better in character than that at Killerby; it is chiefly clayey loam, and grows fine wheat and turnips, and long hay. The pastures are well adapted for cows, but unsuited for sheep, because liable to be flooded. The River Wiske, which still retains its Gaelic name, Uisg (water), being the most sluggish of all the North Yorkshire brooks, and having the shallowest stream-channel, frequently overflows the lower pastures, and large, deep ditches, which have been fatal to many a good cow, intersect the fields to carry off the water.

"The house was everything that an old bachelor or his friends could require; and many a visitor there can bear testimony that within its walls reigned supreme the open-hearted northern hospitality to an extent that Southrons know not. Many a valuable cup and hard-won medal may there be seen; the portrait of many a prize-taker decorates its rooms; and many a pleasant hour has been spent and ancient story told in that quiet Short-horn home, while the genuine old Squire

> Refilled his pipe, 'and showed how fields were won.'

"Shortly after settling at Warlaby, Mr. Richard Booth had quite made up his mind to give up the breeding of Short-horns, and had already sold individual animals from the Strawberry and Moss Rose tribes, when a bantering remark made by a gentleman in the neighborhood, to the effect that 'the Booths had lost their Blood,' incited him to change his purpose, and put his friend's assertion to the proof. The Warlaby herd had for some years past been kept very much in the shade, Mr. Thomas Booth having been latterly intent only on breeding useful animals, without aspiring to the honors, or courting the notoriety of public exhibition; but Mr. Richard Booth felt assured that it contained ample materials to enable him to guard the laurels that had been bequeathed to him."

After giving with such luxury of description the home of Richard Booth and its hospitable occupant, Mr. Carr goes into an enumeration of most of the animals adopted as the bases of his productive herd, for he had now made up his mind again to heartily enter the list in competition with the other breeders of his vicinity for new laurels and honors. He was an enthusiast in his love of Short-horns, and as we before remarked having no domestic cares to withdraw his attention, his whole mind was directed (as a Short-horn breeder's should be, if he means to excel) to the propagation and improvement of his herd, and in it he eminently succeeded.

In glowing rhapsody of almost indiscriminate praise—and we do not say that any portion of his descriptions are untruthful—Mr. Carr occupies fifty further pages with the names of animals which Richard Booth bred, the tribes to which they belonged, the prizes he won, and the applause he drew as a successful breeder. One author relates:

"It has been reported that Mr. Booth refused for his cow Queen of the May, an offer of 1500 guineas,* the highest price ever bidden for a Short-horn. The circumstances—which are given on the late Mr. R. Booth's authority—are these: Two gentlemen from America, apparently agents for an American company, came to see the herd, and when they saw Queen of the May were completely riveted by the fascination of her beauty. After dwelling for some time upon her perfections, they inquired of Mr. Booth whether he would part with her. He replied that he 'would not sell her for the highest price ever given for a Short-horn.' 'That, sir,' said one of them, 'was, I believe, 1200 guineas?' Mr. Booth answered in the affirmative. They consulted together, and asked him whether he would take 1500 guineas, which Mr. Booth declined to do, remarking that if she bred a living calf, and he had the luck to rear it, she was worth more to him to keep, and they relinquished her with regret, leaving on Mr. Booth's mind the impression that, if he had entertained the idea, even that large amount might possibly not have been their final offer."

It appears, among other things, that Mr. Booth had fallen into the recently growing absurd and destructive practice of "training" his animals for the annual "Royal" and district exhibitions. This was no less than loading them with excessive fat in order to win prizes. This mode of "training" injured them for months, or years, and in frequent instances for life, as breeders, bulls and cows alike, and himself, in common with others, severely suffered in consequence. Yet knowing the ill effects of such practice, it is still kept up in England, and we fear that it will yet leap across the ocean, to some extent, in America. We trust not, but there is no knowing to what extremes of rivalry our spirited breeders may venture to win the honors so eagerly sought at our public exhibitions. This system, Mr. Carr says, Mr. Booth "strongly deprecated," but was obliged to fall into it or give up showing his animals in competition at the exhibitions.

At Warlaby, in the enjoyment of an ample estate, surrounded by faithful servants, happy in the fidelity of his old herdsman, "Cuddy,"

---

* A higher price has been offered and refused in the United States for a cow. Both offer and refusal were *bona fide*, as we know.—L. F. A.

who was frequently assisted in his minor duties by his equally faithful and brave-hearted old wife, "Nanny;" his trusty *fac totum*, John White, living on the farm from his boyhood, "who was butler, waiting servant, and valet to him, as well as registrar-general of the births, deaths, and marriages, and all else that transpired in the Warlaby herd," Richard Booth lived, dispensing a wide hospitality to his friends and acquaintances, and, in his charities, ever mindful of the needy.

"When illness had confined Mr. Booth to the house, and Cuddy had become less active, John made it his business, in addition to his household duties, to keep a watchful eye on the cattle—especially the young or ailing ones—in the neighborhood of the house. So admirably did he discharge this self-imposed duty, so methodical were his habits, so retentive his memory, and so scrupulous his observance of his master's orders, that the *active* management of the herd mainly devolved upon his shoulders, and Mr. Booth found him an invaluable auxiliary.

"Last, not least, came doughty Willie Jacques, the farm-bailiff, who had been upwards of forty years in the family. He first lived with Mr. R. Booth at Studley, who sent him to Warlaby in the old master's time, to take the management of the arable land and work people. Willie Jacques' pride was rather in the nameless nondescripts of the farm, the bullocks and half-bred heifers, which converted his marvelous root and clover crops into goodly rounds and lordly barons of marbled beef, than in the pampered aristocrats of the herd, born to consume the fruits of the soil whether earned or not. Proud as Willie was of their triumphs in the show-field, nothing exasperated him like the failure on the part of any of them to contribute their yearly quota towards the increase of the herd. Willie Jacques had a capital head for tillage and general farming, and was always at his post, from which nothing could move him but the Christmas Fat Show at Smithfield. 'I'se seea thrang I canna gang,' was his answer to all invitations. Curt of speech and unceremonious in bearing was Willie Jacques in his sturdy northern independence; but get him upon the subject of his kind old master, and all the frost of his nature melted away, and you found that under that dry, almost blunt manner, a heart as kindly as a child's was hidden. In one of the rooms at Warlaby hung an admirable portrait of this highly respectable and respected steward of the Warlaby estate.

"But there was one other personage, to forget whom in a sketch of Warlaby would be fatal to the character of any historian—a personage who, though seldom visible, has contributed to the visitor, perhaps not the least comfortable reminiscence which an Englishman carries away with him from any place of passing interest; and that is Ann, faithful Ann, that white-bibbed paragon of natty spruceness—the housekeeper. She came, nobody knows how many years ago, to nurse the former housekeeper, an old friend of hers, who was ill, and who died at Warlaby; and Ann continued until Master could find one to suit him, which he never did, and so Ann remained still; and many are the visitors who can testify to the excellence of the pigeon pies, apricot tarts, and other delectable cates, which those brisk and clever hands have fabricated."

This is a delightful picture, and we are happy to chronicle it in such happy connection. "The good old man" died with the resignation of a Christian, October 31, 1864, at the ripe age of seventy-six years, and was buried "beneath the shade of the old gray tower of Ainderby, which looks down upon the scene of his useful and quiet labors. But Warlaby is there still, and his kith and kin retain its hall and herd."

We here take our leave of Mr. Carr and his interesting history, and can only refer those wishing further particulars relating to the recent breeding of the Booth stock, to the book itself. The present Thomas C. Booth succeeded to the Warlaby estate, and a considerable part of the herd, on the death of his uncle Richard. The labors and sagacity of the Booth family—father and sons—whatever merits may be truthfully given to their contemporaries, place them, with the Collings, in the roll of benefactors. As to the improvements made by the Booths in the style or merits of their stock we have little, if anything to say, as so many of their cattle, and their direct descendants, are now alive, both in England and America, that every observer can form his own individual opinion. In their practice of breeding they followed the Collings; that is, breeding chiefly within the blood of their own herds, only going beyond them when they supposed by such course they could supply a deficiency of quality, and that object achieved, returning to their own blood as the polar star of their progress. That they bred eminently fine cattle no one will dispute; but whether they have proved preëminent in *all* the fine qualities which *perfect* a Short-horn, those conversant with them will judge. They have a style, in some respects, peculiarly their own, and as with all other animals of prominent mark, have their warm advocates, as well as those who look upon them with less favor.

CHAPTER V.

THOMAS BATES—HIS SHORT-HORNS AND THEIR BREEDING.

PARTIALLY contemporary in time, but much younger in years, Mr. Bates came onto the stage during the full career of the Collings and the elder Booth. He established himself as a breeder in the later days of the Collings, and obtained his earliest Short-horns directly from Charles, and afterwards from the herds of Robert, which formed the foundation for his ultimate success in breeding.

We have recently been favored with a book entitled "*The History of the Improved Short-horn or Durham Cattle, and of the Kirkleavington Herd, from the Notes of the late Thomas Bates, with a Memoir by Thomas Bell, Brockton House, Eccleshall, Staffordshire.*" The book contains 375 pages, small octavo, compiled by one who intimately knew Mr. Bates, and for many years was a tenant and herdsman on a portion of the very considerable farm which Mr. Bates occupied at Kirkleavington, not far from Darlington.

Of Mr. Bates, we have for more than thirty years past known somewhat, both in his various writings, from what other Englishmen have written about him, and from men on both sides of the Atlantic, who were personally acquainted with him and his herds of cattle, so much as to learn his personal character, his manner of breeding, and the extent of success which he achieved in the long course of his action. From Mr. A. B. Allen, of New York City, who visited England in the year 1841, and for some time was a guest of Mr. Bates, we obtained the first particulars of him as a Short-horn breeder, and through Mr. A., as editor of the "*American Agriculturist*," he was first prominently introduced to the acquaintance of the Short-horn breeders of the United States. A few of his animals had previously—in the year 1834—come to America through the purchases of an importing company formed in the Scioto Valley, Ohio. Not long afterwards he sent over, as a present, to Kenyon College, in Ohio, two or three animals. In 1840 he sold to Mr. George Vail, of Troy, N. Y., a bull and cow, which will be hereafter noticed.

While at his home in 1841, Mr. Bates told Mr. Allen that he intended to write a history of the Short-horns for publication, and had already made many notes for that purpose. That history, however, he never wrote out, nor published. From those notes and various letters and other publications left by him, at a period of twenty years after his decease Mr. Bell has compiled his book, together with various collateral matter drawn from the writings of others, and interspersed with occasional notes of his own, some few of which are original with himself.

Of Mr. Bell's book, its matter and compilation, we have but little to say, as a *literary* labor. It lacks methodical arrangement. It has not even an index, other than the discursive titles at the heads of its several parts, or chapters, and they in no consecutive order of subject, time, or place. Its chronology is deficient, few dates being given, and what there are of them playing hither and thither in ambuscade, as may happen during a period of sixty years, disjointed and difficult to connect. In the absence of quotation marks in the text, we hardly know what is the composition of Mr. Bates, and what the compiler's, except by guess, while the various letters and public addresses of Mr. Bates and others are appropriately marked, but in the same disordered arrangement of time as the other parts of the work; yet, by close examination, we can understand them. The book is not, in fact, a lucid history of either the Short-horns, or even of Mr. Bates, or his cattle breeding, but rather loose memoranda and sketches of history left by Mr. Bates and others. We exceedingly regret that during his life time Mr. Bates himself could not have written out his memoranda—for he was capable of doing it—and left to the world an intelligible general *history* of the Short-horns, as well as those of his own breeding. Such a work should have been done by an Englishman, capable of performing it. To obtain a continuous narrative of Mr. Bates' proceedings one is obliged to skip over numerous pages, and then turn back to keep a thread of his "history," and arrive at a clear understanding of his action. Still, there is much valuable matter scattered throughout the book which, by diligent research, the reader may appropriate and digest into important information. Yet, bating its deficiencies, we are thankful for the work Mr. Bell has given us, as some new facts, through Mr. Bates' version of them, are stated in his memoranda, containing important information, which, if not hitherto secret, or but partially known, throw light on disputed questions, setting previous inaccuracies at rest.

Although from what we had previously learned of Mr. Bates, we deemed him a man addicted to controversy, prejudices, and crotchets, his writings now show him actually to be such, for his biographer has covered nothing of these foibles, although his compilations truthfully illustrate him as of unexceptionable private character, and decided moral worth. The crowning ambition of his life to breed and furnish the world a herd of Short-horns that should exhibit to posterity his skill as a breeder is fully developed. So much for the book. We propose to give from this and other authorities a synopsis of Mr. Bates' life and proceedings in all that is important to be known relating to him and his stock-breeding career, without either partiality or prejudice, and if in the course of our remarks we sometimes touch on his inconsistencies, or censure his assertions, it will only be in the cause of truth and accuracy of historical facts.

With all his partialities and prejudices, Mr. Bates was sound in heart and morals; he blurted out his opinions irrespective of whom they pleased or offended, and if he sometimes made enemies, he had also his warm, attached friends. He was rather tory in his politics, a decided "protectionist," and an advocate of the "corn laws" in principle; a *statesman* to some extent, in his teachings, which his early good education, together with his naturally broad and clear observation of the times, had helped him to become. He was kind to the poor, liberal in his charities, both private and public, a sound adherent of the established church—rather of the "low" order—a companion and associate among the most intelligent classes of men, and like others of generous sympathies, loved the distinction and honors that were frequently conferred upon him. His personal habits were abstemious and temperate; his hospitality was open, genial, and liberal, to peer, or peasant; his hand ever free to the claims of distress; his conversation winning, and open-hearted, abounding in well-told anecdote, and sparkles of wit; his affections kindly, and although a life-long bachelor, he loved children, whose companionship was always a source of pleasure to him. In short, bating his minor eccentricities of character, like very many Short-horn breeders of his own and the present day, Mr. Bates was—a GENTLEMAN—with some oddities.

Thomas Bates was born on one of the estates belonging to the Dukedom of Northumberland, in the year 1775, in the valley of the river Tyne, on a place called Tyneside, at Ovington Hall, of a respectable family, among the elder branches of which had been a Member of Parliament, a Professor in the Colleges, and a Divine of the Church. In his boyhood he was early sent to a grammar school; afterwards spent a considerable time in the University at Edinburgh, and received a good education. Being of rather a slender constitution, and studious in habit, he was intended for the Church; but that calling not suiting his more active temperament, he chose agriculture as a profession. He began his agricultural education at Aydon Castle, in the neighborhood of which lived George Culley, an eminent stock breeder and agricultural writer, from whom young Bates in his frequent intimacies took sound lessons in his newly-chosen pursuit. This period of his life must have been at about sixteen or seventeen years of age; but according to some of his own remarks in later years, he speaks of knowing the Collings and their stock as early as 1782. So early a day, however, we think a mistake, as in that year he could only have been five or six years old. There are other anachronisms of date in some of his narrations of events, inadvertent, possibly, but which, if true, would make him many years older than he is stated. In an article written by him in 1842, he says: "It is *now* above sixty years since I became impressed with the importance of selecting the very best animals to breed from, and for twenty-five years afterwards lost no opportunity of ascertaining the merits of the various tribes of Short-horns." This would put his birth back some years anterior to 1775, the date given by his biographer, as he could scarcely be expected to have much judgment in the way of cattle before he was at least twelve or fifteen years old. There may possibly be an error as to his birth in 1775, as we have heard it remarked by several persons who knew him not long previous to his death in 1849, that he must, from appearances and his own statements, have been at the time of their conversations with him, although active and vigorous, quite eighty years of age. The fact, is now of little consequence; but that at a very early age he had imbibed a passionate love of farm stock, there can be no question.

After a few years at Aydon Castle, and under his majority, he became a tenant farmer under his father on the estate of Park End, in the vale of North Tyne, where he showed his aptitude for farming and improving land, fencing, and various other economies in agriculture. There he remained until the year 1800, when he took the extensive farm and estate of Halton Castle, also in Northumberland, where he began stock rearing and grazing on his own account. It appears that he first adopted the Kyloes, or West Highland cattle, which it was the custom to drive in large numbers from the rougher lands in Scotland down to the richer farms of the north of England, to fatten for market. Soon afterwards, these not altogether suiting his purpose, he made a visit to the Collings, and was attracted by the superior qualities of the Short-horns of their several herds. He saw the "Durham Ox," bred and reared by Charles, and the peerless "White Heifer that Traveled," bred by Robert, and immediately concluded to adopt that blood for his future breeding.

At this point it may be well to mention that Mr. Bates had by gifts from his father and his own earnings come into possession of several thousand pounds, with which to commence and prosecute farming and stock breeding on a considerable scale, and although a "tenant farmer," a comparatively large amount of capital was necessary to establish himself in that branch of business. "At entering on the farm at Halton Castle he received from his father many excellent cattle, and also the improved Leicester sheep. He also obtained some Cleveland bay horses, which at that time had been bred to great perfection on Tyneside. The swine, and even poultry, did not escape his attention; but it was to his herds of cattle that he devoted his greatest attention. He bought cows of Messrs. Colling in 1800, but I can find no record of them."* It appears that so far as the Short-horns were concerned he soon made a determination to obtain the very best animals which his purse would command, of unimpeachable blood, and without regard to the profits he should make from them, establish a herd second to none other, and found an enduring reputation as a breeder. This determination, therefore, may be the key to the various controversies in which he was afterwards engaged, and the acrimony with which some of his future correspondence with other breeders was tainted, and into which he was probably goaded by their accusations upon him. Of positive convictions, and determined purposes, he had the pecuniary means to prosecute his plans, and hesitated at nothing which should honestly accomplish them.

On looking over the Colling herds his attention was peculiarly attracted to the stock descended from the "Stanwick," or first "Duchess" cow (of which Charles had become possessed in 1784), and the bull Hubback, which it did not appear that Colling himself so highly appreciated as to retain it solely to his own use. In a letter written by Mr. Bates to "*The New Farmer's Journal*," in November, 1842, he gives this account: "Having purchased my original cow Duchess [calved in 1800, got by Daisy bull (186)], of this tribe of cattle, of the late Charles Colling thirty-eight years ago." With some notes on several remarkable animals which he had seen

---

* Bell's History, pp. 119-20.

of this stock, he continues: "I selected *this tribe* of Short-horns as superior to all other cattle, not only as small consumers, but as great growers, and quick grazers, with the finest quality of beef. My first Duchess calved at Halton Castle, June 7, 1807. She was kept on grass only, in a pasture with nineteen other cows, and made in butter and milk for some months above two guineas per week." Not knowing the prices of either milk by the gallon, or butter by the pound, at that time, a statement of the quantity of each, which the cow made, would be more satisfactory to readers of the present day.

The pedigree of his original cow, above named, of the Duchess tribe, runs thus: Got by Daisy Bull (186) [Daisy Bull was by Favorite (252), dam by Punch (531), gr. d. by Hubback (319)], out of Duchess, by Favorite (252),—Duchess, by Hubback (319),—(Stanwick) Duchess, by James Brown's red bull (97). This cow Mr. Bates took to his farm at Halton Castle. Finding by the use of Short-horn bulls on his Highland cows how wonderfully it improved their size and quality as feeding animals, he was now fully confirmed of their superior value when in their purity of blood.

The cow "Duchess, by Daisy Bull," had produced Charles Colling a heifer, by Favorite (252), before, and in the same year that Bates purchased her, which heifer Colling retained. The year succeeding that in which Mr. Bates purchased the cow, she produced the bull Ketton (709), also by Favorite, which he retained for his subsequent breeding. Producing no heifer calves to him, Bates sold the cow in the year 1809, to a Mr. Donkin. While in the latter hands she bred several calves, but her heifers, if she had any, left no produce. At seventeen years of age, having done breeding, she was fed off and made an excellent carcass of beef. She was always a great milker.

Having his eye continually on this Duchess blood, at the final sale of Charles Colling's herd in 1810, a two-year-old heifer, "Young Duchess," by Comet (155), dam by Favorite (252), gr. d. by Daisy Bull (186), etc. [this gr. d. being the same "Duchess, by Daisy Bull," previously purchased of Colling by Mr. Bates], was advertised in the herd to be sold. She was a granddaughter of "Duchess, by Daisy Bull," and as will be seen by the pedigree above mentioned, closely interbred to the blood of Favorite (252). This heifer Bates determined to possess, but fearing to openly bid for her himself, (as *Mrs.* Colling, who was as shrewd and knowing a manager in the cattle line as her husband, and had well known of Bates' predilections for that blood, might covertly run her up to an exorbitant price,) he got another party to do the bidding, and the heifer was struck off to him at 183 guineas (a trifle over $900).* Much chagrin was afterwards manifested by the Collings when they found that Bates was the purchaser, and Mrs. C. declared to him that had they known it was his bid that was made, the heifer would have been run up to twice or thrice the amount before he could have taken her! So it appears there was some chicanery practiced in those early days of cattle sales. Bates, however, triumphed on the result of his bargain, as in this heifer he had secured, as it afterwards proved, his grand success and crowning glory as a Short-horn breeder. He called the heifer Duchess 1st, (the first one of her tribe recorded in the Herd Book,) and in his hands she became the founder, on the female side, of his Duchess tribe, which he exclusively bred for thirty-nine years afterwards, and which are continued in the hands of several owners in England and America to the present day.

Mr. Colling had been in possession of the tribe since he bought the original Duchess (Stanwick) cow, in the year 1784, twenty-six years previous to this transfer of Duchess 1st to Mr. Bates, so that the tribe on the side of their dams at the present time shows an unbroken lineage of eighty-eight years.

In 1821 Mr. Bates left Halton, and removed to a farm of 300 acres, at Ridley Hall—whether in Northumberland or Durham, we are not informed—which he had purchased (tenant right, we suppose) in 1818, and remained nine years, until 1830; but the place not altogether suiting him, and being rather inconvenient of access, he purchased Kirkleavington, an estate of about 1000 acres, in the valley of the Tees, and removed there in that year. He had now, by various manipulations and profitable trades in the disposition of his farms and otherwise, together with a legacy from an aunt, become possessed of about £20,000 ($100,000), which afforded him ample means with which to prosecute his cattle breeding and other labors, and gave him leisure to take part in the political, as well as economical questions of the day, touching the agricultural interests of the country.

Kirkleavington is thus described: "It is pleasantly situated on rising ground in the vale of Cleveland, and mostly on the new red sandstone formation. It contains some excellent grass land. It had been the seat of the Percys, and afterwards belonged to the Strathmore family, and was many years occupied by the Maynards, well

---

* The only bull of the pure Duchess blood in Colling's possession at the 1810 sale—Duke (226)—was sold to Anthony Compton, Carham Hall, Northumberland, for 105 guineas.

DUCHESS 1st, BY COMET. (155).

known in Short-horn history."* To Kirkleavington, in the midst of the famed Short-horn localities, which surrounded it, he brought his cattle stock of the several families of which it was at the time composed. In possession of Duchess 1st, by Comet (155), in the year 1810, he had worked industriously on by the use of the "Ketton" bulls, with her breeding. Down to the year 1819 that cow had produced him four heifer calves, viz.: Duchess 2d and 3d, by Ketton 1st (907); Duchess 4th and 5th, by Ketton 2d (710); and one bull [Cleveland (146)], by Ketton 3d (349). These Kettons were solely of the Duchess tribe, and as closely interbred as may be imagined, which their pedigrees will show. Yet it appears that Mr. Bates was not altogether satisfied with the exclusive use of the Duchess blood in his bulls. He once remarked to a gentleman who told us the fact, (and we have seen the same statement under his own name,†) that he at one time offered Robert Colling 100 guineas ($500) to have his 1st Duchess, by Comet (155), served by his "White bull" (151), whose dam and granddam were both by Favorite (252). "White bull" was of the "Princess" tribe, closely related to the Duchess, but strangers on the remote d m's side to the blood of the latter, she running back several generations to "Studley bull" (626). Colling refused the offer, and Bates was disappointed.

Down to the year 1831 Mr. Bates had bred thirty-two Duchess cows, and in the production of all he had used his bulls of purely Duchess blood with the exceptions of Marske (418),‡ which was sire to Duchess 7th, 8th and 9th, and Young Markse (419),§ which was sire to Duchess 11th. Still, having no other resource that suited him for a bull outside of his own herd, and holding an abiding faith in the value of the Duchess blood beyond any other than what was contained in "Colling's White bull" (151), and which latter blood, in the crosses that he particularly liked, had hitherto been out of his reach, he bred on with his Duchess bulls—after the Kettons—Cleveland (146); The Earl (646); The 2d Earl (1511); The 3d Earl (1514); and 2d Hubback (1423),|| down to the year 1831, in which

---

* Bell's History, p. 131.

† Bates' letter to "Mark Lane Express," written in 1842.

‡ Marske was bred by Robert Colling, calved in 1806, got by Favorite (252), dam by Favorite (252),—by Favorite (252),—by Punch (531),—by Hubback (319),—by Snowdon's bull (612),—by Masterman's bull (422),—by Harrison's bull (292),—by Studley bull (626), a pedigree full of the best blood.

§ Young Marske was got by Marske (418), out of Duchess 4th, by Ketton 2d (710), etc. He was of thorough Duchess descent excepting the cross through Marske, his sire.

|| 2d Hubback was but half *pure* Duchess blood, being got by The Earl (646), out of Red Rose 1st, by Yarborough (705),—The American Cow, etc.

his 32d Duchess (the last one begotten exclusively by the Duchess bulls, with the exception of the Marske and 2d Hubback crosses) was calved.

With the production of Duchess 32d, Mr. Bates halted, and wisely. From the possession of his Duchess 1st, in 1810, for a period of twenty-two years, we find but thirty-one of her *female* descendants recorded in the Herd Books. There were, meantime, sundry bulls dropped from them, but mostly sold to other breeders, excepting those which he had used in breeding, and even they had been, during some seasons, let out for service to various parties. The simple fact was, the Duchess cows, as a whole, had not been prolific, or constant breeders, through abortions or other causes, and whenever they passed a year or two without breeding, he fed off and slaughtered them.* The bulls descended from them showed no lack of virility, and Bates still contended that the tribe had increased in their fineness of quality, were admirable feeders, and good milkers when breeding. He was at a stand how further to proceed, and was really—unhappy. He had little faith in the blood of his neighboring breeders, however good many of their *individual* animals might have been, (a crotchet of his own, perhaps,) and although he had tried one or two of their bulls on some of his other tribes of cows, he did not, except in two or three individual cases, risk his Duchesses with them. From his occasional attacks on their blood (for he was prone to speak his mind freely of what he either liked or disliked) he had somewhat aroused their ire, and could find no relief in anything they had to offer him, if indeed, any offer of their assistance was made. He would not go to the Booths, as they contended that four crosses of well-bred pedigree bulls, on *good*, well-bred cows, originally without recorded pedigrees, were sufficient for the establishment of standard blood. Nor would he go to Mason, Wetherell, Maynard, or any other of the old breeders for a bull, as he found some flaw or other, more or less, in their pedigrees, or with being tainted late in the last century with the "Alloy" (Galloway) blood of Charles Colling, through the "Grandson of Bolingbroke" (280).

Hearing that Mr. John Stephenson, living at Wolviston, about twelve miles distant, had some stock descended from the Princess tribe of Robert Colling (and of which Stephenson had become possessed through Sir Henry Vane Tempest, and his wife, the Countess of Antrim, who had years before bought it from Colling), he rode

---

* Bell's History.

BELVEDERE. (1706).

over there one day to see whether he could find anything to suit him. In passing a stable on his way to the house, through a window opening into it, he spied the *head* of a bull which immediately excited his curiosity. He went in and there saw Belvedere (1706). He proceeded to the house, met Mr. Stephenson, and asked his price for the bull. He had used him several years, being then, in 1831, six years old, and not caring for further use of him, a bargain was struck. The next day Mr. S. drove the bull to Kirkleavington, and Mr. Bates paid £50 ($250) for him. The bull's pedigree was fully ascertained to the satisfaction of Mr. Bates, being essentially of the blood of Robert Colling's White bull (151), through descents of the same character, and he thus became established for some years, as the future breeding bull of Mr. Bates' herd. His pedigree is thus given in Vol. 3, English Herd Book:

"(1706.) BELVEDERE.—Yellow roan, calved April 6, 1826, bred by Mr. Stephenson, the property of Mr. Bates, Kirkleavington, near Yarm, got by Waterloo (2816), dam Angelina 2d, by Young Wynyard (2858),—Angelina, by Phenomenon (491),—Anne Boleyn, by Favorite (252),—Princess, by Favorite (252) [bred by R. Colling, and own sister to his White bull (151)],—by Favorite (252),—by Hubback (319),—by Snowdon's bull (612),—by James Masterman's bull (422),—by Mr. Harrison's bull [bred by Mr. Waistell, of Burdon] (292),* bought of Mr. Pickering, of Sedgefield, by Mr. Hall."

With the possession of Belvedere, in the next year he had by him two Duchess heifers—33d from Duchess 19th, and 34th from Duchess 29th. In 1833 he had one heifer, Duchess 35th, by Gambier (2046) [by Bertram (1716), bred by Mr. Whitaker, an outside cross altogether from his Duchess tribe]. In 1834 he had two Duchesses, 36th and 37th, by Belvedere. In 1835 he had 38th Duchess, by Norfolk (2377) [bred by Whitaker, got by 2d Hubback (1423), one-fourth part Duchess and the other three-fourths good blood, running back into the Colling stock], and Duchess 39th, 40th and 41st, by Belvedere. In 1837 he had Duchess 42d and 43d, by Belvedere, which were the last heifers of the tribe got by him.

On the introduction of Belvedere to his herd Mr. Bates used him freely on his other tribes in which his crosses will be found on examination of their pedigrees in the Herd Books, up to the year 1837. Having had the use of him now six years, and needing him no

---

* These figures, in the *Herd Book*, are a mistake, being (669), which we have corrected. (669) is Waistell's bull, got by Masterman's bull, in Belvedere's Herd Book pedigree.

further, as he then had several young bulls got by him of Duchess and other families; and determining that his blood go no further *directly* into other hands than his own, he had him slaughtered.

In the year 1838 we find three Duchess heifers, 44th, 45th and 46th, were produced by Short Tail (2621) (calved in 1835, by Belvedere, out of Duchess 32d), and in 1839 three more, 47th, 48th and 49th, (48th and 49th being twins), also by Short Tail. This bull, although fine in quality, was inferior in size and not commanding in appearance, yet Mr. Bates always said he was one of the best getters he had used. He bred him freely to many of his cows outside of the Duchess tribe. In the last named year (1839) he also had one Duchess, 50th, by Duke of Northumberland (1940) (calved in 1835, by Belvedere, out of his own daughter, Duchess 34th, having two direct crosses of Belvedere in him).

The crosses of Belvedere on the Duchess, as well as on the other tribes of cows belonging to Mr. Bates, as he had anticipated, proved eminently successful, as had also those of Short Tail and Duke of Northumberland. The fame of this last named bull has been so widely spread, both in tradition and history, that a further notice of him is scarcely necessary. His pedigree is fully shown in the English Herd Book, and his qualities are familiarly known wherever the Short-horns are intelligently bred.* His dam, Duchess 34th,† was a remarkable cow, both as a milker and in the exceeding symmetry of her form. At a year old she broke one of her legs, and was confined in the stable, most of the time in slings, for the better part of a year. Yet, when recovered, she grew up a stately cow, although from her constant milking and continuous breeding, she was usually low in flesh. She was never but once exhibited at a show, and then at nine years old, took the first prize over one of—if not the very best show cows in England at the time—Mr. Booth's famous Necklace, at four years old.

DUCHESS 34TH OFFERED TO GO TO AMERICA.

There is one fact which—years ago—we had publicly stated, and since repeated, relating to this cow, which was that Mr. Bates early

---

* While Mr. Bates owned Duke of Northumberland (and he died his property) he was at various times offered almost fabulous prices for him, but would not listen to any of them, determined that so good a bull should never go out of his own possession.

† Duchess 34th produced six living calves, viz.: Duke of Northumberland (1940), 2d Duke of Northumberland (3646), and Duchess 43d, all by Belvedere; also Duchess 46th, and 3d and 4th Dukes of Northumberland (3647) and (3649), by Short Tail (2621). Duchess 34th also produced one premature birth, and another bull calf, which lived but two months, making eight calves in all.

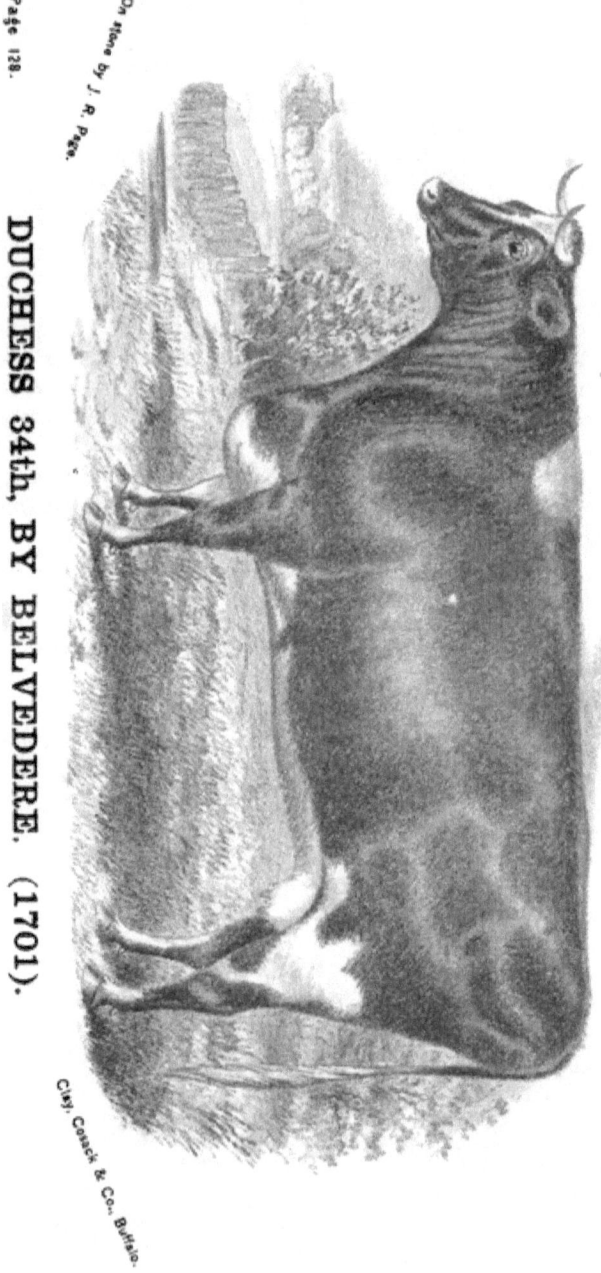

DUCHESS 34th, BY BELVEDERE, (1701).

in the year 1834 offered to sell her, then two years old, to Mr. Felix Renick, to be taken to the United States. This fact has been disputed here—but only on the *negative* testimony of a party who went out with Mr. Renick, and did not personally hear either the offer or its refusal. To set the truth of the fact at rest, which we stated (as received in the year 1841, from Mr. A. B. Allen, of New York, to whom Mr. Bates himself told it), we quote from a letter of Mr. Bates to Mr. Renick, written a year or two after the latter was in England: "Broken Leg (Duchess 34th), I offered you at 100 guineas. If you were to send twenty times that sum for her and her produce, I would not take it now." The full letter is found in "Bell's History," p. 227. She had, when the letter was written, produced the bull Duke of Northumberland (1940) to Mr. Bates, and it proved fortunate for him that Mr. Renick did not take her.

We here temporarily leave the Duchess tribe to notice a new introduction into his herd, viz.:

THE MATCHEM COW,

By which we arrive at another era in the *choice* breeding of Mr. Bates through the infusion of a new cross of blood into his Duchess tribe, and the history is too important to be omitted. We condense it from Mr. Bates' own account, as given in "*The New Farmers' Journal*" (English), dated August 6, 1841. "I purchased her in 1831, she then being four years old, at the sale of Mr. Brown, who had purchased her granddam at public sale many years before. The catalogue of Mr. Brown's sale only stated that the cow was by Matchem (2281),* and her dam by Young Wynyard (2859). The pedigree then traced no further—the original owner of the stock being dead previous to the sale [at which Mr. Brown bought her]—but I have since learned from those who knew the stock for many years, that the greatest

---

* The published pedigree of Matchem (2281), E. H. B., states that he was got by Bonny Face (807) or St. Albans (1412), but the fact has since been generally conceded among the older breeders that St. Albans was the true sire of Matchem. St. Albans was a pure Princess bull, being got by Wynyard (703), out of Nell Gwynn, by Phenomenon (491),—Princess, by Favorite (252),—by Favorite (252), etc., running back through Hubback (319) to Studley bull (626).

An odd story, connected with St. Albans, is related by Mr. Dixon in "*Saddle and Sirloin.*" The bull was at first called "Prince," and fell into the hands of a Mr. Wood, who did not at all appreciate him, and sold him to a *butcher*, whom Mr. Mason covertly engaged to buy him for £20 ($100). Three years afterwards Wood being at Chilton (Mr. Mason's place), he caught a glimpse of St. Alban's *head*, then fifteen years old, and exclaimed: "*Why, this is my old Prince; he was bought to kill.*" Mason, however, better knew the value of the bull. He had re-named him St. Albans, and bred him in his herd, and the bull thus became the sire of a noted progeny.—L. F. A.

attention had been paid to their breeding, and that the former owner had only used bulls of the Wynyard or Princess blood from the time the late Sir Henry Vane Tempest purchased that tribe from the late Robert Colling, now near forty years ago."*

To this Princess blood, as has already been observed, Mr. Bates had always been attached, and now, in this Matchem cow, from her appearance, and what he had learned of her breeding, he hoped for good results in her produce—*after his own manner* of obtaining them. When he purchased her he put her into the hands of his tenants, Messrs. Bell, for whom, including those in Mr. Brown's hands, she bred five, what Mr. Bates called, *inferior* calves, from being put to what he, in his criticising temper, called inferior bulls. He took the cow from the Bells at the price he originally paid for her, £11 ($55), believing that if bred to his own bulls of the Duchess tribe, she would breed first class stock.

Matchem Cow was white in color, of good size and symmetry, and a most excellent milker, to which latter quality Bates was always partial, and strived to promote through the whole course of his breeding. Her sire, Matchem, on his dam's side, run back into the Favorite, Foljambe, Hubback and Maynard blood; so that the cow was considered by Mr. Bates to be a proper instrument to work a fresh infusion of blood into his own Duchess tribe, although the latter had been crossed but a few years before into the blood of Belvedere. The cow came into Bates' herd early in 1833, and in November following she produced a roan heifer calf to Gambier (2046), of which calf we have no account beyond her birth; but Matchem Cow being put to Duke of Cleveland (1937) (by Bertram (1716), out of his 26th Duchess), she produced in November, 1834, Oxford Premium Cow, so called from having afterwards taken the first premium at the "Royal" Show at Oxford in the year 1839.†

---

* In the recorded pedigree of the bull Young Wynyard, he is stated to be bred by the Countess of Antrim. This lady bore that title in her own right of descent, altogether independent of her then husband, Sir Henry Vane Tempest, who was only a Baronet in title, and of course less in rank than his wife, she having the legal right to retain her title irrespective of the name of her husband. It was on her estate of Wynyard that the bull Young Wynyard was bred; and although both husband and wife bred Short-horn cattle, each had them as their own personal properties. The Wynyard bulls and the cows from which they were descended, were through three crosses by Favorite (252), bred back to Hubback (319), and for several generations beyond, to the original "cow bought of Mr. Pickering," about the year 1739, all of Robert Colling's Princess tribe.— L. F. A.

† Two of Oxford Premium Cow's bulls afterwards came to America; one, Locomotive 92 (4242) [by Duke of Northumberland (1940)], for Mr. J. C. Letton of Kentucky; the next, Duke of Wellington 55 (3654) [by Short Tail (2621)], for Mr. George Vail, Troy, N. Y. In January, 1836, Matchem Cow also produced a bull calf by Duke of Cleveland—made a steer; in December of

DUKE OF NORTHUMBERLAND. (1841).

Page 131.

After growing up, fit for service, Mr. Bates bred the 1st and 2d
Cleveland Lads, and 2d Duke of Oxford (9046) (by Duke of Northumberland, out of Oxford 2d, above mentioned) to more or less of
his Duchess cows, until the year of his death, in 1849. Thus the
two families of Duchess and Oxford (Matchem Cow), became incorporated, and the bulls of either tribe were severally used to both classes
of the cows, not only during Mr. Bates' life, but they have been, with
few exceptional crosses by bulls of other good blood, so continued to
the present day, under the more general term of "the Bates blood."
The female descendants have, however, always been kept separate in
both name and classification of Duchess, or Oxford, running back in
their own female genealogies; but now, after so long an interbreeding
of nearly forty years, become almost of identical blood.

Return to the Duchess Tribe.

Following the year in which Duchess 50th, by Duke of Northumberland (1940), was calved, in 1840, came Duchess 51st, by Cleveland Lad
(3407). In 1841 came Duchess 52d, by Holkar (4041) (mainly of
Belvedere and Duchess blood). In 1842 came Duchess 53d, by Duke
of Northumberland. In 1844, Duchess 54th, by 2d Cleveland Lad
(3408), Duchess 55th, by 4th Duke of Northumberland (3649), and
Duchess 56th, by 2d Duke of Northumberland (3646). In 1845,
Duchess 57th, by 2d Cleveland Lad (3408). In 1846, Duchess 58th,
by Lord Barrington (9308) (with three direct Bates crosses in him).
In 1847, 59th Duchess, by 2d Duke of Oxford (9046), and 60th, by
4th Duke of Northumberland (3649). In 1848 came 61st, 62d and
63d Duchess, by 2d Duke of Oxford; and in 1849, 64th Duchess, by
2d Duke of Oxford, being the last of the Duchess heifers calved in
Mr. Bates' possession.

We have been thus minute in enumerating the Duchess tribe while
in Mr. Bates' hands, to show with what pertinacity he adhered to his
own plans of breeding, and how he concentrated in them the strains
of blood which he considered most valuable to effect his purposes.
It was not, as he always remarked, simply to make money out of

---

the same year she produced Cleveland **Lad** (3407); in March, 1838, 2d Cleveland Lad (3408); and
in April, 1839, the heifer Oxford 2d, all three of them by Short Tail (2621). From this last calf
of Matchem Cow, Oxford 2d, with the exception of Oxford 4th, calved in 1843, by Duke of
Northumberland, which is the last calf Oxford Premium Cow produced, all the legitimate race of
Oxford's bulls and cows have proceeded. Having produced ten calves Matchem Cow was put
dry, and after feeding, made a carcass of 850 pounds of beef. Mr. Bates described her as being
remarkably healthy, hardy, and an extraordinary milker.

them—and which, in fact, he never did—but to achieve a success in breeding up a herd which should, in future hands, carry his name down to posterity. In this he succeeded after an anxious labor of forty years, as is fully evinced in the almost fabulous prices at which they have been sold and still sell—$3,000 to $5,000 each, and even more than the latter price for bulls, and much higher prices for cows, when they can be purchased at all, which is seldom; in such close corporation do their owners hold them that such an event in Short-horn history is properly worth recording. Nor, need these prices be altogether called infatuation. Many noblemen, as well as commoners in England, who can wield the purses, and intelligent, enterprising men in America, who have the spirit and means at command, are eager to purchase and breed one or the other, or both the "Duchess" and "Oxfords," and when they feel unable or unwilling to grapple with the "pure Bates" in its fullness, they strive to get all they can of the blood wherewith to cross their herds. Such is the fact, in the year 1872; and although a succeeding generation may call it a folly, yet the additional fact that the use of this blood on both sides of the Atlantic has improved the qualities of many of the Short-horn race, and increased their popularity with their breeders, proves that the result has been both good and profitable.

Notwithstanding the above laudatory remarks, let it be understood by the reader that we take no sides in the question of the superior merit of the "Bates stock" over many others of different strains of blood and breeding. We only write *history*. There no doubt may be, and are, individual animals of divergent blood, and miscellaneous breeding, of pure Short-horn stock equally good—possibly better than the average animals of the "Bates stock," and perhaps equally valuable for practical uses. Of this each one will judge for himself; we wish, in our remarks, to prejudice nothing.

Mr. Bates' other Tribes.

Of the Oxford tribe, from the year 1834 to the year 1849, inclusive, Mr. Bates had bred fourteen females.

Of the Waterloo tribe (the first cow got by Waterloo (2816), dam by Waterloo (1816), being two crosses by that bull, as we find in her pedigree, Vol. 3, E. H. B., which he bought at Thorpe, Durham), Mr. Bell's history gives the following account written by Mr. Bates: "I have seen the gentleman who bred the Waterloo cow, lately, and he stated to me that he and his father had had the breed for fifty years, and that they were well descended all that time, having had a Son of Comet (155), and other blood before the cross of Waterloo (2816)." Of these Mr. Bates bred, from 1832 to 1849, inclusive, from the original cow, twelve females.

Of the Red Rose tribe, springing from the original one he bought of Mr. Hustler, (descended from the "American Cow," previously mentioned,) from the year 1821 to the year 1833, inclusive, he bred eleven females. Taking a premium with the 13th of the tribe, calved in 1834 (the 12th in descent from the original, Red Rose 1st), at the Cambridge Exhibition, she was afterwards called Cambridge Rose, and the successive heifers of the Red Rose family were called Cambridge Rose down to the year 1849, inclusive, of which there were seven in number, making eighteen of the entire number of females descended from the original cow.

Of the Wild Eyes tribe, Mr. Parrington, of the Middlesbro' farm, near Stockton, on the river Tees, a good Short-horn breeder, sold his herd (Mr. Bell says in the year 1831, but this must be a mistake, as the birth of the calf which Mr. Bates bought there with her pedigree in the 3d and 5th Vols. E. H. B., is dated in 1832), and Mr. Bates bought a roan heifer calf called Wildair; but after going to his farm she obtained the name of Wild Eyes. She was got by Superior (1975), dam by Wonderful (700), etc. (This cow has, by some, been confounded with the famous cow Wildair, bred by Robert Colling, but not so, being of altogether different descent from her.) The full pedigree of the tribe is recorded in the cow Wild Eyes 26th, imported by Mr. Cochrane, of Canada, Vol. 9, p. 1008, A. H. B. Of this tribe Mr. Bates bred from his first calf bought of Mr. Parrington from the years 1835 to 1849, inclusive, twenty-nine females.

Of the Foggathorpe tribe, Mr. Bates bought the original cow Foggathorpe, of Mr. Edwards, Market Weighton. She was then ten years old, got by Marlbro' (1189), out of Rosebud, by Ebor (997), etc. Her full pedigree is in Vol. 5, p. 386, E. H. B. From her descended five females, bred by Mr. Bates from the year 1840 to 1850, inclusive—the last calf being dropped after Mr. B.'s death.

Many bulls, and possibly some females, were sold from these tribes, but no females from the Duchess and Oxfords, during the years that Mr. Bates was breeding them. Of the latter two families we have seen no account in other hands previous to his decease. The females were all bred to Mr. Bates' Duchess and Oxford bulls, with few exceptions, and the exceptions possessed much of their blood.

COLORS OF THE BATES HERDS.

It may be of some interest to know the prevailing colors attached to the various tribes of Mr. Bates' breeding; not that we deem any particular color or shades, or admixtures of color, from deep red to pure white, objectionable—all being equally legitimate in Short-horn blood—but there was more uniformity in the colors of Mr. Bates' herd probably than in any other large one of his time.

To trace back the colors of the ancestry of Duchess 1st, by Comet: The original one of the tribe—the Stanwick Cow—was a yellowish red roan; her sire, J. Brown's *red* bull, of course, was red in color. What was the color of her daughter, by Hubback (he was yellow-red and white), we are not informed; but the granddaughter, Duchess, by Daisy bull (his color not given), was red roan, with some patches of white intermixed. Of the other daughter, by Favorite (he was roan), we have no information; but her daughter, Bates' Duchess 1st, by Comet (he was light roan), was red and white, the red largely predominating. The bulls, Ketton 1st, 2d and 3d, which Mr. Bates used for the next seven years in the Duchess breeding, were mostly red, with some white. Marske (418), the next bull, was roan. The next bull, Cleveland, was red and white. Young Marske, red and white. The Earl, yellow-red, some white. The 2d and 3d Earls, both red and white; 2d Hubback, yellow-red and white. These were the bulls used down to the year 1832, when Belvedere was brought into the herd. All the Duchesses descended from these bulls down to the 32d, inclusive, were red and white (the red largely predominating over the white), excepting the 12th, red, and 19th, which latter was yellow-red.

Belvedere was yellow-roan in color. Six of his Duchess heifers were roan; three red and white, and one red; the only Duchess heifer calf got by Gambier (red) was red also; the only one got by Norfolk (roan) was also roan. Short Tail (red and white) got five red and white, and one red, heifers. Duke of Northumberland (red roan) got the first and only pure white heifer ever bred by Mr. Bates of the Duchess family, and another roan heifer. Cleveland Lad (red roan) got one Duchess heifer, roan. Holkar (deep red with little white) got one Duchess heifer, red and white; 2d Cleveland Lad (roan) got one red, one red and white, and one roan Duchess heifer; 2d Duke of Northumberland (red and white) got but one Duchess heifer, red and white; 4th Duke of Northumberland (red and white) got two red heifers. Lord Barrington (red and white) got one Duchess heifer, red; 2d Duke of Oxford (roan) got two roans, one red roan, one red and white, and one red heifer, the last one finishing up all the Duchesses of Mr. Bates' breeding.

Matchem Cow, the original dam of the Oxford tribe, it will be recollected was white, and from her came the lighter colors which followed in her progeny, all of her seven calves, after coming into Mr. Bates' possession, being roans, and red roans. Only one of the heifers of this tribe was white. She was Oxford 3d, by Duke of Northumberland (red roan), out of Oxford Premium Cow, roan; another of them was red and white, by the same bull, and out of the same cow; another was red and white, and all the others roan.

Of the Waterloo tribe, four were roans, four red, three red and white, and one yellow-red and white.

Of the Red Roses, nine were red and white, and two roan, and of their successors, the Cambridge Roses, three were roans, one white, one red and white, and one red.

Of the Wild Eyes, seventeen were roan, two red, six red and white, one yellow-red and white, and two white.

Of the Foggathorpes, the original dam was roan, and of the produce one was white, the next one red and white, and the remaining three roan.

It will thus be seen that of all Mr. Bates' chosen tribes the red and white largely prevailed in his Duchess and Red Roses; the roans in the others, and the whites were seldom found in either. We draw no inferences either of partiality or prejudice which Mr. Bates had in the way of colors, only stating the fact as matter of history. To the present day red, and red and white, prevail in the Duchess, and red and white, and roans prevail in the Oxfords, with now and then a rare exception of white in either tribe, while the other tribes have been so widely scattered and crossed by other and divers bulls, that we can scarcely keep track of their colors as having any fixed peculiarity.

It may be asked, Was Mr. Bates successful in winning prizes on his stock at the various exhibitions of Short-horns held in England during the time of his breeding?

As we find among his numerous communications on that subject, he was, as a rule with himself, opposed to prize exhibitions of his stock at the various cattle shows, for the reason, as he remarked, that there were few men among the judges usually appointed on these occasions, fit for the duty. He once remarked that "there were a hundred men fit for a Prime Minister where there was one competent to act as a proper judge of Short-horns." He did occasionally exhibit, however, and won more or less first prizes; but in some cases afterwards, insisted that his inferior beasts did the winning, while his best ones were overlooked—one of his crotchets, possibly. He only exhibited his stock on a few occasions, and those, in time, a good way apart, except in the years of "The Royal" in 1839, '40 and '41, when he was highly successful, mainly in his Duchess and Oxford animals.

During his whole cattle breeding career Mr. Bates bought, bred and sold, many other good Short-horns, with an eye no doubt to profit, for we cannot well conceive his philanthropy, except in his Duchess tribe, to extend so far as not to turn his labors to the best advantage, while it is quite certain that in the long-continued breeding of his Duchess tribe, other than in the bulls he sold, he played a losing game in a financial way, and won only on the posthumous fame with which his name will long be remembered.

One important item connected with Mr. Bates' success as a breeder should not be omitted. Instead of turning his stock over to the exclusive care of herdsmen, as is the practice of many Short-horn breeders, he looked carefully over them himself—although he always had one or more herdsmen to do his bidding—*personally* saw to all their wants, and knew every small particular relating to them. *He loved his cattle, and almost made companions of them.* They would follow him all around the fields and yards when he went in to look at them. He would fondle them lovingly, talk to and familiarly pat and caress them, while they in return would rub their heads along his body, legs, and arms, lick his hands, and playfully chew the skirts of his coat. So affectionately would they hang about him while he was among them that his herdsmen could not drive them. On one such occasion his cowman not being able to get the cattle away from Mr. Bates, and getting quite irritated, exclaimed: "I wish you'd keep out aft' way. You do fa' mair ill than good, for they won't leave you, and there's no driving them."*

Mr. Bates had another peculiarity which accounted for his usually having a superfluous number of bulls on hand which he did not use, or but seldom. He would neither sell, nor let bulls, except to parties who had first class cows to put to them, remarking that the bulls would do *him* no justice when bred to inferior cows. "One day Mr.

---

* Bell's History.

Wetherell selected two of his bulls at Kirkleavington, which Mr. Bates said he would sell him. Mr. Bates inquired about the herd into which he, Wetherell, proposed to send the bulls. The latter asked, in reply, 'of what consequence is that, so long as you get the money for them?' Mr. Bates rejoined, '*he would not sell any man a bull unless he knew the herd to which he was going*, for if the cross did not answer, *all the blame would be attributed to the bull.*' Mr. Wetherell, on leaving, could not refrain from expressing his opinion in strong terms in regard to Mr. Bates for refusing to sell his cattle at high prices, so long as he got paid for them."* There have been few breeders, we fancy, so fastidious. When a good bargain is offered for a beast they wish to sell, little regard is paid to its destiny.

Much more might be here related of Mr. Bates and his Short-horn career, as we find a great deal written by him, and of him, in sundry English magazines and journals, some of which is copied into Mr. Bell's history. Another pleasant, gossipy writer, "Druid," whose real name was Dixon, now deceased, related much of him in his "Saddle and Sirloin," a book containing various desultory information about cattle and horse breeders in England within the last thirty years. But they would add little to the substantial fund of information which we have already given, or may yet give, touching the Short-horns and their breeders; and we have no space for repetition of what does not immediately concern our history; nor do we wish to overload our pages with matter tending to an undue exaltation of Mr. Bates and his stock over other breeders and their stocks—equally meritorious in their exertions to improve the quality and blood of their herds.

But, it is time we close with Mr. Bates. His character has been sketched, faithfully, as we trust, as a man of unflinching integrity and stern honesty of purpose, and if he sometimes indulged in undue partialities towards his own, and unjust prejudices towards the stock of rival breeders, in which the fallibility of his judgment was exposed, we must remember that both he and his herds were also subjected to the attacks and criticisms of others, which may have tried his patience and vexed his temper.

In a brief memoir of Mr. Bates, highly creditable to his character, in the *Farmers' Magazine* for the year 1850, the writer thus closes: "Active in mind, temperate in his habits, nay, I may say abstemious, for he tasted no intoxicating liquors for some years before his death, and living almost in the open air, he knew little of disease, and seldom,

---

* Bell's History. It is not so stated, but we infer that the bulls were not taken.—L. F. A.

if ever, consulted a physician. A month before death, however, his health began to fail, a disease of the kidneys became painful and harassing, and he went to Redcar to try the effects of the sea air, but which, so far from removing, seemed only to increase the malady. It was sometime before he could be prevailed on to consult a medical adviser, and when he did he refused the greater part of his medicine.

"He gradually sunk and died on the 26th day of July, 1849, and was buried in the church-yard at Kirkleavington. A monument was erected to his memory by a few friends and admirers of his exertions in stock breeding, with the following inscription:

THIS MEMORIAL OF
THOMAS BATES,
OF KIRKLEAVINGTON,
ONE OF THE MOST DISTINGUISHED BREEDERS OF SHORT-HORN CATTLE,
IS RAISED BY A FEW FRIENDS WHO APPRECIATE HIS LABORS
FOR THE IMPROVEMENT OF BRITISH STOCK,
AND RESPECT HIS CHARACTER,
BORN 21ST JUNE, 1776—DIED 26TH JULY, 1849." *

The Sale of Mr. Bates' Herd and their English Successors.

Mr. Bates left a will bequeathing a considerable estate principally to two or three nephews. The only one of these engaged in agriculture was settled in Germany, and had no time or opportunity of attending to a herd, so that it came to be sold on the 9th of May, 1850. One of the nephews of Mr. Bates, living at Heddon, in Northumberland, but then residing in London, who we understand was a lawyer, was made his executor, and wound up the estate, a valuable portion of which lay in his cattle and other farm stock. There were some other difficulties we have learned, arising out of the conditions of the will, with a threat by some of the dissatisfied heirs, to throw it into chancery. The stock was expensive to keep, and troublesome, for one not acquainted with it, to manage. Added to these embarrassments, Short-horn cattle generally were low in price at the time. Rival breeders also had their eyes upon them, and hoped to drive good bargains at the sale; and it is stated that Lord Ducie, who, in the event, became a considerable purchaser, tried an underhanded scheme for a part of it, which, however, the executor detected and foiled. The sale had been widely advertised, and as might be supposed, the final disposition of the herd of such a noted breeder drew

---

* Bell's History.

a large attendance. The animals were arranged in their several tribes, and sold as follows:

DUCHESS TRIBE.

4 Cows,	£322	7s.
3 Heifers,	442	0
1 Heifer Calf,	162	15
4 Bulls,	625	16
2 Bull Calves,	75	12
14	£1627	10

Averaging $581 each.

Of the Duchess females, Lord Ducie bought Duchess 55th, 5 years old, at $551; 59th, 2 years old, at $1,050; and 64th, 9 months old, at $813.

Of the bulls, the same gentleman bought 4th Duke of York (10167), 3 years old, at $1,050.

Grand Duke (10284), 2 years old, was also sold for $1,076.

The other animals of the tribe were sold at lesser prices to different English breeders.

OXFORD TRIBE.

4 Cows,	£288	15s.
2 Heifers,	95	11
4 Heifer Calves,	303	9
3 Bulls,	206	17
13	£894	12

Averaging $313 each.

Of the Oxford females, Col. Lewis G. Morris of Mt. Fordham, N. Y., U. S. A., bought Oxford 5th, 5 years old, got by Duke of Northumberland (1940), for $370; also Oxford 10th, 16 months old (daughter to Oxford 5th), by 3d Duke of York (10166), for $267; and Mr. Noel J. Becar, of New York, bought Oxford 13th, a 4 months' calf of Oxford 5th, by 3d Duke of York (10166), for $330. These cows came to America, and proved successful breeders. No other animals at the sale were then purchased by any Americans.

WATERLOO TRIBE.

2 Cows,	£101	17s.
3 Heifers,	180	12
1 Heifer Calf,	74	11
6	£357	00

Averaging $297.50 each.

CAMBRIDGE ROSE TRIBE.

1 Cow,	£47	5s.
1 Heifer,	73	10
1 Heifer Calf,	26	5
3	£147	0

Averaging $245 each.

WILD EYES TRIBE.

9 Cows,	£328	13s.
7 Heifers,	430	10
2 Heifer Calves,	64	1
4 Bulls,	254	2
3 Bull Calves,	126	0
25	£1203	6

Averaging $241 each.

Of the bulls of the Wild Eyes tribe, Balco (9918) [by 4th Duke of York (16167)], then 15 months old, sold for $813. He was afterwards purchased by Col. Morris, of Mt. Fordham, N. Y., and brought to America.

FOGGATHORPE TRIBE.

2 Cows,	£74	11s.
1 Heifer Calf,	31	10
4 Bulls,	222	12
7	£328	13

Averaging $235 each.

Total amount of sale, 68 animals, £4,558 1s.—$22,240—average $327 each.

What a paltry price compared with what their descendants would bring now, in 1872!

For a herd sustaining the reputation which it had acquired under the long-continued management of Mr. Bates, aside from the adverse circumstances which we have related, the above prices will be considered remarkably low; but it must be remembered that all agricultural values were at a low ebb in England, and cattle of the better breeds had sunk to their minimum depression. Mr. Bates' executor was also but little practiced in cattle management, and the herd had been measurably neglected, both in care and appearance, from what they would have been had their old master been living. Yet most of the animals fell into good hands, who well appreciated their value, and in the space of a few years rose to a reputation, and brought prices never before reached in England.

Lord Ducie's Breeding and Sales.

While we have the herd of Mr. Bates in hand we will trace its history to a recent day, when a part of it fell into the hands of his *American* successors. We have seen that Earl Ducie bought three of the female Duchesses and one of the bulls at the Bates sale. He also bought two of the female Oxfords—6th, 4 years old, and 11th, 9 months old, at $656 each. These animals he added to a herd he had already established, of superior quality and excellence. He was a gentleman of liberal spirit in expenditure; enthusiastic in his love of good stock; and determined to maintain a herd of Short-horns equal to, if not the superior of, any other in England. He purchased good things at liberal prices, never balking at the money value when the creature suited him. His health, however, was delicate, and he lived but about two years after the sale of Mr. Bates' herd. Meantime he had bred his stock with marked judgment and success; the value of good Short-horns had rapidly advanced, and the reputation of the "Bates" stock—particularly the Duchess and Oxfords—had increased in public favor, so that when in the month of August, 1852, Lord Ducie's executors made a sale of his entire herd, the occasion brought together an array of breeders such as had not been gathered in England on any like occasion since the days of the Collings. The sale had been for some time announced, and several American gentlemen crossed the ocean for the purpose of attending it and making purchases, expecting to compete with the elite of England's breeders if successful in effecting them. Nor were the Americans mistaken. They did meet the English breeders on their own soil, outbid and outpurchased them of some of the best animals in the herd, as follows:

Mr. Samuel Thorne, of Thorndale, New York, bought the cows Duchess 59th, by 2d Duke of Oxford (9046), 5 years old, for $1,837; Duchess 64th, by 2d Duke of Oxford (9046), 4 years old, for $3,150; Duchess 68th, by Duke of Gloster (11382), 1 year old, for $1,575.

(Duchess 68th was killed by the falling of a mast on shipboard, while on her passage to America.)

Messrs. L. G. Morris and N. J. Becar, of New York, purchased the cow Duchess 66th, 3 years old, for $3,675, and she (Duchess 66th) was the only one of the Duchess tribe coming to America which left any *female* descendants now living. These gentlemen also purchased the bull Duke of Gloster, 2763 (11382), 3 years old, for $3,412.

Mr. Thorne also purchased of Mr. Bolden the bull Grand Duke, 545 (10284), formerly sold at Mr. Bates' sale in 1850, for $5,000, and brought him to America with his other purchases. A few years afterwards Grand Duke becoming disabled, Mr. Thorne also purchased 2d Grand Duke, 2181 (112961), bred by Earl Ducie, at the price of $5,000, and brought him to America.

Mr. George Vail, of Troy, N. Y., and Gen. George Cadwallader, of Philadelphia, purchased the bull 4th Duke of York (10167), 6 years old, at $2,625, but he unfortunately died on his passage across the ocean.

The other animals of the Duchess, Oxford, and other tribes, passed into the hands of various English breeders. Several of the descendants of the Duchess have since come to America; among them one bull, Duke of Airdrie, 9798 (12730), and his dam, Duchess of Atholl, by 2d Duke of Oxford (9046), in the hands of Mr. R. A. Alexander, in Kentucky, and three heifers, Duchess 97th, 101st and 103d, to Mr. M. H. Cochrane, Compton, Province of Quebec, (Lower Canada.) Of the Oxfords, one, Grand Duke of Oxford, 3988 (16184), was imported by Mr. Sheldon, Geneva, N. Y. Of the Duchess and Oxford *females*, there are now in England and America, some scores in number. The females are held in but few hands in England, and a less number in the United States and Canada. The bulls, however, have been widely scattered, and sold at prices commensurate with the values which breeders partial to their blood place upon their merits.

The sale of Lord Ducie's herd was the highest in price which had taken place since that of Charles Colling in the year 1810, but relatively to agricultural prices in England at the two periods (Colling's at a time of great inflation, and Lord Ducie's at a time of comparative depression), the latter sale was by far the highest, averaging $700 per head for 49 cows, heifers, and heifer calves, and $959 each for 13 bulls, making for the 62 animals the round sum of $46,809, an average of $723 each, within a fraction.

To follow in detail the result, separately, of the Duchess and Oxford tribes, at Lord Ducie's sale, we give a synopsis of each: 8 Duchesses (females) sold for £3,212 10s. 5d., averaging nearly $2,008 each; 4 Oxfords (females) sold for £876 15s., averaging nearly $1,096 each.

In addition to these were the before named Duke of Gloster, at £682 10s. ($3,412), and 4th Duke of York, at £523 ($2,625), and 5th Duke of Oxford to Lord Feversham, at £315 or $1,575.

Mr. Bell tells a story of Lord Ducie after the purchase of 4th Duke of York (10167), at the Bates sale, which is so characteristic of the monopolizing spirit of some of the English Short-horn breeders, that we suppose it to be true. "He sent his agent out to buy the bull 3d Duke of York (10166) (a Duchess bull), then in other hands, that he might slaughter him [Bates fashion], and prevent his blood being used by other breeders, in which he succeeded, and had the bull remorselessly killed, thus supposing he had secured to himself, in his own 4th Duke of York, the only remaining one of the blood; but meeting Mr. Tanqueray shortly after, in London, his Lordship asked him what he was doing in the Short-horn line; to which Tanqueray replied, 'I have just come into possession of 5th Duke of York (10168).' With evident chagrin Ducie answered, 'I had lost sight of *him*.'" So his barbarity, as well as selfishness, in sacrificing a noble beast was thus signally punished.

CHAPTER VI.

Mr. Bates' Influence on the Short-horns—Did he Improve Them?

THAT a sagacious, intelligent man, devoting nearly sixty years of an active life to the breeding of a favorite race of animals, divested of family cares, enthusiastically attached to his stock, selecting his original herd from the best blood of the country, and concentrating all the energies and skill at his command to their highest development, should not succeed in improving their qualities to a greater or less extent, would prove him to be a dullard, or that he worked upon a race of animals incapable of any further development. Neither of these conclusions will be credited to the labors of Mr. Bates, or charged to the qualities of so fine a race of cattle as the Short-horns. During his life no one had greater opportunities to know the origin and lineage of every noted Short-horn in England. In his younger days he was contemporary, acquainted with, and on friendly terms with most, if not all, the substantial and reputable breeders of the country, and after the Collings had retired no one probably knew the pedigrees of the earlier herds of the country any better than, if so well as, himself. In his own private copy of the first volume of Coates' Herd Book, he made extended notes of the ancestry of many of the earlier cattle therein recorded, beyond what the printed pedigrees contained, and these notes, of the bulls, we have had the privilege of copying into our own. At the close of his life he probably knew more about Short-horns than any man in England. He had seen Hubback, Foljambe, Bolingbroke, Favorite, and Comet, and many of their contemporaries, male and female, together with the other most noted bulls and cows of his time. He had been intimate with the herds of the Maynards, the Wetherells, the Booths, the Wrights, the Charges, the Masons, the Hutchinsons, as well as their many younger contemporaries. He knew the superior as well as inferior qualities which their herds possessed. Probably no man in England was a better judge of cattle than he, and at his death he left a herd which challenged the admiration of numerous Short-horn breeders on both sides the Atlantic—and that admiration has not abated with the increasing generations of their progeny. In this assertion we know we are trenching on delicate, if not debatable ground. Yet the prices which they have brought for many years past, and still bring, bear indisputable evidence of the fact, whether those prices are based on sound judgment, or fancy only. We do not assert that for general practical uses the Bates stock are really better than very many animals of more miscellaneously, yet well-bred herds, but in their deeply concentrated blood giving it the power of transmission into others, they are much admired and widely sought.

On Mr. Bates' death the animals of his most cherished blood were quickly appropriated by a few who had long been partial to their merits, and wielded purses to command their possession. £200 to £300 ($1,000 to $1,500) would then buy any Short-horn in England. Three years afterwards it cost £600 to £1,000 ($3,000 to $5,000) as we have seen, to buy the same animals, or their produce, in close competition between Englishmen and Americans, and prices both in England and America have since ranged even higher for both bulls and cows of favorite strains of their blood.

The above remarks are made with no invidious reflection upon the valuable stock of other breeders, or their herds. There are many herds, as well as individual animals, both in England and America, of the highest excellence; but with the exception of the Booths, there has been no herd of Short-horns so closely interbred as that of Mr. Bates, and containing so strong and deep a concentration of blood, and the bulls from which have stamped more strikingly their several individualities upon stranger herds. Not that these cattle in themselves shew such marked superiority over many others, but from their long compacted genealogy and careful breeding, they impress their own characteristics upon their progeny in a greater degree than others which, through their divergent crosses, have not been so compactly bred. Hence their highly estimated value, as certified by the auctioneer's hammer, as well as in private sales. Let the public, if they will, call men fools, or enthusiasts, who pay those exhorbitant prices, but when we see veteran breeders, life-long in the pursuit, as well as those of less experience, doing so, it may well be supposed there is something in it beyond mere assumption, caprice or fancy. Who in England ever produced such bulls with their *in-and-in* bred crosses as, early in this century, did Charles Colling in Comet (155), by Favorite; thirty years later, as did Bates in Duke of Northumberland (1940), by Belvedere; or, still thirty years afterwards, as did Richard Booth, culminating in Commander-in-Chief (21452), by Velasco—and all of them with cows to match? And yet, with all this emphasis, we do not say that there have not since been equally good bulls as these, and cows also, bred in both England and America; but they have not yet achieved the *notoriety* of the others, although a future day may prove that some of them do excel even Comet, Duke of Northumberland, or Commander-in-Chief.

The critical reader may here make a note, and accuse us of writing up the Bates and Booth blood of cattle. Not a word of it. We only state facts that cannot and will not, on mature examination, be contradicted. Almost every herd of note, in either England or America, has more or less of these bloods in their veins. In no well-bred Short-horns whatever can be traced so many crosses back as into the bull Favorite (252), bred by Charles Colling. His blood was the foundation of the bulls of the elder Booth, afterwards of Bates, in both bulls and cows, and also many other of the contemporary, and through them of numerous later English and American herds. Let the pedigrees be traced and the fact will so prove.

If the brothers Colling, one in his thirty, and the other in his forty years' career of breeding, were pronounced by their contemporaries to be "improvers," why not the elder Booths and Bates, Mason, Lord Althorpe, and numerous others of the elder, and their younger followers, making their original selections from the Colling bloods, and appropriating the best cows they could secure from others, and breeding them with skill, adhering almost throughout to the original blood, and their better qualities have been improvers also? Charles Colling may not, during his life-time, have bred a finer one than the Stanwick Cow (his original Duchess), or the "beautiful Lady Maynard"—as he himself acknowledged—which he bought of his elder contemporary, Mr. Maynard; but he had the sagacity to keep their blood as compact as possible by breeding in-and-in their progeny to a depth and endurance which stamped it almost in perpetuity through the successive bulls and heifers proceeding from them, thus transmitting their qualities down to present generations. The elder Booth copying from him, and procuring Colling bulls, which he used upon cows of his own selection for their superior merits from other breeders, did the same, and so following, did Bates, only that the latter had the good fortune to obtain some of the Colling cows, which Booth did not; the latter, as we have already stated, selecting his original cows from neighboring herds, looking only to their good qualities, without

Page 146.

On stone by J. R. Page.

COMMANDER IN CHIEF. (21451).

Clay, Cosack & Co., Buffalo.

any regard to pedigree, other than the fact that they were true Short-horns. Thus his pedigrees ending in such cows are shorter than those of the Bates' Duchesses, as well as of several other breeders whose pedigrees run back to the earliest Short-horn records.

Still, with all their excellencies of quality, the styles of the Booth, and Bates, and some other herds have been and are still different in some of their valuable as well as fancy points. Each one adopted his own standard of excellence, each strived to attain it, and both of them succeeded to a greater or less extent. We do not propose to institute a comparison of their qualities. Rivalries and competitions ran high between the elder Booths, Bates, Mason, and other of the elder breeders while living, and it is not impossible that equal rivalries and competition may now exist among the admirers of their different bloods, as well as in the bloods of other distinguished breeders. It is a noble, a praiseworthy competition, and so long as honorably conducted, altogether commendable.

CHAPTER VII.

THE ELDER SHORT-HORN BREEDERS CONTEMPORARY WITH THE COLLINGS AND THEIR IMMEDIATE SUCCESSORS.

Of the elder breeders, we regret that no clear history of their labors reach us except incidentally, as we find occasional references to them in the scanty agricultural publications of their day, and trace the pedigrees of their stocks in the earlier volumes of the English Herd Books. John Maynard was the senior of the Collings in breeding, Charles having bought in 1786 or '7, his cows Lady Maynard, and her daughter, Young Strawberry, from Maynard's herd. There were the Blackets, the Aislabies, the Milbanks, the Pennymans, the elder Stevenson, and others, anterior to the Collings, whose names have been incidentally mentioned in our previous pages, who bred famous cattle, but of them we have been able to glean few particulars. The first volume of the English Herd Book, published in 1822, contained the names of but about one hundred and forty breeders, including the Collings, Booths, and Thomas Bates.

Among the immediate contemporaries of the Collings, and the elder Booth, was Christopher Mason, of Chilton. He bred largely, possessed a valuable herd, purchased and used bulls from the Collings, and many noted animals of the present day are found descended from his stock. He was among the first class breeders of his time, and made a large, if not final sale of his herd in the year 1829, of which Lord Althorpe (afterwards Earl Spencer) purchased quite a number. The larger breeders, whose names are in the first Herd Book, aside from those already named, were Lord Althorpe, of Wiseton; Messrs. Alderson, of Ferrybridge; Bower, of Welham; Champion, of Blythe; Charge, of Newton; Coates (first editor of the Herd Book), of Carlton; Compton, of Northumberland; Curwen, of Cumberland; Earnshaw, of Ferrybridge; Gibson, of Northumberland; Hutchinson, of Stockton; Hustler, of Acklam; Ibetson, of Denton Park; William Jobling, of ———; Anthony Maynard, of Morton-le-Moor; J. C. Maynard, of Harlsey; Col. Mellish, of ———; Ostler, of

Audley; Parker, of Sutton House; Parrington, of Middlesbro'; Robertson, of Ladykirk; Rudd, of Marton; Seymour, of Woodhouse Close; Simpson, of Babworth; Smith, of Dishley; Spoors, of Northumberland; Sir Henry Vane Tempest, of Wynyard; Thomas, of Chesterfield; Col. Trotter, of ———; Wiles, of Bearl; Wetherell, of Kirkby-Malery; Whitaker, of Greenholme; White, of Loughborough; Wright, of ———, and Wright, of Cleasby.

Aside from the above list appear the names of many small breeders, some with only one, and others representing only a few pedigrees each.

All the breeders above named reared and sold animals of repute, and many of them of marked distinction. We can name but a few of the sales that were made and the prices their animals brought; and even those we can name are found only in fragmentary reports given in the agricultural journals of the time, or since recorded on the recollection of contemporary breeders. Some of the older ones of these breeders sold cattle to the Collings; other younger ones obtained some of their animals from the Collings, either directly, by purchase, or indirectly by hiring their bulls.

At the time of Lord Althorpe's death, in 184-, his herd numbered about one hundred and fifty. His legatee, Mr. Hall (the cattle having been left to him), soon afterwards disposed of them at public sale. One bull brought 400 guineas ($2,100), another 370 guineas ($1,942), and some of the cows 200 guineas ($1,050) each.

Lord Althorpe (afterwards Earl Spencer) was a liberal breeder, and enthusiastic in his attachment to the Short-horns. He many years kept, and had at his decease, probably the largest herd in England. He was a bachelor, or if married, left no children, and his estate and title descended to his brother, who had no taste for cattle, which is probably the reason why the elder brother gave his herd to Mr. Hall. Lord Althorpe corresponded frequently with Mr. Bates, visited him at his home and bought some cattle of him. With how much skill his Lordship bred his animals we are not informed, although he paid much personal attention to them during the leisure time he could withdraw from state affairs. As we find many excellent Shorthorns which trace their pedigrees into his herd, there can be little doubt that he bred many first class animals.

Mr. Jonas Whitaker, of Greenholme, Otley, although a large cotton manufacturer, was an extensive breeder, and had many fine cattle. All, or nearly all, of our American Col. Powel's importations in the year 1824, and afterwards, came from Mr. Whitaker's favorite tribes, together with many others afterwards purchased by American breeders and brought to the United States.

Sometime after the sale of Robert Colling, Col. Trotter, who was a purchaser there, sold three cows from that stock to Col. Mellish for £2,210, equal to $3,683 each. Col. Mellish afterwards sold one of them to Major Bower, of Welham, for 800 guineas ($4,200).

In view of such authenticated sales we can have no doubt that many of the successors of the Collings, the elder Booth, Maynard, Wetherell, and their contemporaries, sold many choice animals at extraordinary prices, showing the right estimate still maintained of their excellence. We regret that we have been confined to such a limited early account of individual sales. Yet if we had them it would hardly be necessary to multiply the many decided evidences of Short-horn values.

Succeeding the efforts of the Collings and their contemporary breeders, the merits of the Short-horns gained widely in public estimation and popularity, not only in the counties comprising their ancient homes, but they were eagerly sought by the larger land-owners among the nobility and gentry of neighboring, and even distant counties, as well as tenant farmers—the former to encourage the improvement of the breeds of neat cattle on their estates at large, and the latter to improve and render more valuable their own individual herds as the most profitable stock they could rear. Thus the number of pure-bred animals increased in a more rapid ratio than ever before, while their crosses upon the common and baser breeds multiplied indefinitely, both as grazing and dairy stock.

It would be an exhausting, if not impossible labor, to enumerate all the various breeders of *established* Short-horn blood in Great Britain since the days of the Collings. The names of the most prominent among their contemporaries, and immediate successors, have already been given, and for those who have since entered the ranks the pages of the English Herd Book must be examined. But to show their extent, these breeders can be numbered by many hundreds, among them the Royal household, every order of nobility—titled women as well—and descending in rank through every intermediate class of ownership to the well-to-do tenant farmer. Not that we ignore other valuable breeds of cattle which, from time immemorial, have existed in Britain and elsewhere, and have maintained and still maintain their advocates and breeders; nor do we claim a *universal* favor towards the Short-horns beyond all others; but they have developed such prominent qualities of excellence as to render them beyond any other breed, both in pure bloods and grades, the now most widely predominating stock of any *distinct race* of cattle. Never were the prices paid for choice animals in England so high as now, and never were animals of choice and fashionable blood so eagerly sought. For many years past they have, in large numbers, been exported to the neighboring continent and to various English colonies—in the latter, mostly to Australia and the Canadas—while men in the United States for fifty years past have purchased and brought out hundreds of their choicest breeding, and still are annually drawing from the British herds their most cherished blood. Strangest of all, English breeders are now almost annually sending to America to purchase and take home to the land of their ancestors some of the descendants of the cattle which years ago they parted with, declaring in such instances, a positive improvement over many of their own animals which they kept at home. And this improvement in the American cattle they consider derived from our fresher pastures and the skill with which they have been bred. Such a concession may be considered no mean tribute to the enterprise of our American breeders! Thus, for the present, we take leave of the Short-horns in England, and proceed to their successors in America.

PART SECOND.

HISTORY OF THE SHORT-HORNS.

CHAPTER VIII.

THE SHORT-HORNS IN AMERICA.

THE date of the first arrival of *purely-bred* Short-horns in the United States is uncertain. Tradition has informed us that a few Short-horn cattle were introduced here from England soon after the Revolutionary War, which separated the American colonies from the mother country, the treaty of peace between the two countries being made in the year 1783. We have no recorded evidence of the fact from any printed chronicles of the time, although men not long ago living, and some still alive, have stated on what they believed good authority, that such was the fact. The best evidence at our command will be given, and if it be not such as will commend the purity of the blood of these animals to breeders of good Short-horns at the present day, they will at least have the benefit of what knowledge exists, and draw their conclusions as best they may from the material which we have gathered.

We have also heard that about the year 1775 a Mr. Heaton emigrated from England to New York, then a provincial city, and followed for some years the occupation of a butcher. It is also said that in 1791 he returned to England and brought back with him several Short-horn cattle from the herd of George Culley, a cattle breeder living near Grindon, in Northumberland. He was probably induced to this enterprise by knowing the deficiencies of the common cattle then bred in the United States, which, in his mind, and truly so, much needed the improvement which the Short-horn blood could impart to them. What became of the cattle, neither tradition nor written history of the day give us an account; but it may be supposed that the males and females were bred to some extent among themselves, and that the bulls were also bred upon the common cows in the places where they were kept. In 1796 it is further stated that Mr. Heaton went again to England and brought out a bull and cow which he bought from one of the brothers Colling and took them to his farm in Westchester county, N. Y., where he then resided. It may be supposed that the Short-horns which he had previously imported had been taken to that place also, but of the fact we have no verified account.

What finally became of the animals and their produce which Heaton brought out, nothing definite is known, only that some superior cattle were many years kept and known in Westchester county, N. Y., after the present century came in, but no pedigrees of them have been traced except in one or two instances through "Brisbane's bull," which was purchased of Mr. Heaton by the late Mr. James Brisbane, of Batavia, N. Y., and brought there by him in the early years of this century. The bull left much valuable stock in the vicinity of Batavia, and was supposed to be a thorough-bred Short-horn. Of the Heaton stock, retained in the vicinity of New York, nothing further is certainly known. It is altogether probable that the people of that vicinity knowing little of either breeds, or blood cattle in those days, let the stock "run out," and they became lost in the common herds of the country.

The Gough (or Goff) and Miller Importations of the Last Century.

We now enter on debatable ground—a subject which has elicited more controversy touching the blood of early American Short-horns than any other which has arisen in this country for the past fifty years by those interested, and the animals of whose herds have been more directly or remotely related to them. We do not suppose that anything we may introduce by way of testimony will decide the question to any exact degree of certainty. Yet the *facts* connected with them are important to be known by all Short-horn breeders who take an interest in the matter; and from them every reader may draw his own conclusions. We do not propose to settle any question of *blood* by what we may submit, but simply to relate history so far as we have been able, by diligent search, to ascertain it.

There have been several published accounts of these early importations, differing somewhat in *date*, which is of little consequence;

but, of more consequence, differing in the *breeds* of the cattle so imported. As they took place nearly ninety, and down to about eighty years ago, the accounts given of them were for many years only of oral transmission, and perhaps of somewhat imperfect recollection by the several parties relating them. We find these accounts recorded in print only after the years 1835 to 1840, at a lapse of nearly or quite half a century after the importations occurred, when probably the importers of the original stock as well as some of the owners of a portion of the descendants of the originals had passed off the stage of action. Yet some of their survivors, venerable in age and character in Kentucky and Ohio, still remain, whose recollections run into the earlier years of the present century, and from these several accounts our history is drawn.

According to these accounts in the year 1783 a Mr. Miller, of Virginia, in connection with Mr. Gough, made an importation—into Baltimore (probably)—of some English cattle, of two different breeds. We infer that the cattle were taken into the fine grazing section of Northern Virginia, in the valley of the South branch of the Potomac river, where they were bred together, as well as the bulls bred to the native cows of the country. They were designated, one as the "Milk breed," the other as the "Beef breed." The former were described as having short horns, heavy carcasses, compact in shape, red, red and white, and roan in color, the cows excellent milkers—in all probability, Short-horns. The latter were longer horned, rangy in form, fatted well *at maturity*, not so smoothly built as the others, and the cows producing less milk than the others. These were, probably, the old fashioned, unimproved stock, coarser and rougher in appearance, but still of the Short-horn race then common in the Holderness district of Yorkshire. Sometime afterwards one, or both, of the previously named gentlemen—whether in conjunction, or separately, is not related—about the years 1790 to 1795, made other importations of nearly the same classes of cattle, a part of, or all of which, probably went into the South branch valley, or elsewhere not far distant from the first importation. We hear nothing of these cattle or their descendants as *Virginia* stock; but two years after the first importation, in the year 1785, two sons, and a son-in-law (Mr Gay) of Mr. Matthew Patton, then a resident of Virginia, took into Clark county, Kentucky (as related by Dr. Samuel D. Mentin, still living there), one of its fine blue-grass localities, a young bull, and several heifers, half-blooded (and they could only have been calves, or less than yearlings), of their then called "English" cattle. These animals were said to have been purchased of Mr. Gough. It is not necessary to further note these animals, as they were but *grades*, only to show the spirit of enterprise among some of the early cattle breeders of the State, in obtaining better stock than Kentucky then afforded for their improvement.

In 1790, the elder Mr. Patton removed from Virginia to Clark county in Kentucky, and took with him a bull and cow directly descended from the Gough and Miller importation of the "Milk" breed, also some half-blooded cows of both the "Milk" and "Beef" breeds. The "Beef" breed were "long-haired, large, coarse, slowly coming to maturity, and fattening badly until fully grown, yet tolerable milkers." The "Milk" breed (of which the bull and cow first named were of pure descent) were short-horned, coming early to maturity, and fattening kindly. Their milking qualities were extraordinary. It was not at all uncommon for cows of this breed to give thirty-two quarts of milk daily. The Short-horn bull, red in color, with white face, rather heavy horns, yet smooth and round in form, was called Mars. He is recorded by number 1850, American Herd Book. The cow was called Venus, white in color, with red ears, small, short horns, turning down. She bred two bull calves to Mars, and soon afterwards died. Mars got many calves on the native cows in Kentucky, which were said by the old breeders to be both excellent milkers and good fattening animals. Mars remained with Mr. Patton until the death of the latter in 1803, when the bull was sold to a Mr. Peeples in Montgomery county, Ky., in whose possession he died in 1806. Of the two bulls descended from Mars and Venus, one was taken to Jessamine county, Ky., the other to Ohio, probably the Scioto valley; but as all this breed, or breeds, in their various intermixtures after their introduction into Kentucky, were called "Patton stock," they became commingled, the shorter horned, and refined ones, with the longer horned and coarser ones, and were, for many years afterwards, universally known by that name only.

In the year 1803 Mr. Daniel Harrison, James Patton and James Gay, of Clark county, Ky., bought of Mr. Miller, the importer, living in Virginia, a two-year-old bull, descended from a bull and cow of his importation. This bull was called Pluto (825 A. H. B.), and said to be of the "Milk" breed. He is described as "dark roan or red in color, large in size, with small head and neck, light, short horns, small-boned, and heavily fleshed." He was bred mostly to "Patton" cows, and produced some fine milkers. He was taken to Ohio about the year 1812, and died soon afterwards.

In the year 1810 Capt. William Smith, of Fayette county, Ky., purchased of the before mentioned Mr. Miller, of Virginia, and brought to Kentucky a bull called Buzzard, 304 (3254). He was coarser, larger, and taller than Pluto, but not so heavy. He was bred in different herds many years, and also used by the Society of Shakers at Pleasant Hill, Mercer county, Ky., in 1821, and for some years afterwards.

In the year 1811 the bull Shaker (2193 A. H. B.) was bought of Mr. Miller aforesaid, and used some years both by the Pleasant Hill, Ky., and Union Village, Ohio, Societies of Shakers. They afterwards sold him to Messrs. Welton and Hutchcraft, of Kentucky. He was of the "Milk" or Short-horn breed. This account we have from Messrs. Micajah Burnett, of the Pleasant Hill, and Peter Boyd, of the Union Village Societies, and although they each differ in some non-essential items, the identity of the bull is fully recognized.

These four bulls, viz.: Mars, Pluto, Buzzard, and Shaker, appear to have been purely bred from the Gough and Miller importations previous to the year 1810. From these bulls, but not on *equally pure* bred cows of those importations, descended many animals whose pedigrees have been recognized and recorded as Short-horns in the earlier volumes of the English Herd Book, and of consequence, since in the American Herd Book, as the latter is founded on the English publication, as standard authority, in all matters of Short-horn genealogy.

During the years above mentioned several other bulls from the Gough and Miller Virginia stock were brought into Kentucky and Ohio—some with names and some without names, other than those of their owners—as "Inskip's bull," "Peeple's bull" (Mars, probably), "Witherspoon's bull," "Bluff," and others.

Some pedigrees in the Herd Books run back into several of those bulls, which, as many pure-bred crosses have since been made upon their descendants, and been recorded in the English Herd Book, must be classed in the family of Short-horns.

From the above accounts it is understood where and how the "Patton stock" originated. There can be no doubt that some of the original importations of Gough and Miller were well-bred cattle of the Short-horn or Teeswater breed (which were identical in original blood), but without pedigrees; also that others of them may have been of the Holderness variety—coarser and less improved—of the same race. In the various accounts which we have gathered from different quarters in Ohio and Kentucky, some of them were rough animals, tardy in arriving at maturity, others fine both in figure and quality, and most of the cows descended from them proved excellent milkers. Their colors were more or less red, white, and roan, which are true Short-horn colors.

These accounts are about as accurate and as much to the point as the English traditions relating to the ancient Short-horns, or Teeswaters in their native land, and may be received as a fair basis on which to found the genealogy of all the pedigrees which trace back into the "Patton" blood, and are found recorded in both the English and American Herd Books. We have had accounts of, and have seen many admirable animals of this descent, since crossed with well-bred Short-horn bulls, among the Kentucky and other Western herds, which, aside from their Patton origin, would be considered, by accurate breeders, equal in blood and quality to many cattle of later importation and unquestionable descent.

With this meager and perhaps unsatisfactory narrative, we are obliged to dismiss the Gough and Miller importation, and "Patton stock" of Kentucky. Besides what has been published in the agricultural and other papers regarding them, all of which are condensed in the above account, we have had the opportunity of conversing with several aged cattle breeders of the blue-grass region of Kentucky more than thirty years ago on the subject, and they clearly corroborated the accounts according to their recollection, as we have given them. A few of these venerable men are still living and have attested to the great excellence of one or more of those bulls as possessing many strikingly good points of the well-bred bulls of the present day.

Various Other Importations.

Soon after the last American war with England, in the year 1815, it is stated that Mr. Samuel M. Hopkins, then a resident at Moscow, in the Genesee valley, N. Y., imported a Short-horn bull called Marquis (408), and a cow called Princess, said to be of the stock of Robert Colling. Mr. Hopkins also, in 1817, brought out a bull, Moscow (9413). A few descendants from these, afterwards crossed by Short-horn bulls from Col. Powel's herd, purchased by the Holland Land Company for the benefit of the settlers on their lands in Western New York, were carefully bred many years at and near Batavia, in Western New York, some of the blood of which is still found in good herds.

In 1815 or '16 a Mr. Cox, an Englishman, brought into Rensselaer county, near Albany, N. Y., a Short-horn bull and two cows, which were placed upon the farm of Mr. Cadwallader Colden. They were there bred for several years, but had no recorded pedigrees. They were afterwards crossed with the later bulls imported in 1822, by a Mr. Wayne, viz.: Comet, 1383, and Nelson, 1914, A. H. B. Some of the descendants of the Cox cows and bulls became the property of Mr. Bullock, of Albany county, which were bred to these bulls, and many good animals sprung from them. These latter were locally called the "Bullock stock." We first saw several of them in the year 1833. They were large, robust animals, good, although not remarkably *fine* in quality, but compared with others of later importation, true Short-horns.

"THE KENTUCKY IMPORTATION OF 1817."

We now come onto fair ground in the introduction of genuine Short-horns in the United States; and although frequent debates and controversies have occurred touching the purity in blood of the *Short-horns* of that importation, to a candid mind there can be little doubt of their legitimate descent. The story of their purchase, arrival in Kentucky, and subsequent breeding, has been often told in various publications—among others, in the first and second volumes of the American Herd Book; but as these volumes may not be at the reader's hand, a full repetition of their history will be given.

Col. Lewis Sanders, a gentleman of character, position, and engaged in active business, then in the prime of life, lived at Grass Hills, Ky., in the year 1816. We have had the pleasure of his personal acquaintance, having first met him about the year 1850, in Cincinnati, Ohio, and on two or three occasions afterwards—the last time in the city of New York, in the winter of 1859-60, he then being upwards of eighty years of age, and a few years previous to his decease. In our first interview he particularly related the account of his importation of cattle from England into Kentucky in the year 1817, of which we then made a memorandum. Of his truthfulness no one knowing him ever entertained a question. The best and most succinctly *written* account of that importation was by Mr. Brutus J. Clay, of Bourbon county, Ky., a large farmer, Short-horn cattle breeder, and a gentleman of unquestionable character, published February 1, 1855, in the *Ohio Farmer*, at Cleveland, Ohio. In prefacing his account Mr. Clay introduces a letter from Col. Sanders to Mr. Edwin G. Bedford, an extensive and experienced Short-horn cattle breeder of Bourbon county, Ky.:

"I was induced to send the order for the cattle (in the fall of 1816), by seeing an account of Charles Colling's great sale in 1810. At this sale enormous prices were paid; one thousand guineas for the bull Comet. This induced me to think there was a value unknown to us in these cattle, and as I then had the control of means, determined to procure some of this breed. For some years previous I was in the regular receipt of English publications on agricultural improvements, and improvements in the various descriptions of stock. From the reported surveys of counties, I was pretty well posted as to the localities of the most esteemed breeds of cattle. My mind was made up, fixing on the Short-horns as most suitable for us. I had frequent conversations on this matter with my friend and neighbor, Capt. William Smith, then an eminent breeder of cattle. He was thoroughly impressed in favor of the old Long-horn breed. To gratify him, and to please some old South Branch feeders, I ordered a pair of Long-horns; and was more willing to do so from the fact, that this was the breed selected by the distinguished Mr. Bakewell for his experimental, yet most successful improvements. I forwarded to the house of Buchanan, Smith & Co., of Liverpool, $1,500 to make the purchase, expecting to get three pair only, with instructions to procure a competent judge and suitable agent, to go into the cattle district and make the selection, the animals not to be over two years old, and no restriction as to price. At the time, the Holderness breed was in highest repute for milkers. I directed that the agent should be sent to Yorkshire to procure a pair of that breed, then to the river Tees, in Durham county, for a pair of Short-horn Durhams, then to the county of Westmoreland for a pair of the Long-horns, etc.

"The agent sent from Liverpool, J. C. Etches, a celebrated butcher of that place, went as directed, and purchased six pair instead of three. It being soon after the war, all kinds of produce had much cheapened, and the stock sold lower than was expected.

"After the cattle were shipped from Liverpool, on the vessel Mohawk, bound to Baltimore, Md., where the cattle afterwards landed, I sold one-third interest in them to Capt. William Smith, and another third to Dr. Tegarden, of Kentucky."

It appears that there were twelve animals in all purchased and shipped—eight Short-horns, four bulls and four heifers; and four Long-horns, two bulls and two heifers. No pedigrees came with the cattle, as it was five years previous to the publication of the first volume of the English Short-horn Herd Book. There was simply an invoice of the cattle, which only partially described them. This invoice Col. Sanders gave, as follows:

"No. 1. Bull from Mr. Clement Winston, on the river Tees, got by Mr. Constable's bull, brother to Comet," afterwards (155) E. H. B. The name of this bull was San Martin, afterwards (2599) in E. H. B.

"No. 2. Bull, Holderness breed, from Mr. Scott, out of a cow which gave 34 quarts of milk per day." The name of this bull was Tecumseh, afterwards (5409) E. H. B.

"No. 3. Bull from Mr. Reed, West-holme, of his own old breed." This bull is probably the one called Comet, afterwards 1382, A. H. B. Said to have been got by either Comet (155), or his brother North Star (458), E. H. B.

"No. 4. Bull, Holderness breed, from Mr. Humphreys, got by Mr. Mason's bull, of Islington." No Herd Book record appears to have since been made of this bull, and we know not what became of him. Mr. Clay states that one of the bulls "was sold to Capt. Fowler, who afterwards sold him to Gen. Fletcher, and was taken to Bath county, Ky., where he died."

Of the females, the invoice states that

"No. 7, was a heifer from Mr. Wilson, Staindrop, Durham breed.

"Nos. 8, 9, 10, were heifers from Mr. Shipman, on the river Tees, of his own breed.

"In the division of the Short-horns above named, Col. Sanders became owner of the bulls San Martin and Tecumseh." Col. Sanders states that Comet became the property of Dr. Tegarden.

"Of the Shipman heifers, No. 7 became the property of Captain Smith, and was called the 'Durham Cow.'

"Of the four remaining, two were retained by Col. Sanders. One of which was called 'Mrs. Motte,' and the other named the 'Teeswater Cow.'"

The other fourth heifer died in Maryland, never having reached Kentucky.

This disposes of the Short-horns of the importation.

"Of the Long-horns, Capt. Smith was the owner of one of the bulls, called 'Bright.' Dr. Tegarden took the other, and called him 'Rising Sun,' which, by some strange mistake, is recorded in the English Short-horn Herd Book as number (6386).

"Of the Long-horn cows, No. 11 was called the 'Long-horn Cow,' and No. 12, 'Georgia Ann,' the property of the gentlemen who owned the Long-horn bulls."

The Long-horns were bred together, and left some produce. A Long-horn bull, from Capt. Smith's cow, was sold to Mr. George Renick, of the Scioto valley, in Ohio, where he was bred for some years. The original Long-horn bulls were bred to some extent to other cows than those which were imported with them, but they did not prove popular with the cattle breeders of Kentucky, and after a trial of some years they gradually run out, as many years ago no trace of them, in pure blood, could be found in the vicinity of their importation. Through the bull taken to Ohio by Mr. Renick (but whether from *pure* Long-horn heifers or not we have no information), several cattle with marked characteristics of the blood were bred in the Scioto valley. We recollect, in 1821, when just verging into manhood, taking a horseback journey from Columbus to Circleville, in the vicinity of which latter town the Renick brothers owned large landed estates, we saw a herd of a dozen or more Long-horned cattle grazing in a field by the side of the road. Their singular appearance, grazing on the rich blue-grass, or lying under the shade of the majestic trees, attracted our attention. We rode up to the fence, hitched our horse, and went into the field to view them. They had every appearance of being either thorough-bred, or high grades of the Long-horn breed, with long drooping horns, pushing forward beyond their noses, or falling below their jaws, light brindle in color, with white stripes along their backs, as we now see their portraits in the books. They were long-bodied, a little swayed in the back, not very compact in shape, but withal imposing animals to the eye. We made no inquiries about them at the time, as we then knew little of breeds of cattle. Thirty years afterwards being again at Circleville, and having a better knowledge of breeds, on inquiry for cattle of that character, we could find no trace, nor even a recollection of them among the older farmers of the vicinity.

We have diverged into this somewhat extended episode of the Long-horns to explain why and wherefore it has since become a subject of more or less controversy with doubters of the integrity of the Short-horn blood of the 1817 importation, that the Long-horn blood became to some extent amalgamated with the true Short-horn blood of the stock which came into Kentucky with them. It is certain that the bull "Rising Sun" got into the English Herd Book (6386), as "imported into the United States of America." It is also certain that some pedigrees of crosses between the Long-horned and Short-horned cattle have crept into the Herd Books, both English and American; but, as the Long-horns in England have for a long series of years been considered a valuable race, and their reputation, through the skill and perseverance of Bakewell, their distinguished breeder, stood high, and many pure Short-horn crosses have since been made upon the Kentucky Long-horns, little, if any, injury can be imputed to animals now existing which may inherit the remote fraction of Long-horn blood traced into their veins.

To return to the Short-horns of the 1817 importation, and the evidences, in absence of pedigrees to them, touching their purity of blood, which has been challenged. In addition to the testimony of Col. Sanders in the employment of his agent, Mr. Etches, the latter, in a letter to Mr. Affleck, published in the *Western Farmer and Gardener*, writes: "I have been a butcher twenty-eight years in Liverpool, and am a breeder of fine stock. I was the purchaser of the Short-horn stock for Messrs. Buchanan, Smith & Co., which went to America in 1817—six in number, three bulls and three heifers [eight he ought to have said, as there were four of each sex, including the two Holderness, which were also Short-horns, in fact]. *Every animal was pure of its kind.*" They were selected in Durham or Yorkshire—perhaps in both, near the river Tees, the ancient home of the race.

Mr. Etches was afterwards the purchaser of Short-horns for other American importers—for Mr. Letton, of Kentucky, of the bull Locomotive, 92 and (4242), also for Mr. Vail, of Troy, N. Y., of the bull Duke of Wellington, 55 and (5654), and the cow Duchess, page 172, Vol. 1, A. H. B., all three of them from the herd of Mr. Thomas Bates.

The late Gen. James Garrard, of Kentucky, whose word no one would question, states that "when in England many years ago, he saw Mr. Etches, who assured him that the Short-horns which he purchased for Col. Sanders were as good of their kind as were then to be had in England."

Further, we now quote from the second volume of the American Herd Book, edited in the year 1855:

"In 1848, Mr. Stevens, of New York, was in England. He thus writes: 'I saw Mr. J. C. Etches in York, and was introduced to him by Mr. Thomas Bates, the noted Short-horn breeder. In answer to my questions, Mr. Etches remarked: 'I purchased for Mr. Sanders, of America, in 1817, some Short-horn cattle, of different persons, near the river Tees. These cattle were thought by myself and others to be very fine animals.' In answer to the question by me if he knew the pedigrees of any of these cattle, Mr. Etches turned to Mr. Bates, and said: 'Mr. Bates probably knows something about the pedigree of the Shipman heifers, and I refer to him.' Mr. Bates replied, that he well recollected of Mr. Shipman's selling a heifer to go to America She was called 'Mrs. Motte,' after a sister of either Mr. or Mrs. Shipman. Mr. Maynard had a cow by a son of Hubback (319), which cow he called Starling. This cow (Starling) had three daughters. One of these daughters Mr. Maynard kept. One he sold to me (Mr. Bates), and the other he sold to Mr. Shipman, who called her 'Starling,' after her dam, and when he bought her she was in calf to 'Adam' (717). The produce was a heifer, which he called 'Mrs. Motte,' and afterwards sold to Mr. Etches.' As Mr. Bates owned a sister of the dam of Mrs. Motte, he knew her pedigree, and as a sale to go to America was a remarkable thing in that day, the fact made a strong impression on Mr. Bates' mind. See pedigree of 'Young Starling,' in page 543, Vol. 2, Coates' Herd Book. Mr. Shipman's 'Starling' (dam of Mrs. Motte), was *full* sister to one of the Starlings named in said pedigree. (Of course her pedigree was the same.)

"Mrs. Motte's pedigree thus stands:

"Mrs. Motte, got by Adam (717), dam Starling, by a son [by Favorite (252)] of Mr. Maynard's old Yellow Favorite (cow); gr. d. by a son of Hubback (319), g. gr. d. by Manfield (404), g. g. gr. d. (Young Strawberry), by Dalton Duke (188). Here this pedigree, at page 543, Vol. 2, ends; but referring, in Vol. 1, page 508, to the pedigree of Young Strawberry, the cow last named above, it will be seen that she goes further back, in carrying out the pedigree of Mrs. Motte, thus: g. g. g. gr. d. Favorite (bred by Mr. Maynard), by Mr. R. Alcock's bull (19). Then, in pedigree of this cow, Favorite, Vol. 1, page 308, it will be seen that Mrs. Motte's pedigree continues further back, thus: g. g. g. g. gr. d. by Mr. Jacob Smith's bull (608), g. g. g. g. g. gr. d. by Mr. Jolly's bull (337). There are few, if any, better pedigrees than Mrs. Motte's—granting it to be correct—in the English Herd Book.

"As the other two heifers, and the bulls, were purchased in the same neighborhood, and at the same time, it may be inferred, that if their pedigrees were not equal in length, their blood may have been as good. But it is not proposed to argue the question. Facts are submitted.

"In the succeeding importations, by Mr. Powel, of Philadelphia, some of which found their way into Kentucky, in 1824-'5 (the pedigrees of which were unquestioned), the descendants of the 1817 importation were bred to these bulls, and were afterwards bred to the Ohio and Kentucky importations of later years; and as they have been bred upon by *fresher* unquestionable Short-horn blood for more than thirty years, there is but a fractional part of the 1817 blood to be traced in any living animal claiming descent from it. These *descendants* stand upon record as having frequently been successful competitors among the prize cattle in the States, where they have been exhibited by the side of those possessing none else than pure Short-horn blood.

"Since writing the above, I have been favored with a letter from Mr. H. H. Hankins, of Bloomington, Clinton county, Ohio, who was one of the agents sent by the Clinton County Cattle Company to England, for the purchase of Short-horns, in 1854. It is thus:

'DEAR SIR—Yours, asking for information relative to the Sanders cattle importation of 1817, is at hand. I was, when in England, in the immediate neighborhood of the river Tees, where Mr. Etches purchased the cattle, *i. e.*, the Short-horns. Before I left Ohio, I had learned the names of the persons of whom the stock had been bought, and also their locality. I made inquiry of many who are now breeding Short-horns on the Tees, respecting the persons of whom the cattle were bought. I found several who knew them from character, but were not personally acquainted with them; but was recommended to call on an old gentleman, of good character, living near Darlington, who had been a breeder of Short-horns at the time Mr. Etches bought them for Col. Sanders. His name is Timothy Lanchester. He told me that he had been an intimate friend of Messrs. Robert and Charles Colling, and most of the other old breeders in Durham. I gave him the names of the men of whom Mr. Etches bought the cattle for Mr. Sanders. He at once said that he knew them well, and gave me a certificate, a copy of which I send you. I was recommended to this old gentleman by the Messrs. Emerson, Harrison, and others, who spoke highly of his integrity and knowledge of the old breeders in that vicinity. The certificate is as follows:

'I, Timothy Lanchester, of Haughton Leskeine, near Darlington, Durham, England, born in the year 1771, do hereby certify, that I was well acquainted with Matthew Shipman, Clement Winston, Thomas Reed, and Mr. Wilson, who were cattle breeders on the river Tees, and who, it is said, sold some Short-horns to a Mr. Etches, of Liverpool, which were to be shipped to the United States, in the year 1817.

'They were gentlemen of the highest character, and their fine Short-horns were considered equal to any in the country at that day. The importance of keeping pedigrees was not so much thought of at that day as at the present; since which time there has been a public record of the Short-horns kept in England, by which may be traced, some of them, to the herds of the above-named gentlemen. I was engaged in breeding Short-horns at the date above alluded to, and have been more or less interested in Short-horns up to the present, and have been familiar with most of the breeders of Short-horns in England, from the days of the Collings down to the present time, and I have never heard any one doubt that the Messrs. Shipman, Winston, Reed and Wilson, possessed as pure Short-horns as existed at that day.

'Given under my hand, at Darlington, England, the 6th day of March, 1854.

(Signed)   TIMOTHY LANCHESTER.'

'I could have had a number of other certificates from younger breeders, but I preferred to take one from this old and much esteemed gentleman, who had personally known those old breeders.

(Signed)   H. H. HANKINS.

'BLOOMINGTON, OHIO, March 25, 1855.'"

To pursue the 1817 importation exhaustively, we quote further from Vol. 4, American Herd Book, edited in the year 1859:

"I herewith publish a list of the produce, by name, of the three cows of Col. Sanders' Kentucky importation of 1817, together with the produce of some of their daughters. The record will be gratifying to many who are interested in that blood, and valuable for future reference. For these papers I am indebted to Mr. H. H. Hankins, of Clinton county, Ohio, who received them from Dr. S. D. Martin, of Clark county, Ky. They are as follows:

"*Produce of Mrs. Motte, Kentucky importation 1817.*

Year of Births.	Color & Sex.	Name.	Sire.	Owner.
1818,	B.	Paul Jones (4661),	Imp. Tecumseh (5409),	
1819, Red	H.	Lady Munday,	Imp. San Martin (2599)	Gen. Garrard.
1821, "	H.	Lady Kate,	Imp. Tecumseh (5409),	T. P. Dudley.
1823, "	H.	Miss Motte,	Imp. San Martin (2599)	Col. Sanders.
1824, "	H.	Sylvia,	do.	Gen. Garrard.
1826, "	B.	Den. de la Motte (1914)	do.	Dr. Martin.
1827, r. & w.	B.	Stonehammer,	do.	Ohio Shakers.
1828, "	B.	Accommodation (2907)	Cornplanter (3492),	Walter Dun.
1830, "	B.	Partnership (6277), (?)	Accommodation (2907)	

"*Produce of the Durham Cow, Kentucky importation 1817.*

Year		Color	Name.	Sire.	Owner.
1818,	—	B.	Wickliffe's bull, 1099,	Got on passage,*	Robert Wickliffe.
1819,	—	B.	Wellington,	San Martin (2599),	Mr. Carr.
1820,	—	H.	Smith Heifer,	do.	Gen. Garrard.
1821,	—	H.	Lady Durham,	do.	B.W. & E.Worthen.
1822,	—	B.	Lafayette, 1755,	Paul Jones (4661),	Col. Sanders.
1823,	—	B.	Napoleon, 1899,	San Martin (2599),	Major Gano.
1824,	—	H.	Beauty,	Lafayette, 1755,	Col. Sanders.
1825,	—	B.	DeKalb (steer),	Napoleon, 1899,	do.
1826,	—	B.	Dead,	do.	do.
1828,	—	H.	Hadassah,	do.	do.
1829,	—	H.	No name,	do.	Major Gano.

"* The Herd Book pedigree of Wickliffe's bull, says: 'Got by San Martin (2599)'.—L. F. A.

"*Produce of the Teeswater Cow, Kentucky importation 1817.*

Year of Births.	Color & Sex.	Name.	Sire.	Owner.
1818,	Red B.	Mirandi (4488),	Got on passage,*	Judge Haggin.
—	H.	Miss Haggin,	San Martin (2599),	Dr. Warfield.
—	H.	Hetty (Haggin),	do.	W. R. Scott.
—	B.	Kentuckian (1733),	do.	
—	H.	———,	Mirandi (4488),	Judge Haggin.
—	H.	Pink,	Munday's bull, 727,	S. Smith.

"In regard to the produce of this cow, Dr. Martin says: 'I cannot give the dates of their birth, nor do I suppose I have given them in their proper order' (of sex or name).—ED.

"* The Herd Book pedigree of Mirandi, says: 'Got by San Martin (2599)'.—L. F. A.

"*Produce of Lady Munday, by San Martin (2599), out of Mrs. Motte.*

1821,	—	B.	Cornplanter (3492),	Tecumseh (5409),	Hector Lewis.
1823,	—	B.	Champion, 325,	do.	Gen. Garrard.
1824,	—	H.	Tulip,	Mirandi (4488),	do.
1825,	—	H.	Dead,	do.	do.
1826,	—	H.	Beauty,	Sportsman, 998,	do.
1827,	—	B.	Denton (3583),	Champion, 325,	do.
1828,	—	B.	Misfortune, 716,	Sportsman, 998,	do.
1829,	—	B.	Comet, 355,	do.*	do.
1830,	—	B.	Drone,	do.	do.
1831,	—	H.	Drucilla,	Duroc, 454,	do.
1832,	—	B.	Slider, 979,	do.	do.

"* The Herd Book pedigree of Comet, says: 'Got by Cornplanter (3492)'.—L. F. A.

"*Produce of Lady Kate, by Tecumseh (5409), out of Mrs. Motte.*

1824,	—	H.	Duchess,	San Martin (2599),	H. Blanton.
——,	—	B.	Mohawk (4492),	do.	James Munday.
1827,	—	H.	Nancy Dawson,	do.	Mr. McClure.
1829,	—	H.	Eleanor,	Stonehammer,	T. P. Dudley.
1830,	—	H.	Amanda,	Accommodation (2907)	T. G. Brent.
1831,	—	B.	Oscar,	do.	T. P. Dudley.
1832,	—	B.	Backway (?),	do.	Mr. Goodloe.
1833,	—	B.	Dan Webster,	Tariff, 1023,	Mr. Dudley.
1834,	—	B.	Southard, 994,½	Pontiac (4734),	do.
1836,	—	H.	Dead,	Tariff, 1023,	do.
1837,	—	H.	Miss Biddle,	Nic Biddle,	T.P.& J.W. Dudley.
1838,	—	B.	Echo,	Geo. Reynolds, 1610,	do.

"In 1838, Lady Kate broke her leg, and was slaughtered at 17 years old.

"*Produce of the Smith Heifer, by San Martin (2599), out of the Durham Cow.*

1824,	—	B.	Sportsman, 998,	Cornplanter (3492),	Gen. Garrard.

"This cow had no other calf, being soon afterwards killed by the goring of an ox.

"*Produce of Sylvia, by San Martin (2599), out of Mrs. Motte.*

Year of Births.	Color & Sex.	Name.	Sire.	Owner.
1826,	— B.	Exchange, 482,	Champion, 325,	Gov. Trimble, Ohio.
1828,	— B.	Duroc, 454,	Sportsman, 998,	Messrs. Renick, do.
1830,	— H.	Nymph,	do.	Gen. Garrard.
1831,	— B.	President, 2046,	Cornplanter (3492),	do.
1832,	— B.	Proclamation (4838),	Denton (3583),	do.
1834,	— H.	Octavia,	do.	do.
1835,	— H.	Virginia,	Exception (3746),	do.

"*Produce of Lady Durham, by San Martin (2599), out of the Durham Cow.*

Year	Color & Sex	Name	Sire	Owner
1833,	— H.	Susan Munday,	Mirandi (4488),	James Haggin.
1834,	— H.	Laura,	Oliver (2387),	Ben. Warfield.
1835,	— H.	Lady Macallister,	Pontiac (4734),	J. N. Brown, Ill.
1836,	— H.	Phœnix,	Oliver (2387),	Ben. Warfield.
1837,	— H.	Lily,	Alonzo, 209,	E. Worthen.
—,	— B.	Commodore (3448),	Mirandi (4488),	———
—,	— B.	Daniel Boone,	Son of Mirandi (4488),	———
—,	— B.	Kentucky, 1734,	Tariff, 1023,	———

"(A part of the numbers attached to the bulls in the above tables, I have looked up and placed there myself.—L. F. A.)

"Dr. Martin, in a note, adds: 'I have no list of the produce of the Durham Cow's heifer Beauty, by Lafayette, 1755, except one heifer called Beauty, by Prince Regent, 877.'

"Thus it will be seen that the three imported cows produced thirteen heifers, besides sundry bulls, and that four of those heifers produced fifteen heifer calves, besides bulls—twenty-eight known females. Supposing the eight other heifers (for the 'Smith heifer' only produced one calf, and that a bull) had produced three heifer calves each, making twenty-four, there would be in the second generation of the imported cows, including 'Beauty, by Prince Regent,' forty breeding cows—and those well cultivated in their breeding faculties during their lives, as their liberal proprietors, both in Kentucky and Ohio, would be sure to do, we can well imagine that their numbers, at the present time, would swell to an extent much beyond what the pages of the Herd Books represent.

"Had all the names of the heifer descendants of the 1817 importation been preserved by the breeders of their produce, many of the uncertainties resting upon some of their recorded pedigrees would be explained. The same remarks may be applied to the produce of some other importations of well-bred Short-horns many years ago.

occasional pedigrees or memorandums of which have been hunted up and recorded in the present volume.

"With these tables of produce of the three cows of the original Kentucky importation in 1817, and some of their heifers, it is to be hoped that those breeders interested in their blood, whose cattle pedigrees do not trace back, *by name*, on the dam's side, will be able to substantiate their claim to an undisputed genealogy."

It will thus be seen that all Short-horns tracing their pedigrees back through well-bred bulls into animals of both sexes named in the foregoing tables, may be called pure Short-horns, admitting that the 1817 importation were such. Alluding back to Mr. B. J. Clay's letter from which we have so largely quoted, he remarks: "In 1817 [other accounts say 1818] Mr. James Prentice, of Lexington, Ky., imported two bulls, John Bull, 598½, and Prince Regent, 877, A. H. B., one of the celebrated Durham improved breed, and the other of the improved '*Milk*' breed. John Bull was a deep red, fine size, good form, with delicate down-pointed horns. Prince Regent was pied, white, with some red spots. They were purchased by Nathaniel Hart, of Woodford, and John Hart, of Fayette counties, for $1,500, and produced some good stock."

These bulls were considered good Short-horns, but like the importation of 1817, they had no written pedigrees. Many excellent Herd Book animals now trace their genealogy into John Bull and Prince Regent, of the Prentice importation.

Those pedigrees which trace through well-bred bulls since the Gough and Miller importation, or Patton tribe, may have a slight fraction of unknown blood; but it may possibly be doubted whether they now have more outside blood in their composition than some other Short-horns of English birth and Herd Book pedigrees which have since been imported.

As intimated, there may be some trivial errors in the foregoing accounts of the early Kentucky Short-horn herds, caused by the various sources from which they are derived, but in the main they may be considered correct. Many years ago, between 1830 and 1840, a committee for the purpose of compiling and issuing a Short-horn Herd Book in Kentucky was appointed, consisting of the late Messrs. Benjamin Warfield of Fayette, Samuel D. Martin of Clark, and Robert W. Scott of Franklin counties—the two last mentioned still living. They obtained probably all the information then in existence relative to the subject in hand. We understood that Dr. Martin was charged with the possession of the documentary matter pertaining to their proposed labors, but the project was never carried out. It is chiefly from such material that our information, at second hand, has been derived.

In November, 1817, Mr. Samuel Williams, of Massachusetts, then a merchant, residing in London, England, purchased of the celebrated breeder, Mr. Wetherell, and sent to his brother, Stephen Williams, of Northboro', Mass., the bull "Young Denton" (963), 16 months old. (This pedigree in Vol. 2, E. H. B., says Mr. Wetherell sold him to Col. Powel, near Philadelphia, Pa., but that is an error.) The bull arrived in Boston, Mass. He remained in that State until the year 1827 or '28, when he was taken to Maine, where he died April 16, 1830. We saw the bull in Massachusetts in the year 1822, then owned by Mr. Williams. He was a fine animal.

In 1818 Mr. Cornelius Coolidge, of Boston, imported the bull Cœlebs, 349, and cow Flora, by Son of Comet (155), both bred by Mr. Mason, of Chilton. From them descended many good animals whose pedigrees are in the American Herd Book.

About the year 1820-'21, Mr. Law, of Baltimore, or Washington, D. C., imported the cow Rosemary, by Flash (261), bred by Mr. Curwen. Rosemary afterwards passed into the possession of Col. Powel, of Philadelphia, Pa., and from her many distinguished animals of Kentucky and other States are descended. Mr. Law may at the same time have imported another animal or two. If so, we have no account of their names.

In 1821 the late Colonel John S. Skinner, of Baltimore, imported for Governor Lloyd, of Maryland, the bull Champion (864), the cows Shepherdess, by Magnet (302), and White Rose, by Warrior (673); all these were bred by Mr. Coates, the first editor of the E. H. B. Shepherdess afterwards became the property of Colonel Powel. What became of White Rose is not known. She was the dam of Wye Comet (1591), by Blaize (76), got in England, but born in America, the property of Mr. Law. He was afterwards owned and used by Col. Powel, and finally by Mr. Watson, of Connecticut.

In 1822 Mr. Williams, of London, before named, also sent to his brother the cow Arabella, by North Star (460), bred by Mr. Wetherell. From her came numerous descendants whose pedigrees are found in the several volumes of the American Herd Book.

In or about the year 1822 several cows were imported into Boston by Messrs. Lee, Orr, Monson, and perhaps others, chiefly from the stock of Mr. Wetherell, before mentioned; among these were Tuberose, by North Star (460), owned by Mr. Monson, and Harriet, by

Denton (198), owned by Mr. Orr. Both these cows had full pedigrees, and left several good descendants. The writer purchased Harriet in the year 1834, then 14 years old, and unfortunately, past breeding. She was a fine cow, mostly white in color.

In 1823 Admiral Sir Isaac Coffin, of the British Navy (Massachusetts born), sent out to the Massachusetts Agricultural Society the bull Admiral (1608), and cow Annabella, by Major (398), from the herd of Mr. Wetherell. Both animals left many descendants.

In 1823 Gen. Stephen Van Rensselaer, of Albany, N. Y.—through Col. Skinner, as we understood—imported from the herd of Mr. Champion, the bull Washington (1566), and the cows Pansy, by Blaize (76), and Conquest. The latter of these cows never bred, but Pansy had several descendants by Washington, whose produce have since been bred and distributed into many States of the Union.

In the year 1822, and during some years afterwards, the late Mr. Charles Henry Hall, a merchant of New York, who had previously lived and done business in different countries of Europe, imported several Short-horns, selected from some of the best herds in England, and among them the cow Princess, by Lancaster (360), bred in 1816, by Robert Colling. Mr. Hall resided on a small farm at Harlem, then a village, just out of New York city, on Manhattan Island. He kept and bred a few of his Short-horns there, but the larger portion of them were taken to his farm in Greenbush, near Albany, where they were for several years kept and bred. This gentleman was not particularly mindful of keeping the pedigrees of his stock, although purely bred, and through this inattention much of the correct lineage of his herd was lost. We knew Mr. Hall personally for some years while breeding his cattle, and after he had disposed of his herds. In answer to our inquiries of their blood relations, his answers were only that "they were all purely bred," but, preserving few memoranda of their breeding, he could not give particulars. Some of them—the Princess family, for instance—have been registered correctly in the American Herd Book; others as only tracing to his imported cows and bulls. This much, however, is certain: Mr. Hall assured us at different times that he had his animals selected with great care in England, and he paid liberal prices for them. We saw many of their descendants between the years 1833 and 1840, and they had every appearance of well-bred Short-horns, with high milking qualities.

During the above years of Mr. Hall's importations, several gentlemen of New York, chiefly through his influence, imported some valuable Short-horns, selected as were Mr. Hall's, chiefly, as we understood, through the agency of Mr. Ashcroft. These were bred in the neighborhood of the city, on Long Island, and in Westchester county; but their pedigrees, on account of their owners not knowing their importance, were sadly neglected. There can be no doubt, however, of the integrity of their blood. Some of their descendants are in the American Herd Book, tracing to the original importations.

In the year 1824, the late Col. John H. Powel, of Powelton, near Philadelphia, Pa., a gentleman of large wealth and public spirit in agricultural improvement, began the importation of Short-horns, and continued it for some years. His selections were mainly, if not altogether, from the herd of Mr. Jonas Whitaker, already mentioned, of Otley, in Yorkshire. He bred them with great attention and care on his home estate, and sold many of their descendants into neighboring districts of Pennsylvania and New Jersey. Some also went into New England, others into Kentucky and Ohio. In the cows, he aimed at securing large milkers, for dairy purposes, in which one of his families, the Belinas, were famous for their yields of both milk and butter. In 1831 he imported the bull Bertram (1716), bred by Mr. Whitaker. We saw him in his stable at Powelton, in August of that year, then 3 years old, a few months after his arrival. In color he was red, with a little white, a compact, massive form, short in the leg, of fine touch, good hair, and altogether an imposing animal. Many distinguished animals of our American herds trace into his blood. Col. Powel bred him for some years in his herd. We saw at the same time several of his imported cows, among them Belina, by Barmpton (54), a famous milker, which yielded at the rate of 20½ pounds of butter per week. These cows struck us as being of excellent quality, with indications of giving large quantities of milk, and were in rather low condition. They were good in form, long in body, straight on the back, broad in the hips, with fine heads and horns, excellent coats of hair, with large, well-shaped udders and teats.

In the year 1828, Mr. Francis Rotch, of New Bedford, Mass., then in England, sent out to his brother-in-law, Mr. Benjamin Rodman, also of New Bedford, the bull Devonshire (966), and the cows Adeliza, Dulcibella and Galatea, all by Frederick (1060), from the herd of Mr. Whitaker, and with good pedigrees. Descendants from all of them are now found in several good American herds.

In 1834, ourself became the owner of "Devonshire," at 8 years old, which we purchased of Mr. Rotch, then his possessor. He was red roan in color, good size, excellent points, and left us, as well as his previous owners, some excellent stock. He died at 11 years old.

The cows, Adeliza and Dulcibella, both roan in color, we have also seen. They were good cows, prolific breeders, excellent milkers, and lived to be aged animals.

As Mr. Rotch is the only survivor of the enterprising class of American gentlemen who introduced the Short-horns into the United States previous to the year 1834, we may be pardoned for a further brief mention of him. Contemplating this present work, we wrote to him about three years ago at his rural home in Morris, Otsego county, N. Y., asking for some reminiscences of the early American Short-horns to aid us in the undertaking. In his answer, a brief extract from which we give, it will be seen that at the age of more than four-score years, "his eye was not dim, nor his natural force abated." The letter is written in a clear, round hand, unshaken, and legible as when in the prime of his life:

"And now, my dear friend, having poured out the fullness of my heart [his previous sentences were on personal matters only], I must not expose the emptiness of my head, and incapacity of my mind by attempting to render you much assistance in the interesting labor you are about to undertake. Samuel Williams, who was bred a farmer's boy in Massachusetts, and became a leading merchant on the Exchange of London, in his prosperity thought of his brother at home, and presuming no present would be more acceptable than some fine stock, sent him over some Short-horns from one of the best herds—Mr. Wetherell's, in England. I think with them came out one or two heifers for a Boston gentleman. It seemed to me they were not appreciated, and but for me and an old friend whom I interested in the affair, their pedigrees would have been irrecoverably lost.

"When in England, in 1828, and making an importation for my brother-in-law, Mr. Rodman, I arrived at Otley just in time to attend the exhibition of stock, which was then the great and leading show of the North for Short-horns. My sudden arrival as an *American*, created much interest and kindly feeling which showed itself in the strong wish that I should not go away without obtaining the animals I selected, though not intended for sale. * * * * *

"How I would work for you were I ten years younger! How I should enjoy it! But it is too late. The decay of intellect, judgment, and memory in old age is sad, and much more sad when it is recognized by the individual himself. I do but cumber the earth."

Mr. Rotch still survives, at the venerable age of eighty-five years, still hale and vigorous, enjoying the temperate pleasures of his quiet home in the valley of "The Butternuts," and although retired from breeding his favorite blooded stock, takes a lively interest in whatever appertains to their prosperity and value.

In the year 1830 Mr. Enoch Silsbey, of Boston, Mass., imported the bull Boston (1735), and cow Agatha (*alias* Boston Cow), by Sir Charles (1440), both bred by Mr. Curry, of Northumberland, Eng. These animals left many descendants, now in several good herds.

The foregoing memoranda completes the earlier era of Short-horn importations to the United States. The prices for which they could be sold was low compared with their actual value. The spirit in cultivating improved breeds of cattle pervaded few districts of country, and those districts widely separated. Communications between the different breeders were few, and inconvenient, and little of a common, or of rival interests, existed. New England, with a lean soil, for the most part, a rigid climate, and a popular opinion generally prevailing among her farmers that Short-horns were great consumers of food, and tender in constitution (both egregious mistakes, when the proper treatment and early maturity of the race were considered), looked upon them as interlopers, and introduced by "fancy gentlemen" only, to have something on their farms more extraordinary than their humbler, harder-working neighbors.

The Kentuckians, and some few stock breeders in Ohio, most of them large landholders, with a rich soil, a mild climate, and abundant forage, had readily ascertained their worth, and breeding on the early "Patton" blood with the 1817 bulls, and cows exclusively with their own bloods, and afterwards with purchases from the later Baltimore and Philadelphia importations, not only held their own, and carefully kept records of their pedigrees, but industriously increased both in blood and quality their cherished herds. Still, for several years there was a comparative interregnum in Short-horn progress, and aside from the few New England and New York breeders, assisted east of the Alleganies by the persistent efforts of Col. Powel, with his fine herd at Powelton, who kept their pedigrees intact, their efforts would have succumbed but for the occasional demand for stock from Kentucky and Ohio. The cattle going westward then had to be traveled on foot, over hilly and mountainous roads for hundreds of miles' distance, and through a period of several weeks' journey to reach their new homes. There were no railways, and hardly a canal by which cattle could be transported, except the Erie, through the interior of New York, which was distant and out of thought for a Kentuckian or southern Ohioan to traverse.

Down to the year, say 1832-3, most of the Short-horn breeders of the States north of Pennsylvania, understanding the importance of true lineage in their stock, had kept correct records of their pedigrees, and registered many of them in the English Herd Books. Col. Powel had done the same. Yet several parties to whom some of these breeders had sold more or less of their stock, deplorably neglected to keep correct pedigrees of either them or their increase, and through such neglect they were irrecoverably lost. After the first interest in their possession had passed away some of the cows were crossed with mean, or native bulls, their descendants became grades, devoted only to common uses, and ultimately even thoroughbred cows, in common with grades, were fed off and driven to the shambles.

CHAPTER IX.

THE LATER SHORT-HORN IMPORTATIONS.

We now arrive at a new era in American Short-horns, dating in the year 1833; many of the Kentucky breeders being convinced by a thirty years' trial, first on the Gough and Miller, or "Patton" stock, and again on the importation of 1817, and their better known successors, that there was a decided improvement in the neat cattle they were rearing, they felt the necessity of still further progress, and also that the material needed should be obtained from a source where the best specimens then existed. The late Mr. Walter Dun, an enterprising Scotch gentleman, residing near Lexington, Ky., in 1833, sent out a commission to a friend, Mr. William Douglass, living in the south of Scotland, with ample funds at command, to go into Yorkshire and purchase several Short-horn cattle, the animals to be of the best quality, without regard to any reasonable price to be paid for them.

The entire correspondence between the parties connected with this transaction has been submitted to us for examination. The instructions were faithfully executed, and six animals sent out in accordance with them. The importation consisted of the bull Symmetry (5382), and cows Caroline, Daisy, Multiflora, Red Rose, and White Rose. The cows are recorded in Vols. 2 and 7, A. H. B. Some of the bulls occurring in their pedigrees were not recorded in the English Herd Book at the time of their purchase, but we have carefully examined the original certificates sent to this country with, and relating to them. The lineage of that importation, may be found in Vols. 2 to 10, inclusive, of the American Herd Book. There need be no question of the purity of their descent. The cattle were shipped at Liverpool, Eng., September 5, 1833, bound to Philadelphia, Pa., and safely arrived in Kentucky on the 26th November following, where they were heartily welcomed both by the owner and the Short-horn breeders generally. They were there bred successfully. Their produce, in the course of years, became widely disseminated, and are now numerously found in many of the good herds of Kentucky, Ohio, and other States.

Although later in point of time the efforts of Mr. Dun did not cease with the importation of 1833. Breaking through the chronological order of dates, in order to complete his introduction of Short-horn stock to America, we follow out his transactions.

In the year 1836 Mr. Dun in connection with Mr. Samuel Smith, of Fayette county, Ky. (son of Mr. William Smith, who was connected with the Kentucky importations of 1817, previously mentioned), sent another order to England for Short-horns. In compliance with the order the bulls George (2059), Comet, 356 (1854), and bull calf Otley (4632), together with the cows Adelaide, by Magnum Bonum (2243), Beauty of Wharfdale, by Brutus (1752), Jewess, and Mary Ann (dam of Otley), by Middlesbro (1234), arrived in Kentucky. These animals were also selected in England by Mr. Douglass, before mentioned. They were placed on the separate farms of the proprietors and successfully bred.

In the year 1838 Mr. Dun on his own account made another importation, consisting of the cows Premium, by Maximus (2284), with her bull calf Otho, 794, and Young Charlotte, by Thorp (2757), with her bull calf Tarick, 1022. These animals did not arrive in Kentucky until the fall of the year, after the death of Mr. Dun, which occurred August 4, 1838.

Mr. Smith, the partner of Mr. Dun, had died a few months before the latter gentleman's death occurred. His entire herd was sold at public auction a few months afterwards, and the *joint* remaining stock of the two were sold with them under the orders of their several executors, September 11, 1838. The list of the partnership animals, their purchasers and prices, were as follows:

Cows.

Adelaide, sold to R. T. Dillard and C. R. Ferguson,	$1,375
Beauty of Wharfdale, sold to F. S. Read,	755
Adeline, sold to J. Kinnard and Thomas Wallace,	1,030
Young Adeline, sold to R. P. Kenney,	440
Mary Ann and calf Otley, 10 days old, sold to R. G. Jackson and B. P. Gray,	2,100
Prudence, sold to E. S. Washington,	755
Jewess (barren), sold to J. Matson and J. Spear,	276

At the same sale many other thorough-bred Short-horns and grade animals, upwards of thirty in number, belonging to the estate of Mr.

Smith, were disposed of, all the animals bringing good prices. Among the former were

    Cow Cleopatra, sold to C. C. Morgan, for $1,230
    Cow Ellen, sold to R. T. Dillard and C. R. Ferguson, for........ 1,235
    Bull Oliver Keen, 5 months old, sold to W. S. Hume, for 1,000

For the imported bull Comet, 356, which had, previous to the sale, become the sole property of Mr. Dun, $3,000 was offered by Mr. Gray, one of the purchasers of Mary Ann. The offer was refused, the herd of Mr. Dun remaining in the possession of his family under charge of his executor, Mr. John G. Dun.

The young imported bull Otley (4632) had been previously sold for $2,100 to Messrs. Wasson and Shropshire, of Bourbon county, Ky.

"The Ohio Company for Importing English Cattle."

Excited somewhat, probably, by the recent Dun importation, in the year 1834 several spirited cattle breeders of the Scioto valley and neighboring counties in Ohio, associated and selected an agent—the late Mr. Felix Renick, of Chillicothe—who, with two assistants, Edwin J. Harness and Josiah Renick, proceeded to England early in that year for the purchase of a herd of Short-horns. It was a propitious time. The prices for good stock of the kind in England were then low. Mr. Renick bought some from Mr. Whitaker, at Otley, Yorkshire, who had previously sent out many cattle to Col. Powel. He had a large herd of his own, his acquaintance with other breeders was extensive, and Mr. Renick had good facilities for making selections from some of the best herds, and at prices within the means at his disposal. During Mr. Renick's stay in England he purchased nineteen Short-horns—bulls and heifers. They were from various eminent breeders living in or near the valley of the Tees. All the animals were thorough-bred, and, with one or two exceptions, which could not be then readily obtained, had excellent pedigrees. They were duly shipped and arrived in Philadelphia during the summer, and driven over the mountains into Ohio, where they were kept on Mr. Renick's farm, near Chillicothe, and bred as the joint property of the Association.

In the succeeding years, 1835 and '36, two further importations, selected from equally good herds as the previous importation of 1834, were made by the same Association. These animals arrived in New York, and were transported to Ohio, *via* Erie Canal to Buffalo, thence by Lake to Cleveland, and from there to Chillicothe, where they joined the earlier importation. The cattle were thus kept until October, 1836, when the entire herd, consisting of the several importations and their produce, were sold at public auction. There were seventy-five bulls and cows comprised in the entire herd, according to the printed catalogue at the time. The number of produce was not large, as many of the females were only young heifers when imported, and the limited increase in but two years is thus readily accounted for.

At the sale a large attendance congregated, chiefly from Ohio, with some from Kentucky, and a few breeders from other States. The bidding was eager and spirited; prices went high, as many of the bidders were stockholders, buying their own goods, yet several outside parties made purchases at equal prices with the others.

As this was the most important and numerous sale ever made in America, down to that time, a full account, copied from *The Scioto Gazette*, October 26, 1836, is herewith given, with purchasers names and some other items added:

BULLS.

Matchem (2283), Abm. Renick, Clark county, Ky.,	$1,200
Earl of Darlington (1944), Batteal Harrison, Fayette county, Ohio,	710
Young Waterloo (2817), R. D. Lilly, Highland county, Ohio,	1,250
Duke of York (1941), R. R. Seymour, Ross county, Ohio,	1,120
Greenholme Experiment (2075), J. M. Trimble, Highland county, O.	1,150
Comet Halley (1855), R. R. Seymour, Ross county, Ohio,	1,505
Goldfinder (2066), Isaac Cunningham, Bourbon county, Ky.,	1,095
Whitaker (2836), William M. Anderson, Ross county, Ohio,	855
Nimrod (2371), Elias Florence, Pickaway county, Ohio,	1,040
Duke of Norfolk (1939), Robert Stewart, Ross county, Ohio,	1,225
Duke of Leeds (1938), John Crouse, Jr., Ross county, Ohio,	575
Windham (2845), Charles Davis, Ross county, Ohio,	500
Davy Crocket (3571), Peter L. Ayers, Ohio,	490
Snowdrop (2654), Stewart & McNiel, Ross county, Ohio,	480
Independence (2152), Hagler & Peterson, Ross county, Ohio,	400
Perry (not recorded), by Reformer (2505), out of Teeswater, W. H. Creighton, Madison county, Ohio,	400
Goliah (2068), Isaac Cunningham, Bourbon county, Ky.,	300
Logan (2218), Elias Florence, Pickaway county, Ohio,	750
John Bull (2161), William Renick, Jr., Pickaway county, Ohio,	615
Paragon of the West (4649), presented by the company to their agent, Felix Renick, Ross county, Ohio.	
Powhatan, 828½, with his dam Flora, Geo. Renick, Ross county, O.	
Rantipole, 885 (2478), Arthur Watts, Ross county, Ohio,	810
Reformer (2505), unsound. J. T. Webb, Ross county, Ohio,	48

Cows.

Gaudy, by a son of Young Albion (15), J. M. Trimble, Highland county, Ohio,	$810
Blossom, by Fitz Favorite (1042), R. R. Seymour, Ross county, O.	1,000
Flora, by a son of Young Albion (15), and her bull calf Powhatan, 828¾, George Renick, Ross county, Ohio,	1,205
Lily of the Valley of the Tees, by Young Rockingham (2547), Thos. Huston, Pickaway county, Ohio,	950
Matilda, by Imperial (2151), Arthur Watts, Ross county, Ohio,	1,000
Calypso, by Bertram (1716), Strawder McNeill, Ross county, Ohio,	325
Young Mary, by Jupiter (2170), and cow calf Pocahontas, E. J. Harness, Ross county, Ohio,	1,500
Lady Blanche, by Prince William (1344), not a breeder, Charles Davis, Ross county, Ohio,	250
Teeswater, by Belvedere (1706), and her cow calf Countess, by Comet Halley (1855), John J. Vanmeter, Pike county, Ohio,	2,225
Duchess of Liverpool (pedigree not obtained), Wm. M. Anderson, Ross county, Ohio,	570
Lady Colling, by Magnum Bonum (2243), not a breeder, J. T. Webb, Ross county, Ohio,	205
Beauty of the West (pedigree not given), Asahel Renick, Pickaway county, Ohio,	900
Lilac, by Rantipole, 885 (2478), Elias Florence, Pickaway county, O.	425
Lady of the Lake, by Reformer (2505), R. R. Seymour, Ross Co., O.	
Lady Paley, by Rantipole, 885 (2478), Alex. Renick, Ross county, O.	510
Poppy, by Rantipole, 885 (2478), Harness Renick, Pickaway Co., O.	610
Pink, by Duke of York (1941), Wm. Trimble, Highland county, O.	575
Mayflower, by Duke of York (1941), Batteal Harrison, Fayette county, Ohio,	405
Lucy, by Duke of York (1941), Geo. Ratcliff, Pickaway county, O.	505
Moss Rose, by Stapleton (2698), Jonathan Renick, Pickaway Co., O.	1,200
Calestina, by Atlas (1660), T. Huston, Pickaway county, Ohio,	930
Malina, by Atlas (1660), Isaac Cunningham, Bourbon county, Ky.	1,005
Illustrious, by Emperor (1974), Abm. Renick, Clark county, Ky.	775
Lady Abernethy, by Physician (2426), Thomas Huston, Pickaway county, Ohio,	815

On the 1st April, 1837, a meeting of the company was held at Chillicothe to close up their affairs and dispose of some remaining animals, which were not taken at the sale, and others not then offered. The following were thus sold on 15th April, 1837:

Bulls.

Acmon (1606), M. L. Sullivant, Columbus, Ohio,	$2,500
Comet Halley (1855), George Renick & Co., Ross county, Ohio,	2,500
Hazlewood (2098), A. Trimble and R. R. Seymour,	700

Bouncer, 13209, John Walke, Pickaway county, Ohio,............ $453
Powhatan, 828½, Harness Renick, Pickaway county, Ohio,........ 500
Santa Anna (3½ months old, not recorded), C. Vance, Ohio Co., Va. 425

Cows.

Flora, by a son of Young Albion (15), M. L. Sullivant, Columbus, O. 1,300
Matilda, by Imperial (2151), Allen Trimble, Highland county, Ohio, 1,220
Fidella, by Comet Halley (1855), 7½ months old, Allen Trimble, Highland county, Ohio,...................................... 610
Elizabeth, by ———, and calf, J. & W. Vance, Champaign Co., O. 1,450
Charlotte, by ———, Joseph G. White, Ross county, Ohio,...... 630
Arabella, by Victory (5566), and calf, Arthur Watts, Ross county, O. 1,200
Blush, by ———, J. H. James, Urbana, Ohio,.................... 1,015
Emily, by ———, Asahel Renick, Pickaway county, Ohio,........ 875
Victoress, by Norfolk (2377), M. L. Sullivant, Columbus, Ohio,.... 700

Thus closed the sales of these memorable importations. The company reaped a large profit on their investment, and conferred a lasting benefit on the neat stock interests of the country, as well as awakened a spirit through various other States for forming associations of like character and results.

At a period of thirty-five years, from the time of the Chillicothe sales, the pedigrees of hundreds of the descendants of most of those animals can be found recorded in the American Herd Book, while others, through various causes, so far as public records are concerned, have become almost, if not wholly, extinct.

After the sales of the Ohio Company, importations multiplied apace. Agricultural prices in products had been gradually strengthening for the few past years, and meats bore good rates in both our home and foreign markets. Money had been unusually abundant for two years past, owing to the rival and conflicting measures of political parties in the general government, and a consequent false estimate of the ability of the people to extend their credits and plunge into all sorts of speculation. The farmers throughout the country felt rich, and among other items of speculative value it is no wonder that the noble race of Short-horn cattle became an attractive object with portions of the agricultural community as well as many men of means whose tastes sympathized in their pursuits. Thus importations of them were sought, commissions were sent to England, and several new purchasers went out to select and bring cattle here where prices ruled high and sales were rapidly made, particularly in Kentucky and Ohio.

It is difficult at this space of time (now thirty-five years since, with the notices and dates of their arrival only chronicled in the scattered agricultural periodicals of the day, and the memories of living men not exact), to enumerate the names of all the animals imported, or the parties owning them from the year 1836 to 1842. It is sufficient to say, however, that the importing parties were many, and their animals numerous. The accounts, so far as we have been enabled to gather them, (but perhaps not in exact chronological order,) will be given.

About the year 1835 or '36, Mr. Thomas Weddle an Englishman, emigrated with his family from Yorkshire, Eng., into Western New York, and brought with him a dozen or more good Short-horns, all having good pedigrees, and chiefly from the herd of Major Bower, a well-known breeder of Welham, Yorkshire. Among them were the bull Charles (1816); Welland 1084¼, and one or two others. Among the cows were Crocus, by Romulus (2563); Primrose, by Pioneer (1321); Daisy, by Ebor (3681), and several more. Mr. Weddle bred his herd several years, selling as opportunity presented, at good prices; yet, not accustomed to the business, he was careless in the records of his herd, and although he had the ability, from the pedigrees of his originals, to perpetuate the genealogy of their increase, the lineage of many of them was irrecoverably lost, or if not entirely so, they could only be traced to the importation in general terms. In the course of a few years, Mr. Weddle going into other pursuits than farming, his herd was sold and dispersed; some of them going into Kentucky, and others remaining in New York.

In the year 1835 or '36, possibly a year or two earlier, Mr. Ezra P. Prentice, of Albany, N. Y., began breeding at his villa farm, near the city, a small herd of Short-horns selected chiefly from the stock of Gen. Van Rensselaer, already noticed. In 1838, '39, '40, '41, he imported a number of choice Short-horns from various herds in England. Among them were the bulls Fairfax, 61 (3754); O'Connell, 118; and cows Appolonia, by Albion (2965); Aurora, by William (2839); Catherine, by Sir Robert (5181); Esterville, by Alfred (2987); Flora, by Imperial (2151); Moss Rose, by Barden (1674); Princess, by Henry (4008); Splendor, by Symmetry (2723); Susan, by Dutchman (3669); and Violanta, by Charles (1815). He bred his stock, both of American birth and imported, with great skill and decided success, selling many animals into New York, and several other States, until the year 1850, when at a public sale he disposed of his entire herd. Mr. Prentice was greatly attached to his stock, but the city had encroached upon him, rendering the necessary accommodations for his cattle stock impossible, and with reluctance he parted with his herd, then nearly forty in number, and one of the best, at the time, in the country.

About the same time, 1835 or '36, or soon after Mr. Prentice, Mr. George Vail, of Troy, N. Y., began breeding Short-horns at his villa farm, near that city. He purchased some imported animals, and others, selecting them with care and judgment. In the year 1839 he imported direct from Mr. Thomas Bates, of Durham, Eng., the bull Duke of Wellington, 55 (3654), got by Short Tail (2621), out of Oxford Premium Cow, by Duke of Cleveland (1937); the first one of the Duchess and Oxford crosses combined, which had been brought into America. With him came the cow Duchess, by Duke of Northumberland (1940). Although called Duchess, she was not, on the dam's side, of *the* Duchess tribe so long identified with Mr. Bates' breeding, but running, after her dam, by Belvedere (1706), into another family. This cow, after producing the bulls Meteor, 104, and Symmetry, 166, (both by Duke of Wellington, 55,) died, leaving no female progeny.

During several successive years Mr. Vail made importations from Mr. Bates' and Mr. Bell's herds, of crosses with the Duchess and Oxford bulls, and various families of their well-bred cows, down to the year 1851. Among them were the bull Earl Derby, 456; and the cows, Cecelia, by 3d Duke of Northumberland (3647); Hilpa, by Cleveland Lad (3407); Lady Barrington 3d, by Cleveland Lad (3407); Arabella, by 4th Duke of Northumberland (3649); Yarm Lass, by 4th Duke of York (10167); Yorkshire Countess, by 3d Duke of York (10166); Agate, by 3d Duke of York (10166); Boukie, by 4th Duke of York (10167; Bright Eyes 3d, by Earl of Derby (10177); Frantic, by 4th Duke of York (10167).

To the above named were added some from other importations. Mr. Vail was enthusiastic in the love he bore to his cattle; he bred successfully, making many and frequent sales until the month of October, 1852, when he disposed of his entire herd.

About the year 1836, Mr. Erastus Corning, of Albany, imported the cow Wildair, by Anthony (1640). She bred successfully, and her descendants are now found in the American Herd Book. There may have been another or two heifers, and possibly a bull in the importation, but of them we have no particular account.

Sometime between the years 1835-40, Messrs. James Gowen, Dennis Kelley, and perhaps another or two associates in the neighborhood of Philadelphia, Pa., either jointly or severally imported from England, or purchased from Mr. Whitaker's importation in some of those years, some Short-horn bulls and cows, which were said to be of good quality and full pedigrees. Several progeny descended from these animals, and a few stray ones, through the hands of other parties whose stock run into them, have been hunted up, and their pedigrees recorded in the American Herd Book. But from the neglect or indifference of their proper owners, many of their pedigrees, together with the cattle themselves, have been lost, and only occasional traces can now be found of them.

A striking instance of the self-sufficiency of some men, in their own pretensions in one of these cases, as well as in some others of past days in the matter of pedigrees may be given. When a certain party was asked if he put the pedigrees of his cattle in the Herd Book, he scornfully answered: "No! if *my word* is not good enough evidence of their pure breeding, no Herd Book record can make it any better." We fancy that most cattle breeders would rather have a clean Herd Book record than the bare assertion, from the imperfect memory of *any* man. Through such lofty assumptions many otherwise valuable pedigrees of good Short-horns in this country have been lost.

In the year 1836 Messrs. Edward A. Le Roy and Thomas H. Newbould, at Avon, Livingston county, N. Y., imported from England the bull Windle, 185 (5667), and the cows Dione, by Monarch (4494); Lady Morris, by Priam (4758); Netherby, by Gambier (2047); and Venus, by Magnum Bonum (2244)—a choice selection. The stock was carefully bred for eight or ten years, occasional sales during the time being made from them. Soon afterwards these gentlemen making sale of their farms the stock was likewise sold, and the herds scattered.

About the same time as the above, the late Mr. Peter A. Remson, of Alexander, Genesee county, N. Y., imported the bull Alexander, 4, and the cows Adelaide, by Cupid (1894); Lavinia, by a son of Scipio (1421); and Prettyface, by Henwood (2114). Mr. Remson bred them for some years, and sold several of them and their produce while at Alexander. On selling his farm in 184–, he soon afterwards removed the few remaining ones to another farm, which he occupied in Maryland, where, within two or three years, they were finally sold, and further traces of them lost, except as some of the pedigrees of their descendants have since appeared in the American Herd Book.

In August, 1837, Mr. Jonas Whitaker, of Yorkshire, Eng., before named, imported a herd of 15 bulls and 19 cows and heifers into Philadelphia, Pa., and placed them on the farm of Col. Powel, at Powelton, near the city. They were a good herd, and in high condition, with good pedigrees, as we saw them a few days previous to the sale. They had been widely advertised, and at the day of sale drew a numerous attendance of Short-horn breeders from the surrounding States, and some from the more distant States of Ohio and Kentucky. The prices for the bulls averaged $353, and for the cows $480, amounting in the aggregate to $14,215. Several of the cattle went to Kentucky, some to Ohio, and others to Pennsylvania, and the States adjoining.

Mr. Whitaker repeated his importations to some extent in 1838-9, but the average prices falling off in the latter year he made no further importations. The late Mr. William Neff, of Cincinnati, Ohio, purchased several animals at Mr. Whitaker's sales, and successfully bred them. Many American recorded pedigrees trace to his herd.

At the last sale, in 1839, eight cows sold for $3,672, being an average of $459 each. The bull Sir Robert (we have not his pedigree number, if recorded) sold for $700. Several other animals were sold at the same time, but we have not seen any report of their prices.

In 1837 to 1839, Messrs. James Shelby and Henry Clay, Jr., of Kentucky, made importations of several fine cattle, some of which they kept and bred for a time, and others were sold soon after their arrival in Kentucky. In 1837 they imported ten cows and one bull, Don John, 426. At a sale of Mr. Clay, Jr., in Lexington, in the autumn of 1839, the following females were sold at a public auction with prices attached:

Victoria, 2 years old,	$835
Victoria, 3 " "	745
Venus, 5 " "	210
Fanny, 1 " "	520
Duchess, 4 mos. "	340
Jane, 9 " "	300
Daphne, 5 " " (sick,)	230
Beauty, 2 years " (doubtful breeder,)	176
Average, $419½ each.	

About the year 1837 or '38, the late Mr. Henry Whitney, of Morristown, N. J., imported two Short-horns. We have no account of the individual animals or their names, but from the records of their produce in Vol. 1, A. H. B., we infer that one of them was the bull

Birmingham (3152), and the other was the cow Ringlet, by Belshazzar (1704). Whether any other cattle were imported by Mr. Whitney we have no information.

About the same time as the above, the late Mr. William Gibbons, of Madison, N. J., imported the bull Majestic (2249), and the cow Volage (bred by Mr. Whitaker), by Charles (878). The cow bred the bull Zero 190 (by Majestic). Of her and her breeding we have no further account, as Mr. Gibbons took little fancy to cattle of any kind, his taste running to blooded horses, of which he bred several of high repute in the turf annals of his time.

Dr. Samuel D. Martin, Pine Grove, Clark county, Ky., in addition to a herd of Short-horns which he had some years before established, in the year 1839, in conjunction with Messrs. Hubbard and J. P. Taylor, sent an order to England and imported four cows and a heifer calf, viz.: Beauty, by Laurel (2181), bred by Mr. Parker; Jessy, by Plenipo (4724), bred by A. L. Maynard; Leonida, by Red Simon (2499), bred by Mr. Peacock; Sprightly, by Fitz Roslyn (2026), bred by Mr. Paley; and the calf Rosalie, by Cadet (1770), bred by Mr. Paley. Three of the cows were in calf before leaving England. Sprightly produced twin bulls: Specie (5289), and Speculation (5263), by Mendoza (4456); Beauty produced Bullion (3240), by Lofty (2217); and Jessy produced the heifer Jessamine, by Leonidas (4211). These cows all proved good animals, and excellent milkers. Many of the produce are recorded in the American Herd Book.

It is probable that about those years some other importations of a few Short-horns were made by gentlemen living in our Eastern cities, which were placed on their country places in their several vicinities, but as they were simply amateurs, caring little or nothing for pedigrees, and the novelty of their possession soon abating, the cattle themselves, and their produce, pedigrees, and history, were ultimately absorbed, or lost in the common stock of the country.

In the year 1837 or '38, Mr. John F. Sheaffe established a choice herd at his farm and country residence at New Hamburgh, Dutchess county, N. Y., on the Hudson. They were chiefly descendants from the New England importations. To them in 1843 he added several cows which he imported, among which was Seraphina, by Wharfdale (1578). The other names are not now recollected.

In 1848 Mr. Sheaffe imported the bull Duke of Exeter, 449 (10152), then a calf, bred by Mr. John Stephenson, Wolviston, Eng., a valuable animal, chiefly of the Princess tribe of blood. This bull made a marked impression by way of improvement on his produce. He was mainly yellow-red in color, and a remarkably fine handler. At two and a half years old, at the final sale of Mr. Sheaffe's herd, he became the property of the writer, and for two years longer bred with signal success. He died at six years old of inflammation in the kidneys.

Mr. Sheaffe bred his herd successfully until 1850, when, going on a prolonged absence to Europe, the stock were sold, and distributed into several hands, who have since placed the pedigrees of their descendants in many pages of the American Herd Book.

In 1838 the late Dr. John A. Poole, of New Brunswick, N. J., imported the cows Fanny, by Charley (1817); Maria, by Henwood (2114), and possibly others. Dr. Poole's house was burned in 1842, and his Short-horn papers were destroyed.

In 1843, and partially contemporary with Mr. Sheaffe, Mr. James Lenox, of New York, owning a fine country residence and farm adjoining Mr. Sheaffe, imported several good Short-horns. Among them were the bulls King Charles 2d, 84 (4154); Prince Albert, 133 (4809); and cows Daffodil, by Sampson (5081); Gayly, by Sir Thomas Fairfax (5196); and Red Lady, by Hubback (2142); all from the herd of Jonas Whitaker, of Yorkshire. He bred them for several years. Although managing his stock by proxy, they were skillfully and successfully bred, but selling the estate and removing altogether to the city, his herd was dispersed into different hands, who still keep their pedigrees in the Herd Books.

In the spring of 1839, Rev. R. T. Dillard and Mr. Nelson Dudley, of Kentucky, went to England and selected for the Fayette, Kentucky, Importing Company, a superior lot of Short-horns. After their arrival home they were placed on the farm of David Sutton, near Lexington, and in July, 1840, were sold at auction, as follows:

BULLS.

Carcase, 312 (3285), calved in 1837, sold to B. Gratz,	$725
Æolus, 200 (2938), calved in 1836, sold to R. Fisher,	610
Eclipse (9069), calved in 1837, sold to R. Fisher,	1,050
Crofton (3523), calved in 1839, sold to J. Downing,	155
Prince Albert, 2065, (calf of Victoria,) 2 mos. old, sold to J. Flournoy,	350
Washington (not recorded), calf,	85
Nelson, 741, sold to P. Todhunter,	610
Orlando, 3225, (calf of Lady Eliza,) sold to H. Clay, Jr., Bourbon Co.,	305
Trojan, 11080, (calf of Lily,) sold to Wheeland & Co.,	150
Bruce, 289, (calf of Avarilda,) sold to M. Williams,	315
Milton, 713, (calf of Miss Maynard,) sold to James Gaines,	285
	$4,640

Average, $422 each.

Cows.

Victoria (dam of Prince Albert), sold to R. Fisher,	$1,750
Miss Hopper, sold to Thomas Calmes,	270
Elizabeth, sold to A. McClure,	505
Maria (calf of Elizabeth), sold to J. B. Ford,	310
Miss Luck, sold to H. Clay, Jr., Bourbon county,	800
Fashion, sold to G. W. Williams,	440
Zela (calf of Fashion), sold to G. W. Williams,	445
Splendor, sold to B. Gratz,	650
Tulip, sold to A. McClure,	700
Britannia, and heifer calf Dido, sold to H. T. Duncan,	375
Isabella, sold to R. Fisher,	355
Lady Eliza, sold to H. Clay, Jr., Bourbon county,	660
Lily, sold to T. Calmes,	390
Nancy, sold to C. J. Rogers,	730
Avarilda, sold to John Allen,	920
Beauty, sold to H. Clay, Fayette county,	700
Flora (calf of Beauty), sold to H. Clay, Fayette county,	410
Miss Maynard, sold to A. McClure,	1,005
Jessica, sold to Joel Higgins,	330
Rosabella, sold to William A. Warner,	465
Average, $610 each.	$12,210

Of these animals Mercer county took 5; Scott county 5; Fayette county 8; Jessamine county 4; Clark county 2; Bourbon county 5. Where the remaining 2 went the account does not state.

Under the depression of the money market of the country at the time, although at lower prices than paid at some previous sales of the kind, the result may be considered a good one.

In the *Franklin* (Ky.) *Farmer* of June, 1839, it is stated that Lewis Shirley, of Louisville, Ky., imported from England, and brought there the bulls General Chasse, calved in 1834; Liverpool, calved in 1838; and another, called Young Matchem, all having good pedigrees. Only a few pedigrees in A. H. B. trace their lineage to these bulls. It is also stated in the same paper, that Mr. Shirley in the autumn of 1839, sold the bull Velocipede (imported in 1836) to Kendall & Co., Elkton, Ky., for $1,500; and the bull Liverpool to a company in Nelson county, Ky., for $1,000.

In February, 1840, Messrs. Wait & Bagg brought to New York from England, seven Short-horns, bulls and cows. One of the cows, Empress, by Cyrus (3538), was sold to Mr. George Vail, Troy, N. Y., and in the succeeding year they took others of the importation to

Kentucky. Pedigrees of their descendants are frequently recorded in the pages of the American Herd Book.

With the year 1840, under the continued depression of the financial interests of the country at large, the spirit so active during several previous years in cultivating the Short-horns gradually waned, and further importations ceased. For several succeeding years the prices of meats were unprecedentedly low. Mess pork fell to $10, and even less, per barrel, in our principal markets, and the dressed carcasses of swine were dull of sale at $2.50 to $3.00 per hundred pounds, while beef of good quality was worth even less, and a drug throughout. As a consequence, there was little or no encouragement for breeding Short-horns. Under this depressed condition of affairs hundreds of well-bred bull calves were castrated for steers, and many cow calves spayed and reared for the shambles. Prices for even the best blooded animals were merely nominal; public sales were scarcely made at all as in past years, and private sales infrequent. Nor was the depression for a few years only, but continuous down to nearly or quite the year 1850. One hundred to two hundred dollars per head would buy the choice of almost any herd, bull or cow, in the country. As a specimen of the times, the writer received a commission from the firm of A. B. Allen & Co., Agricultural Merchants in New York city, in October, 1850, to select fifteen or twenty good breeding Short-horns, bulls and heifers, to fill an order for the Island of Cuba, where an experiment was to be tried with them on the high ranges of country near its eastern coast. We went into the Scioto valley of Ohio, and from the herds of some of its best breeders purchased several beautiful (in calf) heifers, of two to three years old past, red, red and white, and roan in color—as all white was objected to—for $50 to $100 each, and several bulls at like prices. Some of them were descendants of the Kentucky importation of 1817, with several crosses of the Ohio Company bulls and their descendants of the 1834 importation in their pedigrees, and others, pure descendants from the latter. Every animal was of our own selection. We paid the full price asked for them, and could have quadrupled the number, or even more, at the same prices. In Kentucky, New York and New England, Short-horn values were no better, and many breeders who had begun rearing them but a few years before became disgusted with their stock, turned their choice bred cows into the dairies, put them to common bulls, and sold off their calves remorselessly to the butcher. During this depressing period numerous good pedigrees were lost, as not being worth preserving, and many valuable families of this lordly race became almost, if not wholly, extinct. A newly imported animal, although Short-horns were then suffering under depressed prices in England, would hardly pay the expenses of transportation across the ocean from any sale which could be made of it here.

Still, the low prices of meats in the markets were not all the difficulty. The taste of our stock breeders had at the time been but scantily cultivated. Shrewd, discriminating men knew the value of Short-horns, and the immense improvement they were capable of giving to the common herds of the country; but when the great mass of farmers were either too dull or too ignorant to buy, there was little or no encouragement to breed them. Thus the choice herds so highly prized but a few years before lay dormant. It was but a repetition of the result of many valuable enterprises in the agricultural world— a spasm, an excitement incident to the trial of a new thing, followed by an indifference, a mistaken and culpable neglect on the part of the many; but still kept alive by the hopeful foresight of the few who held persistently on to their herds, anticipating a brighter day when their anxious efforts would be amply rewarded, as the sequel will show.

CHAPTER X.

Revival of the Short-horns in America.

The year 1852 dawned upon a more cheerful prospect in agricultural pursuits than that of the last ten or twelve years preceding it. Meats had gradually increased in price, as a foreign demand to a considerable extent had opened for our surplus provisions; our farmers had measurably recovered from their depressed condition, and a spirit of improvement in their neat stock now gradually revived among the cattle growers of the country, particularly in the States of New York, Ohio and Kentucky. Those Short-horn breeders who had tenaciously held on to and cherished the blood of their favorite herds—and taken in the aggregate, there were quite a number of them—gathered their choice things together with renewed care, and with cheerful hope of better times in the future, set themselves about their improvement both by accelerated increase and painstaking in their breeding. Had not the Short-horn race, by their inherent qualities of excellence, borne up against the neglect under which many of them for years past had suffered, some of them in their depressed appearance and careless breeding would scarcely be recognized as high-bred cattle at all, although the aristocratic blood of many generations still coursed through their veins and remained intact as ever. Yet by the still hopeful interest, and care of their breeders under the exercise of a discriminating judgment, the neglected herds rapidly resumed their wonted comeliness of form and robustness of condition, and showed their excellence as of old.

About the year 1852 a demand for them gradually sprung up, and on a deliberate survey of the situation a new impulse was directed to further importations from abroad. Anticipating a movement of this kind, in the year 1849 Mr. Ambrose Stevens, of Batavia, N. Y., went to England and purchased the valuable bull 3d Duke of Cambridge, 1034 (5941), by Duke of Northumberland (1940), then eight years old, of his breeder, Mr. Thomas Bates, of Kirkleavington. This bull was of the Duchess, Princess, and Waterloo tribes combined. After his arrival in America he became the joint property of Col. J. M. Sherwood, of Auburn, N. Y., and Mr. Stevens, and was kept several years, until he died on Col. Sherwood's farm. He did much valuable service as a sire.

At the same time with 3d Duke of Cambridge came the bull calf Duke of Exeter, 449 (10152), bred by Mr. John Stephenson, for Mr. J. F. Sheaffe, New Hamburgh, Dutchess county, N. Y., previously mentioned.

With the above named bulls were brought out from the herd of Mr. Stephenson the yearling heifers Princess 2d, by General Sale (8099); Princess 3d, by Napier (6238); and Red Rose 2d, by Napier (6238). The latter was sold to Col. Sherwood, and soon afterwards Red Rose 2d gave birth to Red Rose 4th, by Earl of Chatham (10176). Red Rose 2d was a remarkable milker (a small cow, from her early breeding, and thin in flesh from heavy milking), having made 49 pounds of butter in 25 successive days in May and June, 1851, when 4 years old, with her second calf. To the above may be added Red Rose 3d, by General Sale. This heifer died without produce.

With these also came out the bull Lord Vane Tempest, 669½ (10469), sold to Col. Sherwood.

In the year 1850 were imported the bull Earl of Seaham, 1499 (10181), the joint property of Mr. Stevens and Col. Sherwood, afterwards purchased by Rev. John A. Gano, of Bourbon county, Ky., in whose possession he died, leaving some valuable descendants.

With Earl of Seaham came also the bull Wolviston, 1109, afterwards sold by Mr. Stevens to Mr. Ashton, of Canada West.

With the above bulls were imported the cow Princess 4th, by Napier (6238); Waterloo 5th (bred by Thomas Bates), by Duke of Northumberland (1940); Wild Eyes 5th (bred by Mr. Bates), by Short Tail (2621). The two last named cows died after their arrival in America, without issue.

In 1851 Mr. Stevens imported the bull calf Earl Vane, 464, by Earl of Chatham (10176), and the cow Princess 1st (5 years old), by Napier (6238); and in 1852 came out the cow Lady Sale 2d, by Earl of Chatham (10176). Sold to Col. Sherwood.

In the same year Col. Sherwood imported the cow Tuberose 2d, by Earl of Antrim (10174).

All the above animals of the Stevens-Sherwood importation (excepting the three bred by Mr. Bates) were bred by Mr. Stephenson, Wolviston, Eng., and of his Princess tribe.

In some year, shortly previous to 1848, a Mr. Oliver, of Westchester county, N. Y., imported the bull Marius, 684, bred by Earl Spencer, England. He was exhibited at the New York State Agricultural Show, in Buffalo, 1848, by Colonel L. G. Morris, and there sold to Mr. David Harrold, of South Charleston, Clark county, Ohio, into which State he went and did good service for some years. Our impression is that one or two heifers were brought out with the bull, but of the fact we have no particular account.

About the year 1851 or '52, Mr. Lorillard Spencer, of New York, imported the young bull Augustus, 225 (1125), bred by G. D. Trotter, Middlesex, Eng.; Duke of Atholl, 44 (10150), bred by Thos. Bates; and Woldsman, 1108 (11056), bred by Mr. Topham, Spilsby, Eng., and the heifers Faraway, by 3d Duke of Oxford (9047); Jean, by Chevalier (10050); Sonsie 8th, by 2d Cleveland Lad (3408), and possibly one or two others. . These he bred for a few years with some others acquired at home, when he finally disposed of his herd, and gave up further Short-horn breeding.

In the month of May, 1850, the sale of the late Mr. Bates' herd was held in England, by his executors, as related in a previous chapter, at which Messrs. Morris and Becar, of New York, were present, and bought three Oxford cows and heifers, viz.: Oxford 5th, by Duke of Northumberland (1940); Oxford 6th, by 2d Duke of Northumberland (3646); Oxford 13th, by 3d Duke of York (10166). Of these, Oxford 5th and 10th, were taken by Col. Morris, and Oxford 13th by Mr. Becar. Col. Morris also bought of another party the bull Balco, 227 (9918), bred by Mr. Bates.

These gentlemen also purchased of another party in England, the bull Romeo (13619) on joint account.

Col. Morris further purchased of various others the bulls Marquis of Carrabas (11789); The Lord of Eryholme (12205), and Billy Pitt (9967); also the cows Beauty of Brawith, by Emperor (6973); Bloom, by Sir Leonard (10827); and Romelia, by Flageolet (9130).

Mr. Becar also bought of other parties the cows Actress, by Harkaway (9184); Apricot, by 3d Duke of York (10166); Garland, by Pestalozzi (10603); Lady Barrington 12th, by 4th Duke of York (10167); and Lady Booth, by Chilton (10054). These animals were all shipped to America, where they were established on the farms of their respective owners, and most, if not all the females bred successfully, producing a numerous progeny.

At the great Tortworth Court sale of the herd of the late Earl Ducie, in the year 1853, noticed in a preceding chapter, Messrs.

Morris and Becar bought the bull Duke of Gloster, 2763 (11382), and the cow Duchess 66th, by 4th Duke of York (10167), which they brought home and bred with their previously established herd, until the death of Mr. Becar, which most unfortunately occurred in the year 1854, in the full maturity of his vigor and usefulness. Mr. Becar was a native of France, and emigrating when a young man to the city of New York, he established himself as a merchant, which occupation he for many years successfully pursued. He married an American wife, whose family held large possessions of land on Long Island, and were among its most intelligent farmers. In possession of one of those attractive farms Mr. Becar cultivated alike its acres and his Short-horns with assiduity and success, during the few years which he devoted to the pursuit. Soon after his death, his late partner, Col. Morris, purchased his interest in the herd, and a few months afterwards (selling out meantime many valuable young bulls to various breeders in different States) he transferred them in one entire sale to Mr. Samuel Thorne, at Thorndale, Dutchess county, N.Y.

Anticipating a year or two of time, we follow the herd of Messrs. Morris and Becar into the hands of Mr. Thorne, and merging them in his own recently well-selected herd, we must pass to an account of that gentleman's Short-horn importations and breeding.

In the year 1850 Mr. Jonathan Thorne, of the city of New York, having on his extensive farm, at Thorndale, a couple of Short-horn cows recently bought of Mr. Vail, at Troy, sent out to his son, Edwin Thorne, then in England, to purchase and send him a Short-horn bull. The order was filled by the importation of St. Lawrence, 1005 (12037), bred by Capt. Pelham, of the Isle of Wight. The young bull, calved only in the previous November, arrived in America early in the spring of 1851, and was taken to Mr. Thorne's farm, where he remained until of breeding age. He was afterwards sold to the late Dr. Elisha Warfield, near Lexington, Ky., where he did good service in his herd for some years.

In the summer of 1852, Mr. Thorne received, on an order which he sent to Mr. Robert Bell, of England, two heifers, Forget-me-not 2d, by 4th Duke of York (10167), and Countess, by 3d Duke of Oxford (9047); also from J. S. Tanqueray the young cow Ellen Gwynne, by Sir Harry (10819). This last named cow (pregnant before shipped), after her arrival in America, produced the bull calf Young Balco, 1124, got by Balco (9918), and soon afterwards died from a quantity of nails found in her stomach, after death.

In the spring of 1853, Mr. Samuel Thorne (son of Jonathan)—having assumed charge of the farm and Short-horn stock—in company with the late Mr. F. M. Rotch, residing in Morris, Otsego county, N. Y., sailed for England in quest of some Short-horns, "as good as could be found, without regard to the prices to be paid for them." In the ensuing October Mr. Thorne brought out the bul Grand Duke, 545 (10284), bought of Mr. Bolden, and two cows Duchess 59th and 68th, bought at Lord Ducie's sale, previously noticed; also the cows Peri, by Grand Duke (10284), bought of Mr. Bolden; Frederika, by Upstart (9760), and Lalla Rookh, by The Squire (12217), bred by Mr. Townley; Aurora, by 3d Duke of York (10166); Mystery, by Usurer (9763); and Darling, by Grand Duke (10284). The vessel on which the cattle were shipped for America had a tempestuous passage. Duchess 68th was killed outright by the falling of a mast, and Peri had one hip knocked down, two ribs broken, and lost one horn. This accident, however, did not prevent her from breeding successfully after her arrival in America. The bull Harry Lorequer, bred by Mr. Fawkes, also purchased by Mr. Thorne, and embarked on the same ship, was lost by stress of weather.

The cow Duchess 64th, which was purchased by Mr. Thorne at the same (Lord Ducie's) sale, with the before named Duchesses, was left in England until the succeeding year, having meantime dropped her calf, 2d Grand Duke, 2181 (12961), which, by previous arrangement, was the property of Mr. Bolden. She soon after came to America. Her calf, 2d Grand Duke, became the property of Mr. Thorne, afterwards, in the year 1855, soon after the accident, which rendered his previous Grand Duke (10284) useless, at the price of 1000 guineas, the same which Mr. Thorne paid for the latter at the time of the Ducie sale.

All efforts to restore the usefulness of Grand Duke having failed, he was slaughtered in the year 1857, and made upwards of 1400 pounds, net weight, although in only moderate condition.

The ten animals (exclusive of 2d Grand Duke) of Mr. Thorne's first purchase in 1853, comprising Grand Duke and the three Duchesses, cost 3,600 guineas—upwards of $18,000—probably the most costly purchase ever made by an American down to that time, though several purchases of *cows* have since been made at higher prices.

Mr. Thorne's next importation was made in the year 1854, consisting of nine cows and heifers, viz.: Lady Millicent, by Laudable (9282); Sylphide, by Pestalozzi (10603); Cypress, by Lord of

Brawith (10465); Agnes, by Lord of Brawith (10465); Cherry, by Lord of Brawith (10465); Constantia, by Lord of Brawith (10465); Diana Gwynne, by Duke of Lancaster (10929); Lady of Atholl, by Duke of Atholl (10150); and Dinah Gwynne, by Balco, 227 (9918). These all came out in good condition and proved successful breeders, with the exception of Sylphide, which produced nothing after leaving England.

In November, 1855, as before mentioned, Mr. Thorne brought out the young bull 2d Grand Duke, also the bull Neptune, 1917 (11847), bred by Mr. John Booth. The bull Duke of Dorset, bred by Lord Feversham, was also bought by Mr. Thorne, but not shipped until the summer of 1856. He unfortunately died on the voyage to America.

In the summer of 1856 Mr. Thorne purchased at the sale of Sir Charles Knightly, in England, the cows Blouzelind, by Earl of Dublin (10178); Elgitha, by Balco (9918); and Mrs. Flathers, by Earl of Dublin (10178); also heifers Buttercup 2d, by Horatio (10335), and Miss Buttercup, by Master Butterfly (13311), both bred by and purchased of Col. Townley, at the price of 1,000 guineas—over $5,000 for the five; also the cows Dewdrop, by Financier (9122); Darlington 6th, by 4th Duke of Oxford (11387); and Maria Louisa, by Hopewell (10332), bred by and purchased of other parties. These animals all arrived safely at Mr. Thorne's farm, bred successfully, and left many descendants.

In 1857, Mr. Edwin Thorne, then in England, purchased and sent out to his brother Samuel, the bull Grand Turk, 2935 (12969), bred by Mr. Bolden, Lancashire.

In the spring of the same year Mr. Thorne purchased, as previously mentioned, of Col. Morris, Mt. Fordham, N Y., the combined herds of Messrs. Morris and Becar—who had imported largely from England—numbering 53 animals, including the Duchesses 66th, 71st, and Duchess (——) (afterwards recorded in E. H. B. as Duchess of Fordham); the cows Oxfords 5th, 6th, 13th, 17th and 20th; Maid of Oxford, Bride of Oxford, Romeo's Oxford, Gloster's Oxford, and Beauty of Oxford, together with bulls imported Duke of Gloster, 2763 (11382); Fordham Duke of Oxford, 2863, and Baron of Oxford, 2525.

In the year 1854, 2d Grand Duke, 2181 (12961), having become useless, was slaughtered at Mr. Thorne's farm, being then eleven years old.

Having some years previous sold some of his Duchess and Oxfords, bulls and females, to Mr. James O. Sheldon, of Geneva, N. Y., which the latter had successfully bred, in the year 1867 Mr. Thorne made a final sale of his entire herd, about forty in number, to Mr. James O. Sheldon, Geneva, N. Y., at the gross sum of $42,300.

About the years 1850 to 1853, inclusive, (for we have been unable to obtain the exact dates of his importations,) the late Mr. R. A. Alexander, of Woodford county, Ky., who had for some years, then past, been a breeder of Short-horns, obtained from different herds in that State, began an extensive importation of Short-horns from England onto his farm, and extending through several successive years. His imported animals were selected from several different prominent breeders. Of these importations, on referring to his catalogue of the year 1856, we find there were eleven bulls, and a much larger number of cows. He was aided in his selections by Mr. Strafford, editor of the English Herd Book, and with the ample means at his command, a choice assortment from some noted tribes was obtained. Among them we find, from the somewhat incomplete catalogues which we have been able to obtain, the following:

BULLS.—Lord John (11728); 2d Duke of Atholl (11376); Grand Master (12968); Baron Martin (12444); Fantachini (12862); Mickey Free, 8626 (A. H. B.); Doctor Buckingham (14405); Duke of Airdrie, 9798 (12730); El Hakim, 2814 (A. H. B.). To these he added some other bulls by purchases from late imported herds into Kentucky.

Cows.—Sweet Mary, by Rufus (6428); Peeress, by Lord Marmion (8244); Nightingale, by Prince Alfred (8422); Victoria, by Diamond (5918); Filbert, by 2d Cleveland Lad (3408); Jubilee, by Lycurgus (7180); Lady Laura, by Laudable (9282); Maid Marion, by Robin Hood (9555); Vellum, by Abraham Parker (9856); Forget-me-not, by 2d Cleveland Lad (3408); Princess 4th, by Revolution (10713); Tizzy, by Robin Hood (9555); Beatrice, by Attraction (9912); Alice Wiley, by Rumor (7456); Lady Barrington 13th, by 4th Duke of York (10167); Duchess of Atholl, by 2d Duke of Oxford (9046); Graceful, by Earl of Dublin (10178); Pearlette, by Benedict (7828); Rose, by Puritan (9523); Buttercup, by Puritan (9523); Victoria 20th, by Broken Horn (12500); Joyful, by Lycurgus (7180); Emma, by Fair Eclipse (11456); Bonny Lass, by Earl of Dublin (10178); Jubilee 2d, by Marquis of Rockingham (10506); Filligree, by Abraham Parker (9856); Lady Gulnare, by Senator (8548); Prune, by Lord Lieutenant (11734); Ferella, by Grand Duke (10284); Grisi, by Grand Duke (10284); Kathleen Bawn, by Holcombe (10384); Bessy Howard, by Fitzwalter (10232); Miss Wiley 2d, by Prince Royal (8428); Jessy 3d, by Duke of Albany (10149); Miss Townley, by Brunel (9999); Coquette, by Monk (11824); Doria Picola, by Duke of Albany (10149); Mary Cattley, by Puritan (9523); Alberta, by Holcomb (10324); Christine Cattley, by De Grey (11346); Lydia Languish, by Duke of Gloster (11382); Sally-in-our-Alley, by Bridegroom (11203); Rosabelle, by Bridegroom (11203); Sunrise, by Abraham Parker (9856); Canny, by Will Watch (12307); Lady Valentine, by Harbinger (10207); Frances Fairfax, by Crusade (7938); Zara, by Bridegroom (11203); Constance, by Bridegroom (11203); Scotia, by Lancaster Comet (11663); Minna, by Bridegroom (11203); Prunella, by Duke of Bolton (12738).

To these numerous selections were added several more purchases from other herds imported into Kentucky, which, with his native bred Short-horns he had for some years previous been cultivating, comprised the largest Short-horn herd then in the United States. Neither money nor pains were spared in the selection of his stock, or in their subsequent propagation. Many sales were made from it, both in Kentucky and other States, and its reputation was among the best in the country.

Mr. Alexander died, unmarried, in the year 1867, in the prime of his life and usefulness. His large Woodburn estate of some 3,000 acres, together with his cattle, sheep, swine, and valuable stud of blood and trotting horses, fell into the possession of his brother, Mr. A. J. Alexander, who still maintains, if not in numbers, yet in their integrity of blood and quality, the descendants of the valuable stock which the earlier proprietor had so carefully collected.

In the year 1852 a number of gentlemen in the Scioto valley, in Ohio, formed an association, sent out one or more agents and made an importation of near 20 Short-horns, bulls and cows. Most of them, 16 in number, were sold at the farm of the late Dr. Arthur Watts, near Chillicothe, at public auction, under the attendance of a numerous company, as follows:

BULLS.

Nobleman, 1932, sold to John J. Vanmeter, Pike county, Ohio,	$2,510
Master Bellville (11795), sold to Abram Maypool, George Renick, Harness Renick, and Alexander Renick, Ross and Pickaway counties, Ohio,	2,005
Lord Nelson, 664, sold to John L. Myers, Fayette county, Ohio,	1,825
Alderman, 204, sold to Alex. Waddle, Clark county, Ohio,	1,150
Gam-boy (11503), sold to M. L. Sullivant, Columbus, Ohio,	1,400
Count Fashion, 381, sold to N. Perrill, Clinton county, Ohio,	2,075
Young Whittington, 1165, sold to Arthur Watts, Chillicothe, Ohio,	450
Rising Sun, 5130, sold to G. M. Herodh, Scioto county, Ohio,	1,300
Isaac, 589, sold to G. M. Gregg, Pickaway county, Ohio,	600

Cows.

Moss Rose, by Stapleton (2698), sold to Alex. Waddle, Clark Co., O.	$1,200
Strawberry,* by ——, sold to Geo. W. Renick, Ross county, Ohio,	1,000
Raspberry,* by ——, sold to Geo. W. Gregg, Pickaway county, O.	1,110
Sunrise,* by ——, sold to John J. Vanmeter, Pike county, Ohio,...	1,230
Mary, by Lord of the Manor (10466), sold to Alex. Waddle, Clark county, Ohio,	1,650
Enchantress, by Leopold, son of D'Israeli (7967), sold to Harness and Alexander Renick, Pickaway county, Ohio,	900
Blue Bonnet, by Earl of Antrim (10174), sold to Felix W. Renick, Pickaway county, Ohio,	1,225
Average, $1,352 each.	$21,630

The above prices may be considered extraordinarily high for the time; but as the competition was among the stockholders of the importation chiefly, if not altogether, their dividend of profit much reduced, to themselves, the prices which they paid for them.

In 1853, The Northern Kentucky Association commissioned Messrs. Charles T. Garrard, Nelson Dudley, and Solomon Vanmeter, who went to England and selected 9 bulls and 15 cows, from among the best English herds, and brought them to Kentucky in July of that year. They were sold at public auction soon after their arrival. The list consisted of the following:

Bulls.

Young Chilton, 1131 (11278), sold to Dr. Breckinridge and B. and W. Warfield, Fayette county, Ky.,	$3,005
Diamond, 416 (11357), sold to Brutus J. Clay & Co., Bourbon Co.,	6,001
The Count (12191), sold to Strawder Goff, Clark county,	2,575
Orontes 2d, 1966 (11877), sold to R. A. Alexander, Woodford Co.,	4,525
Fusileer, 1584, sold to R. W. Scott, Franklin county,	1,425
Senator 2d, 958 (13687), sold to John and Albert Allen, Fayette Co.	2,000
Bellville 3d, 1246, sold to Sutton and Coleman, Fayette county,...	1,500
Challenger, 324, sold to Isaac Vanmeter, T. L. Cunningham, Solomon Vanmeter, and Wm. R. Duncan, Clark county,	4,850
Fortunatus, 1564, sold to Messrs. Vanmeter, Fayette county,	1,800
Yorkshire Maynard, 2401 (14043), sold to Robt. S. Taylor, Clark Co.	1,000

Cows.

Lady Stanhope, by Earl Stanhope (5966), sold to Brutus J. Clay, Bourbon county, Ky.,	$1,500
Lady Fairy, by Laudable (9262), sold to Dr. Breckenridge and B. and W. Warfield, Fayette county,	1,100
Roan Duchess, by Whittington (12229), sold to William H. Brand and John Allen, Fayette county,	900

---

*These cows not having been recorded, unless they have since occurred as dams in other pedigrees, in A. H. B., we are unable to name their sires, their names not being inserted in the catalogue of their sale.—L. F. A.

Goodness, by Orontes (4623), sold to Albert Allen, Fayette county,	$2,025
Gem, by Broker (9993), sold to T. L. Cunningham, Bourbon Co., and S. Vanmeter, Clark county,	825
Equity, by Lord George (10439), sold to R. A. Alexander, Woodford county,	1,000
Necklace, by Duke of Atholl (10150), sold to H. Clay, Jr., Bourbon county,	805
Bracelet, Twin Sister to Necklace, sold to M. M. Clay, Bourbon county,	750
Mazurka, by Harbinger (10297), sold to R. A. Alexander, Woodford county,	750
Lady Caroline, by Newtonian, 745, sold to B. J. Clay, Bourbon Co.	1,825
Duchess of Sutherland, by Captain Edwards (8929), sold to Wm. H. Brand and John Allen, Fayette county,	800
Maid of Melrose, by Lord Marquis (10459), sold to Sam. Humphreys, Woodford county,	2,000
Muffin, by Usurer (9763), sold to D. H. Coulter and W. A. Smith, Scott county,	535
Orphan Nell, by Ruby (10760), sold to John Hill and John A. Gano, Bourbon county,	1,000
Flattery, by 4th Duke of York (10167), sold to Wm. R. Duncan, Clark county,	815

Near the close of the year 1853 an association in Scott county, Ky., made an importation consisting of 4 bulls and 7 cows. They were sold at auction, as follows:

BULLS.

Pathfinder, 805, sold to W. B. Webb and R. D. Ford, Scott Co., Ky.,	$860
Baron Feversham, by Diamond, 416, sold to —— Estell, Madison county,	1,525
Captain Lawson, 310, sold to A. D. Offutt and W. D. Crockett, Scott county,	400
Cunningham, 1415 (12671), sold to S. J. Salyers, Fayette county,	865

COWS.

Yorkshire Rose, by General Fairfax (11519), sold to P. L. Cable, Scott county,	425
Venus, by Fair Eclipse (11456), sold to J. Hill, Bourbon county,	710
Carnation, by Budget, by Bumper (10005), sold to Charles W. Innes, Fayette county,	610
Enterprise, by Fair Eclipse (11450), sold to Jas. C. Lemon, Scott Co.	710
Rosamond, by Sir Charles Napier (10816), sold to Silas Corbin, Bourbon county,	575
Cameo, by Arrow (9906), sold to W. Boswell, Bourbon county,	450
Casket, by Arrow (9906), sold to W. D. Offutt, Scott county,	405

In the year 1853, an association of breeders was formed in Madison county, Ohio, and an agent sent to England who brought out 15 bulls and 9 cows. The selections were of good quality, and they were sold at London, Ohio, at public auction, 27th September the same year, a few weeks after their arrival. We were present at the sale; the stock were in fine condition; a large audience were in attendance, and the bidding spirited. The following is a report:

BULLS.

Thornberry, 1035 (12222), sold to F. W. and H. Renick, Pickaway county, Ohio,	$875
Sheffielder, 961½, sold to J. W. Robinson, Madison county,	1,800
Mario, 683½, sold to Robert Reed, Madison county, Ohio,	1,550
Marquis, 687 (11787), sold to James Fullington, Union county,	3,000
Starlight, 1003 (12146), sold to Charles Phellis, Madison county,	3,000
Beauclerc (not recorded), sold to D. M. Creighton, Madison Co.,	750
Symmetry, 1019, sold to J. G., W. A. and R. G. Dun, Madison Co.,	1,150
Farmer Boy, 2842, sold to Joseph Reyburn, Madison county,	925
Prince Albert, 3284, sold to J. F. Chenoweth, Madison county,	300
Colonel, 350, sold to J. G., W. A. and R. G. Dun, Madison county,	1,350
Sportsman (not recorded), sold to James Foster, Madison county,	700
Prince Edward, 864, sold to M. B. Wright, Fayette county,	475
Rocket, 921½, sold to David Watson, Union county,	425
Splendor, 997½, sold to F. A. Yocum, Madison county,	500
Duke of Liverpool (not recorded), sold to George G. McDonald, Madison county,	555
Average, $1,157 each.	$17,355

COWS.

Victoria,* sold to J. Q. Winchell, Madison county,	$600
Picotee,* sold to Jesse Watson, Madison county,	1,275
Stapleton Lass,* sold to Jesse Watson, Madison county,	1,350
Princess, by Belted Will (6780), and calf, sold to William Watson, Clark county,	690
Miss Hilton, by Headland, sold to David Watson, Union county,	875
Alexandrina, by Magistrate (10487), sold to D. Watson, Union Co.,	560
Blossom, by Teeswater Lad, a son of Lord Barmpton (11708), sold to David Watson, Union county,	650
Yorkshire Dairy Cow,* sold to Joseph Negley, Clark county,	425
Monsoon,* sold to Joseph Reyburn, Madison county,	295
Average, $747 each.	$6,720

In the year 1853, Dr. A. C. Stevenson, of Green Castle, Indiana, imported from England two bulls: Prince of Wales, 876, and Fancy Boy, 492; and four cows: Strawberry 5th, by Deliverance (11347); Bloom and Violet, by Master Bellville (11795); and Miss Welbourn (Vol. 2, p. 485, A. H. B.), by St. John. These animals and many of their descendants are recorded in the several volumes of the American Herd Book.

---

* The pedigrees of these cows did not come out with them.—L. F. A.

About the year 1853 or '54, the late Thomas Richardson, an Irish merchant in New York city, imported several good Short-horns, with various other stock, among which were the bull Duke of Cambridge, 1469 (12746), and cows Bijou, by Crown Prince (10087); Fanella, by Baron Warlaby (7813); Fanny Warlaby, by Baron Warlaby (7813); Harmony, by Crown Prince (10087); Laura, by Hector (13002); Rachel, by Hopewell (10332), and perhaps some others, which he kept on his farm at Westchester. Several of them were recorded in the American Herd Book. Mr. Richardson was a spirited and liberal breeder. His herd was sold a short time previous to his death, which occurred a few years after making his importation.

In the year 1854, the Society of Shakers, Pleasant Hill, Ky., imported the bull Duke of Cambridge, 447. They had previously, in 1840, in connection with the great statesman, Henry Clay, bought for $1,000, the bull Orozimbo, 786, imported by Mr. Shepherd, of Virginia, in the year 1834. This bull the Shakers bred in their extensive herd. In 1840 they also bought 8 cows, imported by Mr. Gambel, at New Orleans, La. Among them were Daisy, by Barnaby (1678), and Splendor, by Symmetry (2723). The names of the six other cows are not given.

In 1854, Messrs. Wilson and Searight, imported from Ireland into Ohio, the bull Lord Eglinton, 1795; Deceiver, 401 (11340), and possibly another or two bulls, together with some cows, among which were White Rose, by Sir Robert Peel (9658); Laura, by Lord Clarendon (10434); Lady Gage, by Deceiver (11340), and some others.

In the year 1854, the Society of Shakers, at Union Village, Warren county, Ohio, imported, chiefly from the herd of James Douglass, of Scotland, 12 Short-horns—6 bulls (including Duke of Cambridge, 447, before mentioned, belonging to the Shakers at Pleasant Hill) and 6 cows. Their names are as follows:

BULLS.—Duke of Southwick, 450; Crusader, 387; Morning Star, 725; Hearts of Oak, 1646; Economist, 2809.

Cows.—Blanche, by Twin (10981); Violante, by Trumpeter (10978); Margaret, by Fitz Adolphus Fairfax (9124); Farewell, by Prince Charlie, 862; Beatrice; Lady Blanche, by Matadore (11800).

The same Society also imported in 1855:

BULL.—Captain Balco, 1316 (12546).

Cows.—Scottish Belle Center, by Kossuth (11646); Bellview, by Capt. Balco (12546); Florentia, by Trory (13901).

Also in 1856:

BULLS.—King of Trumps, 1739; Hawthorn Hero, 1644½.

Cows.—Hawthorn Blossom, by Hudibras (10339); Flora McIvor, by New Year's Gift (10564); Eva, by Prince Ernest (10644); Preserve, by Orphan Boy (11878); Duchess, by Captain Balco, 1316; Heroine, by Capt. Balco, 1316; April Morn, by Capt. Balco, 1316.

These animals were of excellent quality, and the importations since 1854, as those of that year, were chiefly from the herd of Mr. Douglass. No public sale was made of these cattle—most of them being adopted into the extensive herd of the Shakers, and there bred.

In the year 1854 an association was formed in Clinton county, Ohio. Their agents, Mr. H. H. Hankins and another, proceeded to England to make a selection and bring out the cattle. The stock, consisting of 10 bulls and 18 cows and heifers, safely arrived, and were sold by public auction at Wilmington, Clinton county, on the 9th August, as follows:

BULLS.

NAME.	COST. GUIN.	PURCHASERS.	RESIDENCE.	DOLLS
Warrior, 1076,	120	B. Hinkson, H. H. Hankins and others,	Clinton county, O.	$1200
Whittington 2d, 2385,	80	Solomon Brock,	Fayette county, O.	900
The Marquis, 1031,	40	William Bentley,	Clinton county, O.	625
Wellington, 1087,	180	J. G. Coulter, H. H. Hankins and others,	Clinton county, O.	3700
Alfred, 205,	80	D. S. King,	Clinton county, O.	900
Duke of Cornwall, by Albert (8816)	60	David Quinn,	Clinton county, O.	700
Billy Harrison, 263,	125	Jesse Starbuck,	Clinton county, O.	1500
Moonraker, 3175 (bought with his dam Sunbeam),		Thomas Connor,	Fayette county, O.	400
Lord Raine 2d, 665 (calved on passage),		Daniel Earley,	Clinton county, O.	195
Young Sir Robert, 1161 (calved on passage),		Thomas McMillen,	Clinton county, O.	250

COWS.

NAME.	GUIN.	PURCHASERS.	RESIDENCE.	DOLLS
Duchess, by Norfolk (9442),	155	M. B. Wright and William Palmer,	Fayette county, O.	$1675
Emma, by Promoter (10658),	100	Thomas Kirk,	Fayette county, O.	750
Hope, by Duke of York (6947),	50	William Palmer,	Fayette county, O.	1000
Miss Shaftoe, by Captain Shaftoe (6833),	100	Jesse Starbuck,	Clinton county, O.	650
Familiar, by Fitz Leonard (7010),	60	Jesse Pancake,	Ross county, O.	500
Sunbeam, by Twilight (9758), and calf Moonraker,	80	J.G.Coulter (without calf),	Clinton county, O.	450
Young Emma, by Sailor (9592),	60	H. H. Hankins and G. C. Palmer,	Clinton county, O.	450
Miss Walton 2d, by Chilton (10054),	25	John Hadley,	Clinton county, O.	325
Princess, by Lord Newton (——),	40	Hadley and Hawkins,	Clinton county, O.	1060
Moonbeam, by Oxygen (9464),	40	Henry Kirk,	Fayette county, O.	500
Lady Jane, by Whittington (12299),	50	David Watson,	Madison county, O.	500
Lady Whittington, by Whittington (12299),	50	William Reed,	Clinton county, O.	300
Strawberry, by Wiseman (12317),	50	James Fullington,	Union county, O.	675
Louisa, by Crusader (10088), bought with dam, Miss Shaftoe,		James R. Mills,	Clinton county, O.	300
Jessamine, by Y. Chilton (11278),	25	J. O'B. Renick,	Franklin county, O.	475
Victoria (pedigree not obtained),	35	D. Persinger,	Fayette county, O.	1000
Queen (calf of Victoria), by The Marquis, 1031,		H. S. Pavy,	Fayette county, O.	425

In the same year—1854—an association was formed in Clark county, Ohio, and an importation made under the agency of the late Dr. Arthur Watts, of Chillicothe, and Mr. Alexander Waddle, of South Charleston, who proceeded to England and bought 9 bulls and 20 cows and heifers. A public sale was made of the stock on the 6th day of September of that year, which we transcribe from their catalogue:

BULLS.

Buckingham 2d, 297, sold to Wm. D. Pierce, Clark county, Ohio,	$1,000
The Duke, 1029, sold to W. C. Davis, Montgomery county, O.,	625
New Year's Day, 746, sold to C. M. Clark & Co., Clark county, O.,	3,500
Czar, 395, sold to A. J. Paige, Clark county, O.,	1,900
Medalist, 697, sold to Arthur Watts, Chillicothe, O.,	2,100
Lord Stanwick, 668, sold to Alex. Waddle, Clark county, O.,	500
Rodolph, 923, sold to W. C. Davis, Montgomery county, O.,	200
Lord of the Isles, 3090, sold to Alex. Waddle, Clark county, O.,	575
Shylock, 965, sold to John Hadley, Clinton county, O.,	300

COWS.

Aylesby Lady, by Baron Warlaby (7813), sold to A. J. Paige, Clark county, O.,	1,425
Roman 13th, by Will Honeycomb (5666), sold to Jacob Pierce, Clark county, O.,	1,300
Zealous, by St. Albans (7462), sold to Alex. Waddle, Clark Co., O.,	1,000
Dahlia, by Upstart (7960), sold to A. J. Paige, Clark county, O.,	1,100
Nectar, by North Star (9447), sold to James Davis,	600
Lavender, by St. Albans (7462), sold to Arthur Watts, Chillicothe, O.,	500
Lancaster 17th, by Prince Royal (7371), sold to William D. Pierce, Clark county, O.,	900
Roan Lady, by St. Albans (7462), sold to William D. Pierce, Clark county, O.,	1,000
Lancaster 19th, by St. Albans (7462), sold to L. B. Sprague, Clark county, O.,	
Venus, by Lord Byron (11710), sold to Wm. D. Pierce, Clark Co., O.,	1,075
Zenobia, by Crusade (7938), sold to Alex. Waddle, Clark Co., O.,	625
Nell 2d, by Monarch (——), sold to A. Toland,	
Butterfly 13th, by Monarch (——), sold to H. Stickney,	290
Blushing Beauty, by Crown Prince (10087), sold to Alex. Waddle, Clark county, O.,	425
Rose of Panton, by Leonidas (10414), sold to A. Toland,	375
Zephyr, by Beaufort (9943), sold to L. B. Sprague, Clark Co., O.,	400
Easter Day, by Lord Marquis (10459), sold to C. M. Clark, Clark county, O.,	1,125
Blush 17th, by Baron Warlaby (7813), sold to G. Green, Bloomington, Ill.,	470
Rosy, by Royal Buck (10750), sold to G. Green, Bloomington, Ill.,	400
Silk, by Hopewell, sold to Charles Phellis, Madison county, O.,	205

Much valuable stock has since sprung from these animals.

In 1854 the Kentucky Importing Company imported from England and placed on the farm of Mr. Charles W Innes, near Lexington, and in October of that year sold the following Short-horns:

BULLS.

Emigrant, 472, sold to Silas Corbin, Bourbon county, Ky.,	$ 205
Sirius, 4371 (13737), sold to R. A. Alexander, Woodford county, Ky.,	3,500
Macgregor, 675, sold to J. Hill, Bourbon county, and C. W. Innes, Fayette county, Ky.,	600
Earl De Grey, 2801, sold to W. C. Goodloe,	250
Oakum, 763, sold to Bagg, Finley and Rosele, Scott county, Ky.,	
Capt. Stouffer, 311, sold to J. McMeekin, Scott county, Ky.,	167

COWS.

Irene, by Sheldon (8557), sold to J. Hill, Bourbon county, Ky.,	520
Amazon, by Newmarket (10563), sold to H. Clay, Bourbon Co., Ky.,	225
Bessy Howard, by Fitz Walter (10232), sold to R. A. Alexander, Woodford county, Ky.,	650
Lizzy, by Marquis of Carrabas (11789), sold to R. A. Alexander, Woodford county, Ky.,	600
Pine Apple, by Lord Morpeth (13205), sold to W. F. Jones,	510
Ruby, by Gen. Fairfax (11519), sold to R. A. Gano, Bourbon Co.,	215
Commerce, by Concord (11302), sold to J. McMeekin, Scott Co., Ky.,	415
Peeress, by Treasurer (13899), sold to —— Gaines,	275
Winny, by Crusade (7938), sold to Albert Allen, Fayette Co., Ky.,	300
Mary, by Sweet William (9701), sold to W. Simms,	240
Welcome, by Beaufort (9943), sold to J. McMeekin, Scott Co., Ky.,	505
Shepherdess, by Bridegroom (11203), sold to R. Innes, Fayette Co.,	505
Matilda, by Villiers (13959), sold to S. Corbin, Bourbon Co., Ky.,	205
Downhorn, by Liberator (7140), sold to J. McClelland,	405

In the same year, a number of wealthy farmers and cattle breeders of the Genesee valley, N. Y., known as "The Livingston County Stock Association," through their agents, Messrs. David Brooks and S. L. Fuller, purchased in England 24 well-selected Short-horns. They were shipped for America, but during a stormy passage 12 of them were lost, and only one-half the original number arrived at their destination. Among the surviving animals were the bulls Bletsoe, 2548, purchased by Sackett, Barber & Co., and Usurper, 3522, owned by the late Judge Carroll, of Groveland. Also the cows Australia, by Lord Foppington (10437); Hopeless, by Horatio (10335); Lady Ellington, by Broughton Hero (6811); and Music, by Balco (9918). These four cows became the property of the late General James S. Wadsworth, of Geneseo. Also Phœnix 2d, by Horatio (10335), which was owned by J. H. Bennett, of Avon.

Shortly after this importation came out to the same parties the bull Governor, 2922, owned by Messrs. Brooks, Bennett & Co., and two cows, the names of which are not now recollected. Like some other importers, these parties were negligent in keeping records of the names of their animals, or pedigrees. We have been unable to obtain further particulars of these importations. Many of their produce are recorded in the American Herd Book.

In the year 1856, an importation of Short-horns was made by the "Mason and Bracken Counties Importing Company" into Kentucky, of 4 bulls and 12 cows. They were kept and bred by the importers, and sold near Germantown, Ky., on the 1st October, 1859; the herd then consisted of the original importations and their increase, 12 bulls and 17 cows and heifers. The imported ones were:

BULLS.—Vatican (12260) (bred by Earl Ducie), by Usurer (9763); Blandimar (bred by Sir Charles Knightly), by Earl of Dublin (16178); Emperor Napoleon (bred by Mr. Fawkes), by Bridegroom (11203); and Grisset (bred by Mr. Christy), by Duke of Beauford (11377).

COWS.—Julia, by Young Grant; Duenna, by Duke of Cambridge (12742); Light of the Harem, by Nabob (11834); Granny Light, by Bridegroom (11203); Alice, by Harbinger (10297); Diana, by Brennus (8902); Lady Laura, by Grand Duke (12973); High Bank, by Horatio (10335); Hasty, by Horatio (10335); Violet, by Duke of Beauford (11377); Jennie Deans, by Duke of Beauford (11377); Lady Bariscourt, by Jasper (11069).

Several of these animals were selected from choice herds in England and Ireland, and they were, no doubt, valuable cattle. The catalogue from which the above list is taken gives no names of the purchasers, nor prices at which the cattle or their produce were sold. We have made inquiries at the proper quarter for particulars, but have not been able to obtain them. Few of their descendants have found their way into the Herd Books, and we infer that the calamitous financial times during which the sale was made, swallowed many of them in the common ruin, or run them into the shambles of the butcher.

In the year 1857, a number of substantial farmers and stock breeders in the central part of Illinois came together and formed "The Illinois Importing Association." The late Capt. James N. Brown, who, in 1833, had removed from Kentucky into Sangamon county, Ill., brought with him the first established herd of Short-horns known in the State of his adoption. He had bred them assiduously and successfully but recognizing the advantage of an infusion of more popular blood, he induced several others to join him in the enterprise of obtaining it. Himself, together with Messrs. H. C. Johns and Henry Jacoby went abroad as agents, and purchased 10 bulls and 21 cows and heifers, well selected from standard herds in England, Ireland and Scotland. Of these, three bulls and one heifer died on their passage. The remainder, twenty-seven in number, safely arrived in Illinois. They were sold by auction at Springfield, August 27, 1857, as follows:

BULLS.

Defender, 2704 (12687), sold to A. G. Carle, Champaign Co., Ill.,	$2,500
King Alfred, 3053, sold to Brown, Jacoby & Co., Sangamon Co.,	1,300
Admiral, 2473, sold to S. Dunlap & Co., Sangamon county,	2,500
Master Lownds, 3140½, sold to J. H. Spears, Menard county,	725
Argus, 2502, sold to George Barnet, Will county,	2,058
Doubloon, 3833½, sold to Wash. Iles, Sangamon county,	1,075
Goldfinder, 2920½, sold to J. C. Bone, Sangamon county,	725

COWS.

Bella, by California (10017), sold to J. Ogle, St. Clair county,	$750
Caroline, by Arrow (9906), sold to J. M. Hill, Morgan county,	500
Stella, by Snowstorm (12119), sold to Mr. Bohnman, St. Clair Co.,	925
Lady Harriet, by Procurator (10657), sold to J. H. Jacoby, Sangamon county,	1,300
Cassandra 2d, by Master Charlie (13312), sold to H. Ormsby, Sangamon county,	675
Western Lady, by Grand Turk, 2935 (12969), sold to J. N. Brown, Sangamon county,	1,325
Empress Eugenie, by Bridegroom (11203), sold to J. Ogle, St. Clair county,	675
Pomegranate, by Master Charlie (13312), sold to T. Simpkins, Pike county,	975
Lily, by Snowstorm (12119), sold to George Barnet, Will Co.,	550
Constance, by Snowstorm (12119), sold to George Barnett, Will Co.,	700
Empress, by Tortworth Duke (13892), sold to Henry Jacoby, Sangamon county,	1,725
Rachel 2d, by Duke of Bolton (12738), sold to J. N. Brown, Sangamon county,	3,025
Minx, by Lord Spencer (13251), sold to J. G. Loose, Sangamon Co.,	800
Adelaide, by Matadore (11800), sold to R. Morrison, Morgan Co.,	825
Emerald, by Hopewell (10332), sold to J. C. Bone, Sangamon Co.,	2,125
Perfection, by The Baron (13833), sold to E. B. Holt, Scott Co.,	900
Coquette, by Economist (11425), sold to George Barnet, Will Co.,	550
Fama, by 2d Grand Duke, 2181 (12961), sold to J. H. Spears & Co., Menard county,	1,050
Coronation, by Cheltenham (12588), sold to J. A. Pickrell, Madison county,	500
Violet, by Young Scotland (13681), sold to J. H. Judy, Menard Co.,	700

From these animals, in most instances, have since been bred a numerous progeny.

The result of this sale, confined (as may be supposed from the extent of the prices obtained) chiefly to those who had contributed to the funds of the association, testified that the Short-horn spirit was yet buoyant, and in the course of successful continuance.

Just after the close of this transaction came down upon the country the great commercial revulsion of 1857, long memorable in the financial annals of our history. This crisis was severe upon the agricultural interests, as well as the commercial and manufacturing industries of the country, and the values of Short-horn cattle, in common with other commodities, suffered. For a time their sales were dull, and prices, as in 1842, and years afterwards, with some few and noted exceptions, became almost nominal.

In 1861 followed our unfortunate civil war, revolutionizing not only the political and financial policy of many States in our hitherto united country, but temporarily depressing values of all industrial products. As the war grew wilder and more desperate, although all commodities of necessary consumption rose rapidly under an inflated currency, and the restricted labor of the farms consequent on the call of soldiers to the field, an interregnum in the product and sales of Short-horns was widely and disastrously felt among their breeders. In the Northern States they were undisturbed by invading armies; but prudent and considerate men, usually ready for successful enterprises, as purchasers, with the exception of a few spirited breeders of the more fashionable strains of blood, let the Short-horns, as well as other improved breeding animals, severely alone. The Kentuckians, in whose hitherto favored State the Short-horns, early established, had long flourished in their fullness of pride and excellence, as it became ravaged by conflicting troops on either side, hid their cattle away from their spoilers, or drove them into adjoining Northern States, where they could remain secure from danger. All was uncertainty, so far as related to the values of their cherished herds; and thus for four years of civil war, matters remained in doubtful anticipation.

Yet the consumption and disorganization of the war had created a fearful void in meat-producing animals throughout the country, North and South alike, and on the return of peace and a more settled order of things, the Short-horn breeders deliberately cast about and ascertained that their hitherto cherished herds had suffered but little diminution of numbers beyond what their productive increase had made good, and that previous values had now returned with a new demand and widely extended market for their animals. So stood the Short-horn animals of our country at the close of the year 1865.

After the civil war was ended a few importations were again made by some of our enterprising breeders. Mr. James O. Sheldon, of Geneva, N. Y., previously mentioned, in the year 1859, imported the bull Grand Duke of Oxford, 3988 (16184), and the cow Miss Butterfly, by Master Butterfly (14918), both of which he bred in his herd. He had previously become possessed of several animals from the fine herd of Mr. Thorne, and to them had added extensive purchases from the herd of Mr. Alexander, of Kentucky, and soon afterwards of the entire herd of Mr. Thorne. In the year 1868 or '69, he imported eight heifers, selected from some of the best herds in England. The pedigrees are recorded in the later volumes of the American Herd Book, and several of them afterwards passed, at the final sale of his herd, into the hands of Messrs. Walcott and Campbell, New York Mills, Oneida county, N. Y.

Messrs. Walcott and Campbell, who had a few years previous become possessed of many good animals, and in 1870 purchased the large herd of Mr. Sheldon, some 70 or 80 in number, about the same time, or previously, made several valuable importations—bulls and cows—from Mr. Thomas C. Booth, and other noted English breeders. They were purchased without regard to prices, so that their qualities were of a high order. One of the cows, Bride of the Vale, was bred by and purchased of Mr. T. C. Booth, at the price of 1,000 guineas, but on the express condition that she was to be taken to America, as Mr. Booth would not part with a *female* of her tribe to be retained in England. Their importations of several choice selections were continued until into the year 1871, and are recorded in Vols. 10 and 11, American Herd Book.

In 1871, Mr. Lewis Hampton, and some associates, of Clark county, Ky., went to England and selected several valuable cows and heifers from different breeders there, and brought them out as fresh crosses to their already valuable herds. They were sold at auction a few weeks after their arrival in Kentucky, mostly among the associates, and their pedigrees are recorded in Vol. 11, American Herd Book.

In the same year Mr. Edwin G. Bedford, of Bourbon county, Ky., also sent out and purchased (through Mr. John Thornton, of London) several valuable cows and heifers on his own individual account, which he adopted into his long established home-bred herd. Their pedigrees may be found in Vol. 11, American Herd Book.

During the same year, Capt. Pratt, of the ship Hudson, trading between New York and London, brought out in June four fine heifers. In November, afterwards, he again brought out two bulls and six heifers, from the herd of Mr. Torr, and Messrs. Dudding, of Lincolnshire, all superior animals, which were placed on the farm of Mr. L. F. Allen, near Buffalo, N. Y., and all—together with two bull calves, dropped since their arrival from England—afterwards sold, by Messrs. A. B. Allen & Co., to Mr. J. H. Pickrell, Harristown, Ill. Their pedigrees are recorded in Vol. 11, American Herd Book.

There may have been a few other Short-horns imported into the United States in the year 1871, but if so we have no immediate account of them.

IMPORTATIONS OF SHORT-HORNS INTO CANADA.

We would gladly narrate a full and particular history of the Canada Short-horns, their introduction and progress, as has been done with those of the United States, had we the material at hand. But with all our efforts to obtain them our notes are scant. We give such memoranda as we have.

In the year 1833, Mr. Rowland Wingfield, living in the vicinity of Toronto, Canada West (now Ontario), imported from England the bulls Reformer, 898, and Young Farmer, 62, also cows Favorite, by Warden (1563); Favorite 2d, by Henwood (2114); Pedigree, by Mynheer (2345); Countess, by Warwick (2815); and Lily, by Warden (1563). Their produce are now in several herds.

The succeeding year The Home District Agricultural Society imported four thorough-bred bulls—names not ascertained—and spread them in various directions. They were chiefly bred to common cows, as we find no pure Short-horn produce resulting from them.

About the year, 1836, the late Mr. Adam Ferguson imported into the vicinity of Hamilton, C. W., the bull Agricola (1614)—afterwards called Sir Walter by Mr. Ferguson—and cows Cherry, by Dunstan Castle; and Beauty, by Snowball (2674). They were successfully bred by Mr. Ferguson, and their produce are now found in many herds.

In or about the same year of Mr. Ferguson's importation, Messrs. George and John Simpson imported from Yorkshire, England, and brought with them to New Market, C. W., from the herd of Mr. Parrington, Stockton-on-Tees, several good Short-horns, which they bred for some years. The results of their breeding we have not been able to accurately ascertain.

During several years afterwards various other importations were made, both into Lower and Upper Canada, of which we have been unable to gather either dates of the importations, or names of animals brought out. Among these William and George Miller, of Markham, about the year 1850, and in several years since, imported a number of valuable animals—chiefly from Scotland—but as we have had no catalogue, nor full records of their pedigrees, no particular accounts can be given of them.

In the year 1855, Mr. Frederick Wm. Stone, of Guelph, began a series of importations from several noted English herds, which he has continued through intervening years down to nearly the present time.

In 1859 or '60, Mr. N. J. McGillivray, of Williamstown, Glengarry county, C. W., imported a bull and four cows from the herds of Mr. Cruikshank, of Sittyton, and others, in Scotland.

Mr. David Christie, of Brantford, commenced his importations in the year 1864, of several fine Short-horns, chiefly from the herd of Mr. Douglass, of Athelstaneford, Scotland, which he placed with a thorough-bred herd established by him some years earlier. He has since added to his importations, all, or nearly all of which have been recorded in the later volumes of the American Herd Book.

Other parties, comprising the names of Mr. Armstrong, of Markham; Mr. Mairs, of Vespra; Messrs. Wade, of Cobourg; Mr. Mullock, of Waterdown; Mr. Ashton, of Galt; Mr. Ashworth, of Ottawa; Mr. Place, of Beachville; Mr. Petty, of Huron; Dr. Phillips, of Prescott; Mr. John Thomson, of Whitney; Mr. Roddick, of Cobourg, The Quebec Agricultural Society, and probably some others in different localities have made importations. Added to the above names occur John Miller, of Brougham; William Miller, Jr., of Pickering; Simon Beattie, of Markham, and Richard Gibson, who have made valuable importations within a few years past.

But the most striking series of importations, either in number or value, ever made into Canada, were by Mr. Mark H. Cochrane, an extensive manufacturer and merchant, of Montreal, and placed on his large farm of Hillhurst, at Compton, Province of Quebec, beginning in 1867, and continued until and into the early part of the present year, 1872.

In 1867 he shipped from Glasgow, Scotland, his first importation of two animals: the cow Rosedale, by Velasco (15443), and the bull Baron Booth of Lancaster, 7535, American Herd Book.

In August, 1868, he shipped from Liverpool, Eng., seven cows and heifers, and one bull, Robert Napier, 8975, A. H. B.

In June, 1869, he shipped from Glasgow four cows and heifers.

In August following he shipped from Glasgow five cows and heifers, and two bulls.

On August 2d, 1870, he shipped from Liverpool thirty-five cows and heifers, and four bulls; on August 7th, following, he shipped also from Liverpool five cows and two bulls.

In the months of August and October, 1870, he also shipped from Liverpool seven cows and heifers, and three bulls.

In July, 1871, he shipped from Liverpool twenty cows and heifers, and four bulls.

In March, 1872, he also had shipped from Liverpool three cows and heifers, making in all the shipments of the last six years eighty-seven well-bred Short-horns.

Of the whole number a few died, or were killed by accident on their passages; the remainder all arrived safely onto Mr. Cochrane's farm at Compton. The animals were selected by Mr. Cochrane himself, for which he made several voyages across the Atlantic, or with the assistance of Mr. Simon Beattie, of Canada, and Mr. John Thornton, the noted stock auctioneer, of London. No importation of Short-horns ever made by an American have equaled in cost, the stock brought out by Mr. Cochrane. Among them were two Bates Duchess heifers, at the price cost of 2,500 guineas, or upwards of $6,250 each. A considerable number of them were either pure Booth, or containing several crosses of the blood of the Booth tribes; several others were deep in various tribes of Bates blood. The pedigrees of all, or nearly all these animals, and their produce since their importation have been recorded in the later volumes of the American Herd Book, where they can be readily found. Many of them were sold soon after their arrival, and brought into the United States; others have been sold, and still remain in Canada, in the hands of different owners, while a still larger number remain in the home herd of Mr. Cochrane.

Thus concludes our history of the Short-horns, both in England, until a modern period, and in America down to the present time; but as some other important matters connected with them are worthy of notice, we shall occupy a few further pages in their consideration.

The Short-horns as Milkers.

Our history has fully shown that from the earliest period the Short-horn cows, as a rule, were large milkers, and when cultivated with a view to dairy purposes no animals of any breed excelled, and few if any equaled them. When milk has been the main object in their keeping, no cows have made larger yields according to the consumption of food than they.

Even in our own time we have frequent records of cows, in the height of the grass season, giving 24 to 36, and even 40 quarts per day. Numerous notes of the kind may be found attached to the pedigrees of cows in the several volumes of the American Herd Book, and the yields of butter have been correspondingly large. It is not necessary to quote these items, as every one acquainted with the race will call to mind more or less of them. It is true, as a rule, that the cow which is a profuse milker must be comparatively lean in flesh, which detracts from her appearance when by the side of one otherwise equally good, or perhaps inferior in quality, which gives little milk, and runs more to flesh. Yet the large milker, when dried off and fed, may present as fine a form and development as another which never gave more milk than would nurse a calf for five or six months after birth, even in cases where the feeding is equal in quality. It may be added that the heavy milker requires more feed during her dairy season than the other, while the latter carries a heavy carcass of flesh; but the additional food is more than compensated in the milk or butter she yields.

In the wide beef-producing districts of our country where milk is of little object beyond that of nursing a calf to the proper age of weaning, the milking faculty of the Short-horn cow has been partially bred out, but it is capable of being restored in a few generations by the application of bulls descended from herds where the dairy quality has been preserved. Indeed we have seen wonderful milkers occasionally strike out in herds where the cows were only nominal in their yields, abundantly testifying that the dairy quality is inherent in their organization. As thorough-bred cows, from their much higher value for breeding purposes than for dairy use, are likely for many years to be devoted solely to breeding, it is not at all probable, unless for the production of bulls to beget grade dairy cows, that they will be reared with much regard to their lacteal qualities, unless in certain sections of the country where milk, as a matter of necessity, is the chief object. In this view, we have no suggestions to make other than that each party choosing the Short-horns for his stock, should exercise his own judgment in their selection, whether they be greater or lesser milk producers. It is sufficient to say that the Short-horns may be the maximum or the minimum of milkers, as the parties needing them may determine.

As a Flesh-producing Animal.

Nothing of the bovine race ever has, or probably ever can, equal the Short-horns in early maturity, rapid accumulation of flesh, fullness and ripeness of points, according to the amount of food they consume, and assimilating that food to its most profitable use. A century of experience in Britain and half a century of experience in America, with a rapidly growing confidence in their flesh-taking capacity have placed the Short-horns in the foremost rank of all neat cattle. It must be a newly-discovered animal that will supercede the Short-horn wherever abundant forage and rich pasturage are found. With cows of the common, or of inferior breeds, on becoming aged, and their profitable use for the dairy passed, they are, comparatively, almost useless for feeding into a profitable carcass of flesh from the disproportionate amount of forage they consume and the light yields of meat they make. It is not so with the Short-horn. Her broad, well-proportioned anatomy, with sufficient food, takes flesh rapidly, and within a period that would enable the inferior one to reach only a preparatory, or thriving condition, the Short-horn will be fed off and fit for the shambles. Thus, when the native or common cow is done with for the dairy, and becomes comparatively worthless, the other yields a profitable carcass of beef, hide and tallow, as if in her prime of age and usefulness.

Vitality, Longevity, and Fertility.

No cattle, of whatever race or breed, have exhibited more of the above named qualities than the Short-horns. We might mention scores of bulls by name which have proved useful to extreme ages, both in England and America.

Among the English bulls, one of the earliest and most celebrated of the Herd Book animals, Hubback (319), begat calves after he was ten years old. Favorite (252) begat calves at thirteen years. He was ten years old when he sired the celebrated Comet (155). Marske (418) was useful thirteen years, and died at the age of fifteen. And so with many other English bulls, who were the sires of as good stock in their later as in their earlier years. Among the American bulls Washington (1566), bred by Mr. Champion, in England, imported and owned by Gen. Van Rensselaer, at Albany, N. Y., died at nineteen years old, and held his virility to within a year of his death. Oliver (2387), bred by Col. Powel, of Philadelphia, Pa., and owned in Kentucky, got calves at seventeen years old. Old Splendor, 767, A. H. B., bred by Mr. Weddle, in Western New York, got calves after sixteen, and died when seventeen years old. Renick, 903, A. H. B., bred by James Renick, in Kentucky, got calves at fourteen years old, and died soon after, while yet apparently vigorous. Baron of Oxford, 2525, A. H. B., bred by Mr. Thorne, of Thorndale, N. Y., died at fifteen years from the effects of an accident by a fall on slippery ice when in the act of serving a cow—useful to the last.

Among the aged cows may be named "Duchess, by Daisy bull," bred by Charles Colling, in England, who, after many years of successful breeding, made an excellent carcass of beef at seventeen years. Many other cows of English breeding attained the age of fifteen to upwards of twenty years. Among the American cows, one belonging to Mr. John G. Dun, of London, Ohio, the name not recollected, had a calf, at seventeen years. Imported Young Mary, by Jupiter (2170), owned in Kentucky, bred fourteen heifer calves— and one bull—and died at twenty-one years. This is the most remarkable instance of heifer breeding within our knowledge, and more Herd Book pedigrees run into Young Mary than any other half dozen cows of record. Mr. Dun's cow Florida, by Comet, 356 (1854), brought her last calf at eighteen years, and nursed and reared it. The Kentucky cow, Catherine Turley, by Goldfinder (2066), lived until eighteen years old; she was then fed off for the butcher, and when slaughtered was found to be in calf. A well-bred cow of the Union Village Shakers, Warren county, Ohio, brought a living heifer calf after she was twenty-one years old. But it is useless to multiply instances of great longevity. We have related these from many others which might be named, had we opportunity to look them up and record them.

All the Short-horns need is a sufficiency of proper food—not forcing—and sensible treatment in the way of shelter and care to prove them the equals, if not superiors, in fertility and longevity, of any others of the bovine race.

THE COLORS OF SHORT-HORN NOSES.

In the earlier history of them we find that cloudy, smoky, or even black noses in the Short-horns were frequent, and some of the more distinguished breeders had more or less of them among their best animals. But so far as we can discover they were never *fashionable;* on the other hand they were objectionable, as a matter of taste, at least. Yet withal, dark noses were inherent in the race, cropping out, now and then, in almost every herd, even to the present day, and only by the most careful weeding out of the dark-nosed young breeding animals as they occurred, have the orange or drab noses become the rule, and dark the exception.

Some critical people have asserted that a dark nose is indicative of impure blood; that it came in with the Colling cross of the Galloway cow; others that stealthy crosses of the West Highland, or other outside cattle introduced it, but no *proof* exists of either, and the question may as well at once be yielded that the dark nose is inherent in the Short-horn race. We do not advocate a dark nose, either in full, or cloudy, or in streaks, or spots, yet we have seen many Short-horns with unimpeachable pedigrees, and descended from herds long distinguished for their superior quality, which had either dark or cloudy noses. Nor have we ever known that the color of the nose at all governed the otherwise essential good qualities of the animal; yet so long as a good bull or cow can be found with an orange, drab, or brownish nut-colored nose, of equally good quality otherwise, we would not breed from a dark-nosed one—more from the unpopularity of the color than any other exceptional bad quality the creature might possess.

To make our position good in the way of an occasional dark nose cropping out: We once had a choice Short-horn cow, with a perfect orange nose, which we bred to a pure *Devon* bull, with an equally good nose as the heifer, and the produce was a red roan calf with a jet black nose, which a well-bred Devon never has. The black nose of the calf in question came from the Short-horn blood, not the Devon. A pure Short-horn nose of any shade between a *nut*-brown, or deep *drab*, running up to a yellow, may be classed as unexceptionable in that particular. It is so in England. A light *flesh*-colored nose is equally objectionable as a dark one, being usually accompanied with a lighter colored skin, and sometimes a delicacy in physical form or constitution, (although not always so,) beyond those animals with noses of a deeper color, either orange, drab, nut-colored, or cloudy.

For *grade* breeding, that is, for beef or dairy purposes, (and for the most *progressive* purposes of working up toward the pure blood,) a grade bull should never be used, when a thorough-bred one can be obtained; provided the bull be otherwise good, if he have a dark nose it need not be objected to. No matter what the color of the nose, the cow will milk as well, and the steer feed as profitably as if that feature in them were the height of perfection.

Bodily Colors of Short-horns.

The legitimate colors of the race, from their earliest history, have been red, in its different shades, and pure white, either one prevailing to greater or less extent over the entire body, or spreading in various proportions of each in distinct patches, or the promiscuous intermingling of both into either a light or red roan, as accident might govern, giving the animal a picturesque and agreeable appearance to the eye of the spectator. The lighter shades of red are termed "yellow-red," which, among the earlier animals, occasionally run into a pale dun, or drab, mingling with white, as with the deeper reds; but within the last fifty years the dun or drab hues have mostly disappeared and become unfashionable, the full reds of lighter or deeper shades having the preference. Still, the light dun or drab may occasionally crop out in a calf of perfect pedigree without prejudice to its blood or lineage.

Fifty years ago a preponderance of white, and less of red, was the usual color, and in many distinguished animals pure white was equally acceptable as red, red and white, or roan, with the best breeders. In fact, we cannot discover that so late as twenty years ago objection was made to a good animal solely on account of color, either red, in any of its different shades, or their intermixtures with white, or the pure white itself. It has been so in England from the earliest days down to the present time. Any *shade*, in fact, from the deepest to the lightest in the reds, to pure white, and their mixtures, are *legitimate* Short-horn colors, and any choice in preference to more or less of these prevailing in the animal, is simply a matter of taste with the breeder or owner.

There has, of late years, however, grown up in the United States a *fashion* in colors, red being the choice, and *deep* red the prevailing choice. This fashion, we believe, has been mainly induced by the increasing popularity of the "Bates" blood, they having more of it than almost any other distinct family tribe; for we do not recognize it as predominating in any other tribes belonging to the different English, Scotch, or Irish breeders. Thirty years ago we seldom saw a purely red Short-horn, and not many where the red much overrun the white. Red and white, and the roans, were the most common, and pure white was more popular than a full red. In fact, the roans were the most fashionable, and more preferred than any other where a preference for color prevailed at all. Some of the best bulls and cows ever imported into the country were pure white, so late as twenty years ago, while now either at public or private sale a white, or even a light roan bull, unless of distinguished blood, will sell for a much less price than a full red or red roan of equal quality, even when discriminating breeders in the more substantial qualities are the purchasers.

In this partiality or prejudice—for we cannot call it any other—in the United States, we cannot but think it an absurd distinction so far as the true merits of the animal are concerned. A purely red cow may be bred to a purely red bull, and a white or roan calf may be the produce, as is sometimes seen; or, a bull and cow of any other legitimate shades, white, roan, or of distinctly patched colors may be coupled, and grades of color common to neither parent may be produced in the calf. In fact, color in Short-horns is not controllable, or but partially so, except as through a persistent course of breeding to certain colored bulls, on the rule that "like begets like," will the produce inherit the shades belonging to the parents, and then not uniformly. Therefore we say, other qualities being equal, one color is just as good as another, no better, no worse. Still, fashion may rule for a time among breeders, as the color of a person's dress may rule in the fashionable world of people, to be discarded at the next freak of fancy or taste, as those who invent them may dictate.

Let us illustrate: The Collings always bred many more *pure* whites than *pure* reds, (seldom did they breed one of the latter,) while roans of different shades were their prevailing colors. So also with other of the leading breeders of England from time immemorial. The Booths bred without regard to a choice of color; so that their cattle were good, color was a minor object. They seldom had a red animal, but chiefly roans and whites. In Mr. Bates' early *Duchess* stock the red color prevailed, and it has through their close interbreeding, although since crossed by roan bulls, still held its own in their descendants. The importations into the United States from the earliest date to 1857, were chiefly roans, red and whites, and whites, the reds being little cared for, but rather objected to, until the Bates Duchess blood became in demand. Previous to the Bates arrivals reds were decidedly *un*fashionable, some breeders carrying their prejudices against a full red so far as to declare such colors indicative of impure blood and bad breeding!

We incline to the opinion that not many years will transpire before good judges of Short-horns will look more closely to quality than color, convinced as we are that a fashion existing solely on prejudice or partiality, cannot be permanent.

CHAPTER XI.

EXPORTATION OF AMERICAN SHORT-HORNS TO ENGLAND AND SCOTLAND.

AFTER the long series of purchases by American breeders from the British herds which have been enumerated, it is an interesting item to record the progress of the back tidal wave of purchases from our own American herds by English breeders, which have been taken to the land of their origin to re-unite their possibly superior qualities with the long-cherished blood of their ancestors, an event which has been regarded among the British breeders as of novel and especial interest.

Fifty years ago, or more, a pungent writer of critiques in one of the British Reviews opened his article upon an American author with the sneering question: "Who reads an American book?" But at the present day American books have become a welcome commodity in the British market, and receive an admiration and respect equal to those of its own most favored authors.

Forty years afterwards, although the Americans had long been purchasers of English Short-horns, the question might have been as contemptuously asked by the English breeders: "Who buys an American Short-horn?" For many years our American breeders had visited Great Britain, and carefully selected and purchased many choice animals from the most costly and fashionable herds, which they transferred onto their own American farms, and bred with a care and skill equal to any which had been bestowed upon them in the land of their nativity. It was afterwards discovered that much of the best blood of their cherished herds had crossed the Atlantic, and not to be regained except by going to America to re-purchase and import it back at much higher prices than those for which they had originally sold them. But the blood they must have, whatever might be the cost, and they wisely set about regaining it.

In a letter to us of June 12, 1871, Mr. Samuel Thorne, of New York, thus writes: "During a visit to England in the spring of 1861, I was eagerly sought after for 'Duke' and 'Oxford' bulls, and in

May of that year I sent over the bull 'Our American Cousin,' by imported Neptune, 1917, out of imported Lalla Rookh, sold to me by F. W. Welch, of Ireland. A short time after I sent over the bulls 3d Duke of Thorndale, 2789 (roan), 4th Duke of Thorndale, 2790 (roan), 5th Duke of Thorndale, 3488 (white), Imperial Oxford, 4905 (red); also the heifer 4th Lady of Oxford, which afterwards became celebrated as one of the most distinguished cows in England, both as a show animal and breeder. The bull 5th Duke of Thorndale, sickened on the voyage, and died in Queenstown harbor, Ireland, before reaching England. On their arrival in England they were sold at prices varying from 300 to 400 guineas each, in gold coin. In the following year, 1862, I sent out to England Lord Oxford, 3091 (roan), 2d Lord Oxford [not recorded in A. H. B.], Bishop of Oxford [not recorded in A. H. B.], and Duke of Geneva, 3858 (roan). The latter shipment arrived in England safely, and sold for 250 to 600 guineas each, in gold, amounting to a considerable larger sum in our own currency."

Soon afterwards Mr. Ezra Cornell, of Ithaca, N. Y., sold to go to England, the young bull 3d Lord of Oxford, 4958, bred by Mr. Thorne, of whom Mr. Cornell had sometime previously purchased him. He sold for $3,000 in gold, which, with the premium added swelled the sum to a much larger amount in our currency.

About the same time Mr. R. A. Alexander, of Kentucky, sent out to England a few animals of choice blood of the Airdrie (Bates' Duchess) tribe, and possibly another animal or two, the names of which we have not been able to learn, nor the result of their sales.

In August, 1867, Mr. John R. Page took out for Mr. J. O. Sheldon, of Geneva, N. Y., eight young animals, consisting of the roan bull 3d Duke of Geneva, 5563, which sold for 550 guineas, and the heifers 7th Duchess of Geneva (white), sold at 700 guineas, together with 4th Maid of Oxford (red), Countess of Oxford (white), 6th Maid of Oxford (roan), 7th Maid of Oxford (roan), 8th Maid of Oxford (roan), and 5th Maid of Oxford (white). For the six Oxfords he obtained 2,050 guineas, an average of $2,293 each. The entire sale amounted to 3,300 guineas=$17,325, or an average for the lot of $2,615.50 each, which, together with the premium on the gold received for them, not less than 20 to 25 per cent. above American currency at the time, made the handsome sum of nearly or quite $20,000 for eight animals, less the expense of exportation.

In the year 1870, Mr. Sheldon also sold, to be delivered *on shipboard* in the city of New York, the red roan bull calf 8th Duke of

Geneva, 7935, to Messrs. Howard and Downing, in England, for 800 guineas, and to Mr. Cheney, also in England, the (red) heifers 11th Duchess of Geneva, and (red roan) 13th Duchess of Geneva, at 1,000 guineas each, in gold coin. They were taken on board ship and arrived safely at their destination.

In April, 1871, Mr. M. H. Cochrane, Compton, Province Quebec, sold to Earl of Dunmore, in Scotland, the cow 11th Lady of Oxford, by 14th Duke of Thorndale, 8031, for 750 guineas; and to Colonel Kingscote, of England, the red bull Duke of Hillhurst, 9862, at eleven months old, for 800 guineas. Both these animals were delivered at Portland, Me., the freight and charges to be paid by the purchasers.

In November following, Mr. Cochrane also sold to Earl of Dunmore the following heifers: Duchess of Hillhurst (white), and 2d Duchess of Hillhurst (roan), at about a year old, each (both got by 8th Duke of York, 11867, out of imported Duchesses 103d and 101st), for 2,500 guineas; also the cow 8th Maid of Oxford and her heifer calf, for 1,300 guineas; also two cows and their two heifer calves, purchased by Mr. Cochrane, in Kentucky, for which he received 500 guineas. This lot, like the previous one, was delivered at Portland, subject to the exportation charges. The whole ten animals of these two exportations netted Mr. Cochrane the sum of 5,850 guineas, or about $30,712 American currency.

Late in the autumn of 1871, Messrs. Walcott and Campbell, of New York Mills, Oneida county, N. Y., sold to Lord Skelmerdale, England, the young red bull, 1st Duke of Oneida, 9925, for 850 guineas, at eighteen months old; and with him also went out the red bull 5th Lord Oxford, 10382, fifteen months old, to another party there; also to Mr. Cheney the roan heifer 9th Maid of Oxford (two years old), by 10th Duke of Thorndale, 5610; red cow 10th Lady of Oxford (four years old), by 10th Duke of Thorndale, 5610; and roan heifer 13th Lady of Oxford (nine months old), by Baron of Oxford, 2525, all at about the average prices of Mr. Sheldon's sale.

The above are the last sales to go abroad of which we have a detailed account up to the year 1872; and most gratifying they must prove, in the acknowledgment by some of the most enterprising breeders of Great Britain to the excellence and value of *American*-bred Short-horns.

The Style, Figure and Quality, which should Represent a Perfect Short-horn.

To demonstrate this we should, perhaps, have a portrait, model, or diagram of the animal we purpose to describe; but such an one is difficult to obtain, and could we obtain it, objection might be made that it represented a *particular* animal, of certain blood or breeding, whose conspicuity in a work of this character might show partiality in us, the imputation of which we wish to avoid. We shall, therefore, speak of what *should be*, rather than what *is* in any animal with which we are familiar. We have occasionally seen a Short-horn which we considered almost, if not quite, perfect. We have recited the histories of some which seemed *almost* perfect in the eyes of judges of them in the days of the earlier breeders—the Maynards, Wetherels, Collings, Booths, Mason, and their contemporaries, as well as to others now living. But they were not altogether so, as some deficient points in them have been detected. Nor do we think their *standard* of perfection was then so high as it is at the present time. We believe the standard of excellence has improved within the last seventy years, and that the average quality of well-bred Short-horns is higher now than in the years 1800 to 1830, although many animals of surpassing excellence, and known by name, existed in those days, as we have seen by portraits and descriptions of them.

The *mass* of the old Short-horns, as we have seen, were faulty—coarse, many of them, sleazily made up, too prominent in bone, hard in the handling, lacking flesh in the most valuable parts of the carcass, and having too much offal for their net weight. Their shoulders stood too far forward, were too upright and open at the tops; their fore ribs were too flat, with too little flesh on their crops, those points being hollow, or concave, leaving neither roasts nor steaks upon them. That was, perhaps, their greatest fault, and the most difficult to overcome. There were other deficiencies which have been already enumerated and need not be repeated. Yet the *cows* were generally great milkers, and great milkers even at the present day are more apt to fail in those points than in almost any others. The reader will understand that we now speak of the Short-horns of some centuries ago, before their breeders had discovered the capabilities of the race in the extent of improvement to which they have since attained.

But good breeding has corrected most of these, and we now see large numbers of Short-horns existing in the peerless symmetry which in early days were not common to their race.

To the point, then: WHAT is a perfect Short-horn?

We propose to dissect and analyze the creature from the point of its nose to the brush of its tail. In this we are aware that we may run against both tastes and prejudices, as well as fashions; but tastes, prejudices and fashions, are all more or less arbitrary, the results of education, and sometimes absurd when running against *practical excellence*, or true merit, in almost any subject. We propose to speak of *merit* mainly, and permit the reader to interpose his own ideas of taste or fashion, as they may occur.

The muzzle: This should be fine, with a wide, open nostril; a large, but not coarse mouth beneath it, thin lips, light, fine under jaw, devoid of flesh, except a slight pendulous skin underneath. The color of the nose yellow, orange, or a nutty drab. (The colors of the nose are elsewhere discussed.)

The head: Should be well-proportioned in length, breadth, and general symmetry; rather shorter in the bull and longer in the cow, in proportion to the size of the animal of either sex. The cheeks should be lean, and destitute of *much* flesh, giving them a neat, airy appearance. The forehead broad, gracefully narrowing along the face towards the muzzle; the face slightly concave — not *dished*, (like an Alderny,) but a true Short-horn face of elegant and stylish bearing. The hair in the forehead of a bull may be either straight, or curly, without prejudice either way. The eye should be prominent and large, encircled by a broad orange ring, clear of hair, or the hair growing upon it short, and running gradually out into the face and cheeks at a brief distance. The expression of the eye should be mild and gentle, indicating kindness of disposition. A sullen or deep-set eye, is more or less indicative of bad temper, and intractable nature. The style and expression of the eye we consider an important feature of the animal in its qualities of perfection.

The horn: As a rule, should be light, although a heavy one is not particularly objectionable, as it is of no use other than indicating the character of the race. The bases should stand wide on each side at the top of the skull, and bend gracefully forward in an outward curve, and may then incline downward or upward, either way without prejudice to the main qualities of the beast. They should be oval in shape at the base, and so continue some distance from the head; of waxy or neutral tint, inclining, if not strictly of the waxy character, to a creamy, rather than a white shade, and no dark tint or black except at the tips, and even there the less of either the better. The horns of some of the best animals sometimes take an upright form; others a backward and downward curve, which need not be objected to if the creature be otherwise unobjectionable. But a *perfect* horn, in either bull or cow, should have a graceful, outward spread, inclining gently downward or upward at the sides and front, small and fine.

The ear: Should be upright, large, and thin, well covered inside and out, with long, fine hair, and flexible in movement. It is not an important feature, and only noticeable in adding grace and beauty to the general features of the head. The head of a Short-horn gives the animal much of its character for grace and comeliness, if not of general excellence, although we have known many of superlative quality in every other particular, with plain heads—that being the only objectionable point. The Booth heads are inclined to be quite straight in the face, from forehead to muzzle—so much so as sometimes to give the heifers a *steery* appearance. This, however, is a matter of taste only, yet more common in the Booth stock than in the herds of most other breeders.

The neck: Should be strong and well set, of a graceful oval shape adjoining the head, running backward on a level, in the cow, and with a gradually rising crest in the bull, deepening and widening as it approaches the bosom, where it should connect in a smooth expansion, so that it can hardly be seen where the neck terminates or the bosom begins. The neck should be free from hanging skin or dewlap.

The chest: This most important feature, from which spring the brisket, shoulders, and fore ribs, should be deep, broad, and full, indicating robustness and good constitution.

The brisket: Set prominently forward, nearly perpendicular in front, broad, and well let down, or even slightly projecting, towards the bottom, with a thin, pendulous skin underneath, indicating an elasticity of the flesh inclosed within it.

The shoulders: Should be broad and even at the tops, working backward into a level with the chine in the rear, on a direct line, moderately upright, spreading outward as they descend from the top of the chest, smooth at the forward points, and thence sloping gracefully and tapering symmetrically into the fore legs above the knees. The knees should be round, muscular, and stand well apart; the legs below fine-boned, and terminating in hoofs of proportionate size, waxy, brindled or dark brown in color.

The fore ribs: Springing in a well-rounded arch from the spine, should be well expanded, long, and deep, giving abundant space for the well-sized heart and lungs to play, and develop what some may term the "fore flank" at the floor of the chest or sternum, into full breadth and levelness with the belly.

The crops, or spaces behind the shoulders: These should be full, perfected mainly by a sufficient springing outward of the fore ribs from the chine, with a full coating of flesh upon them. The crops in the older Short-horns were one of their most deficient points, but by skillful breeding they have been improved to such extent that they are now, in many animals, of remarkable excellence, and when so developed as to yield acceptable steaks and roasting pieces, add much to the selling as well as consumable values of the beast. In fact, no *perfect* Short-horn will show a depression behind the shoulders, but let a carpenter's *straight-edge* touch the entire space on a line from the shoulders to the after ribs adjoining them.

The spine, or back bone, by whichever name it may be called: Should run on an even level line from the chine to the setting on of the tail, although in some of the choicest animals a slightly depressed *notch* is permitted at the connection of the spine with the tail.

The loin: Broad, full, and level with the spine and hips—for there the choicest flesh usually lies, adding much to the weight and value of the carcass.

The hips: Wide spread, smooth, and on a level with the spine—not falling off and tapering downwards to cause a contraction of the ribs and belly forward. Drooping hips are apt to be narrow, with a "cloddy buttock" in the rear, giving tough and lean meat of little value.

The rumps: Long, full, broad and level, narrowing gracefully from the hips to the pin-bones, or points of the rumps, which latter should be wide apart, giving a proportional symmetry to either sex, and a great advantage and convenience to the cow in parturition.

The tail: Well and strongly connected with the spine on a straight line, small, and tapering gradually to the brush, which should be clothed with a full tuft of long hair.

The hinder ribs: These should spring roundly from the spine, long, deep, and well set back towards the hips, holding the belly up level, as near as may be with the floor of the chest, and by their breadth, giving abundant room for the viscera or bowels to play, and in the cow to spread sufficiently for the growth of the fœtus, while breeding.

The flank: Should be full and low, on a line with the belly and thighs, the skin loosely developed to fill with fatty flesh when perfected for slaughter.

The udder—in the cow: Should be broad, square, and set well forward, with fine, thin hair, wide between the teats, which should be placed well apart, of medium size and length, and gently tapering.

The testicles of the bull: Should be full for his age, equal in size—as near as may be—and lightly haired.

The thighs: Should drop perpendicularly from the pin-bones or points of the rumps, broad on the upper sides, and full throughout, the flesh running well down towards the hocks in the bulls. In the cows, from the rump-points downward the backward slope of the thighs may retreat forward and be thinner than in the bulls, as is the wont of her sex. Still, they should be muscular and strong.

The hind legs: Straight, like those of the horse, standing well apart, with a strong muscular hock, tapering into a fine-boned, flat leg below, and ending in a well-spread, compact hoof, of color like the forward ones.

The twist, or space above the junction of the thighs: Should be broad, full, and clothed with a soft, silky hair in either sex. In cows used for dairy purposes some importance has been given to the "escutcheon," according to Guenon's theory (the hair running both inversely and transversely far upward and outward on the thighs, indicating high milking qualities); but we consider that of minor consequence, as experience has not given anything more than a doubtful belief in its certainty of application. It relates to the lacteal tendency of the cow only, and needs no further discussion here.

The hair: Should be close, long and soft, furnishing a warm winter covering. It will be short enough in the warm season, as nature provides for the changing temperatures.

The touch, or handling quality: Should be elastic, mellow (not flabby), and springing under pressure of the fingers like a light India rubber ball. Good handling is one of the best points in a Shorthorn.

The skin: Moderately thick, strong, and loose, easily moving by action of the hand upon it, and showing plenty of cellular tissue underneath.

The above qualities have been generally accepted by experienced and skillful Short-horn breeders to constitute the necessary points of a perfect specimen of the race.

CHAPTER XII.

Pure Short-Horns—Herd Books—Pedigrees.

The subjects embraced in this chapter are, of necessity, more or less debateable; still we shall strive to treat them with truth, and fairness.

The question may very properly first be asked: What is a "thorough-bred or pure-blooded" Short-horn?

The simplest and most obvious answer may be: An animal which traces its descent through a line of ancestors, on both sides of its parentage, back to the earliest ages in Short-horn history or the fountain-head of its race, whether such ancestry be recorded in the Herd Books or not. To ascertain such fact to an absolute certainty, a close and thorough investigation of every volume (possibly) of the books, both English and American, now thirty in number, and containing over seventy thousand pedigrees, unless other positive testimony is at hand, must be made in order to settle the fact of *indisputable purity* of blood, and even then it cannot *unquestionably* be done, as our previous history has already shown.

The question of purity in descent is a broad and intricate one. Numerous commentators and critics through the papers, pamphlets, magazines and journals, of both past and present days, have from time to time ventilated their opinions upon it, and arrived at widely different conclusions, each one for himself, and apparently satisfied in his own correctness; yet they have *proved* nothing beyond what the Herd Books—and they but imperfectly either investigated or understood—together with some traditions derived from the old breeders have given them. It is unfortunate that the investigations of this subject have, from the beginning, both in England and America, been too much of a *partisan* and in many of them of a *personal* character, as well as exhibiting a prejudice against, or partiality for some of the bloods and pedigrees which they discussed.

Our history in the foregoing pages has related as definitely as could be ascertained, the origin of the Short-horn race; and the Herd Books have recorded their individual progress down to the present time, through the pedigrees which they contain; but it may be well to understand the authority on which those pedigrees were based, and for that a history of the foundation of the English Herd Book should be related.

We have seen that the Short-horns had been more or less cultivated and no doubt greatly improved through some past centuries in the counties comprising the ancient Northumbria, previous to the year 1730, and we have some few records of animals by name, from that time down to the year 1780, when, through the intelligence and enterprise of some of their younger breeders, they began in considerable numbers to take position by partial pedigree, as well as name, in a few individual herds. The records of many animals were kept in the private notes of their breeders, in some instances; in many more instances they were retained only in the memories of their breeders, and in the fallibility of those memories may not in all instances have been correct in *certain facts* of blood or birth. Yet, such were the only records, and they were not reduced to a permanent shape until the year 1822, when the first volume of the English Herd Book was published; thus the pedigrees of the Short-horns remained either in private memoranda or tradition, for more than half a century after some of them had acquired individual names, and reputations as prominent and leading animals of their race. Their progress and increasing numbers through those years had been so rapid, and the chances of error in perpetuating their lineage were so many, that an imperative necessity compelled their breeders to place them in a permanent record.

According to a concise and well-considered narrative, published in "*The Country Gentleman*," under date of July 27, 1871, over the signature "S.," which we consider competent authority, as was received by the writer more than twenty years ago, in England, from some of the then living parties who had been active in the proceedings, we extract as follows:

"The English Short-horned Herd Book was originated as a project some years before its publication. Sir Henry Vane Tempest, a large and capital breeder of Short-horns, held semi-annual agricultural meetings in Wynyard Park, his residence, in Durham county, giving prizes for horses, cattle and sheep. These meetings, like those of the Durham Agricultural Society, always were attended by the leading breeders of that county and Yorkshire. At a meeting in the autumn of 1812, there were present, among others, Robert and Charles Colling, Mrs. Charles Colling, Mr. Bates, Col. Trotter, Messrs. John and

George Hutchinson, Wetherell, Baker of Ellmore, Wright, Stephenson, Hustler, Raine, Mr. Booth and his sons John and Richard, Maj. Rudd, and the two Coateses, father and son. Sir Henry was a breeder of blood horses, and he suggested to the company, what had been before arranged between him and Mr. Coates, the publication of a record for Short-horns, like the Stud Book for horses. The view was at once adopted. All the gentlemen named were breeders of Short-horns, and at least three of them breeders of blood horses, viz.: Sir Henry, Col. Trotter and Mr. Stephenson. That was the start of the Herd Book. Sir Henry, Mr. Coates and Col. Trotter, had, prior to this consulted on the subject, and the movement at Sir Henry's dinner of the day of his show, was in pursuance of arrangement. It was conceded that Mr. Coates was the most proper person to act as editor of the book. He was fitted for that duty by a large knowledge of pedigrees and great interest in cattle, as well as knowledge of breeders. He had also their confidence. Mr. Coates at once went to work. Sir Henry agreed to defray the expense—but, alas, he died the next year, nine months only from this arrangement, when only partial progress had been made. His death delayed the matter, and except that Mr. Coates continued to collect material, there was no advance made. Had Sir Henry lived, the first volume of the Herd Book would have been published years before it was.

"The matter now rested until the first sale of Robert Colling's cattle in September, 1818. In the evening after the sale the project was revived among the breeders present, who were of course numerous, Col. Trotter bringing it up for consideration. As a means of defraying the expenses and giving a guarantee to a publisher, he proposed a subscription. A list was prepared and was largely signed there, and by every breeder then present. As the list was not money, no further progress was made for a year and a half. Through the zeal of Mr. Bates, who had deeply entered into the project, an arrangement was made to hold a meeting to consider the subject; to examine and correct the manuscript pedigrees, and furnish more material. This meeting took place at the King's Head Hotel, Darlington. There were present at it, Robert and Charles Colling, Mrs. Charles Colling, Miss Wright of Cleasby, (her father was one of the purchasers of Comet, and she continued her father's breeding after his death,) Mr. Bates, Mr. Mason of Chilton, Mr. Baker of Ellmore, Mr. Whittaker, Mr. Wetherell and Mr. Coates. Letters had been addressed largely to breeders, requesting information, and replies were obtained giving much material. Mr. Bates had traversed all the

Short-horn region and procured a large number of pedigrees. When the matter in hand was all laid before the meeting, it was clear that there was enough for a good sized volume. The plan of arrangement as it appears in the first volume was adopted, and it was decided to publish as speedily as possible.

"The subscription, started in 1818, had in the next year (1819) largely increased. But a subscription was not money, and Mr. Coates was poor. Therefore, Robert Colling and Mr. Whittaker agreed to advance the funds necessary. Robert was still a breeder, for he had sold only a part of his cattle in 1818. But a second death came to stop the enterprise, and in a month from this meeting and financial arrangement, Mr. Robert Colling died on the 7th of March, 1820. Mr. Bates would have advanced the money required, but there were circumstances in his then personal position, not necessary to relate, which prevented. The death of Mr. Colling occasioned another delay, and for two years and more nothing was done toward publication. In 1822, Mr. Whittaker, then a large breeder, proffered to advance himself alone the money necessary to print the first volume, to be repaid out of the subscriptions; but he made it a condition that the book should be printed at Otley, Yorkshire, near Greenholme, where he had his business and residence. Mr. Coates resided at Carlton, near Pontefract, thirty to forty miles from Otley, while the book could have been printed at Pontefract equally well and cheaper. The necessities of the case, in point of money, overruled the convenience of Mr. Coates, and the book was put into the hands of Mr. Walker, printer at Otley. It appeared in the autumn of 1822. The subscribers numbered four hundred and fifty-five, and the subscriptions were five hundred and five, at a guinea each, or $2,580. These were paid on the delivery of the book, and Mr. Whittaker's advance refunded. Mr. Coates and Mr. Whittaker were always fast friends during life, and Mr. C. was always grateful for the assistance rendered him. And it may be said that all the breeders were kind friends to him as he was to them. There was always some coolness between Mr. Coates and Mr. Charles Colling, from the period of Mr. Colling's success over Mr. Coates in the Shows of the Agricultural Society of Durham. And this would not have been mentioned here, but that their relations were said to have influenced Mr. C. Colling adversely in giving Mr. Coates information for his Herd Book, and Mr. Coates so believed. There was some sale beyond the subscriptions, but the surplus of receipts above the expenses of publication afforded no remuneration for Mr. Coates's labor, time and expenses through years in obtaining material for the book. He was obliged to be much at Otley on expense, when, if the book had been printed at Pontefract, his home, or at Doncaster, near it, that would have been avoided. But Mr. Coates' great point was gained, for now not only were the Short-horns an established and popular breed, and had long been locally, and were becoming generally, but by his exertions they had a record, and he was proud of it. He now stood their herald, to record their genealogies and blazon their escutcheons and their arms."

The number of bulls recorded in the first volume of Coates' Herd Book was 710, with about an equal number of cows, a very few of which are noted as having gone to America. The second volume appeared in 1829, seven years after the first, with 891 additional bull pedigrees, and a proportionate number of cows. We also find in Vol. 2, a number of new English breeders, and a few Americans, added to the contributors of pedigrees in the first volume. The third volume, issued in 1836, still seven years later, and in bulk larger than either of its predecessors, represented a considerable increase of breeders, including a number of Americans, with an addition of 1,298 bull pedigrees, making the number up to 2,897, and a fair aggregate of cows attending them. This third volume, we understand, on the authority just quoted, was issued by a son of Mr. Coates, the elder, and original editor, who had assisted his father in the compilation of the two earlier volumes. Mr. George Coates had died previous to its publication. At seven years later, in 1843, came volume four, with an increase of 3,800 bulls, running their entire number up to 6,700. Volume four contained the pedigrees of bulls only. The next year, 1844, produced volume five, in two parts, containing cows only, increasing the whole number of cows up to, probably, 8,000 or more. The three last books comprised about 1,900 pages, with a considerable number of American breeders and their cattle pedigrees. The mass of well-bred living Short-horns then in England, Scotland and Ireland, together with many others long dead, belonging to breeders who had neglected to record their herds in the first three volumes, came into the fourth and fifth. Those volumes also contained many American pedigrees of dead as well as living Short-horns, fully satisfied, as both British and American owners were, of the necessity of keeping the lineage of their herds before the public, and in a permanent depository.

These five volumes concluded the Herd Book labors of the Coateses —father and son. The proprietorship of the work and compilation of the sixth volume was thereafter transferred to Mr. Henry Strafford, who issued it in the year 1846, in the same style and form, mainly, as had been done by the Coateses. The work has since been continued at intervals by Mr. Strafford, down to the year 1871, until the whole number amounts to nineteen volumes, containing 30,347 bulls, with a much larger number of cows. A considerable number of American pedigrees were entered in the successive volumes edited by Mr. Strafford, until a few years ago, when they were no longer admitted, except such as were necessary to give the lineage of British Short-horns descended from American sires or dams, or were exported from America to England. The later volumes of the E. H. B. also contain the pedigrees of most of the native Short-horns which have since been imported from Great Britain into America.

SHORT PEDIGREES IN THE ENGLISH HERD BOOKS.

We here mention one item connected with the Strafford Herd Book, particularly, which is necessary for the American breeder to understand. No *female* pedigree, except in a few particular instances, is admitted to record in its pages until she has become a breeder, and then only two, three, or (seldom) four of her pedigree crosses are given, with a further reference to the names of either herself or her dam in some previous volume, so that in order to obtain her full pedigree those volumes must be examined. The names of her "produce," however, are placed in tabular form, with date of birth and name of sire given, that the pedigrees of such produce can, with some extra labor, usually be ascertained.

We have given the above particular account of the origin and history of the English Herd Book, as a part of the information with which the American breeder should be familiar; but there is still another history with which, in order to a thorough knowledge of the origin and truth of pedigrees, he should be acquainted.

WERE THE EARLY PEDIGREES IN THE ENGLISH HERD BOOK ALL TRUE SHORT-HORNS?

The question may here be pertinently asked: "What reliance have we that the names, or the pedigrees recorded in the Coates Herd Books were correct, or that they were true Short-horns?" To this we answer: Nothing, but the veracity of the breeders of the cattle whose names and pedigrees they furnished, and the acceptance of them by their contemporaries who were acquainted with their blood and breeding. To several of those animals we have already alluded.

In many of the names and pedigrees mutual questions arose among the men who established the book, as to their correctness. Some averred that possible crosses of the Scotch Kyloe or West Highland blood, or that of other breeds had, some generations back, occurred in them. The Dutch, or Holland blood introduction, of which we have previously spoken, (if it had ever occurred, but which it appears was then mostly or altogether ignored,) was not a source of contention. Of Charles Colling's Grandson of Bolingbroke cross from the Galloway cow, the whole story was then known, and what little there was left of its introduction acquiesced in by the main body of the breeders, as were the pedigrees of all others which could be traced into what were considered good Short-horn herds, be their date either ancient or modern. Yet, much party spirit existed among the English breeders, (as now, both in Britain and America,) and sharp controversies took place in relation to their various pedigrees; but all disputes were finally reconciled into the admission of the pedigrees recorded in the first, and subsequently into the succeeding volumes of the English Herd Book, so that with few exceptions, from that time to this, they have existed as authority for the lineage of their race. True, individual questions may arise among breeders, in tracing pedigrees to a remote source, as to the *entire* purity of their Short-horn descent; still, the Herd Book record must ultimately decide the extent of confidence in blood to which the animal in dispute is entitled, *and no individual opinion or decision can, absolutely, otherwise determine it.*

Another point in the English Herd Book may here be stated. Four crosses of pedigree bulls running back to what, in England, is considered a Short-horn cow, with but fifteen-sixteenths of recorded *pedigree* blood, entitles the animal having that number to a place in its pages. In this age of intelligence where five or six crosses at least in a well-bred English pedigree can easily be obtained, the showing of but three or four gives wide latitude for conjecture and guess-work. The Booths, from grandfather in 1777, to grandsons in 1871, in England, have ever maintained that four crosses of well-bred Herd Book bulls running back to *true Short-horn dams* (which can readily be found there, as large numbers of such exist which have not been recorded in the Herd Books to this date) are sufficient to establish *thorough breeding.* Hardly a single animal of their herds, since they first obtained their original bulls from the Collings, runs back into a *cow* having an ancient Herd Book pedigree, although they have bred many of the best animals the race has produced, and yet their pedigree cattle, both in England and America, are accepted as thorough-bred. We note their practice simply as matter of history, not from any doubt of the integrity of their blood. We have no such precedent in America where only the common native cows of the country, or those of some well-bred race other than the Short-horn can be resorted to. Thus, in America, having English Herd Book authority for example, we, as a matter of course, have been constrained to accept all *English* cattle imported from there *as true Short-horns*, on good authority that they were so. As such, they are entitled to record in our own Herd Books. Let cavilers say what they may, there can be no fairly disputing the question. As to what degree of confidence such pedigrees may be received by the public, it must be simply a matter of choice, or individual preference for them to either accept or refuse. The pedigree, or history of the animal, is the title to either acceptance or rejection, as best suits one's pleasure or judgment. Be it understood, however, that pedigree alone does not determine the excellence, or value of the animal; its form and other good qualities must confirm, to a greater or less extent, the value of the pedigree; otherwise a wide misjudgment may be made in the choice.

Another point—for we may as well canvass the whole question of *pedigrees*, so far as possible. We have seen it intimated, both in England and America, by some who may possibly know something about it, and more frequently by those who do not, that there have been divers interpolations in some of the earlier, or even later English pedigrees, some bulls having been omitted that ought to be in, and others inserted which ought to be left out, and thus the pedigrees measurably falsified. That may, or may not be. Of our personal knowledge we can say nothing of the facts; and in such doubt, we have no authority to decide the matter one way or the other but the Herd Book itself. The pedigrees are in the Herd Book, and being there, and long accepted by the mass of past, as well as living breeders, without the most positive evidence to the contrary of what they contain, we have no right to question them. Inferences, innuendoes, and arguments may be advanced indefinitely, but they *prove* nothing.

Still another point—treating the subject exhaustively while about it. Many people are prone to believe that a long pedigree extending sixty, seventy, or eighty years back, with fifteen or twenty Herd Book crosses in it, is *positive* evidence of purity, and therefore no question can be entertained of its thorough breeding. We shall readily see that such evidence may be of deficient character. Suppose, for instance, we take a daughter of Charles Colling's cow Lady, by

Grandson of Bolingbroke, the Galloway cross so frequently mentioned. This daughter of Lady had one-sixteenth part of Galloway blood, and she being put to a bull having the same amount of that blood, the produce would contain the same fraction of impurity. Or, let the female produce be put to another bull having even a lesser fraction of the blood—for bulls were used with one-sixteenth, one-thirty-second and one-sixty-fourth part of it, and very much less, in a descending ratio, from that day to this—all of them having a taint of it. We ask how many crosses of that tainted blood will have to be made before it is entirely eradicated? We shall not undertake to compute it, and yet to settle the fact, a month's labor or more may have to be exhausted in finding it out; while half the number of crosses in some other animal may carry a pedigree back into its original parents without finding the most distant taint of any other than pure Short-horn blood. We mention this without prejudice to the tainted pedigree, but only to show that its value must be judged by the *qualities* of the animals through which it has run as well as its length, or the number of *pure* crosses it contains.

To further elucidate the matter of blood, let us reckon the degrees of impurity in the number of crosses a pedigree may contain, by taking a continuation of descent from well-bred Short-horn bulls and a common cow, or one of other blood. The

1st cross gives	1-2	blood Short-horn.
2d "	3-4	" "
3d "	7-8	" "
4th "	15-16	" "
5th "	31-32	" "
6th "	63-64	" "
7th "	127-128	" "
8th "	255-256	" "
9th "	511-512	" "
10th "	1023-1024	" "
11th "	2047-2048	" "
12th "	4095-4096	" "
13th "	8191-8192	" "
14th "	16383-16384	" "
15th "	32767-32768	" "
16th "	65535-65536	" "

So, this sixteenth cross contains 1-65536 fraction of impure to all the other parts of good blood. How much damage, let us ask, in ordinary probability, will that do the creature possessing it? And yet the bull or cow possessing this 1-65536 part of impure blood, according to the natural law of descent may, by *an extreme chance*, either beget or produce an offspring which may show in some one feature, or even more, a cropping out of its impurity—a remote chance, indeed. Still, an animal *without the least taint* of impure blood in its veins is better; but to ascertain that fact, *to a certainty*, may be pronounced a sheer impossibility when we consider the various authorities on which the English pedigrees have from time to time been founded.

We do not give the above scale, or analysis of approach to pure blood, as an encouragement to grade or impure breeding, but to demonstrate the almost impossibility of tracing *pure* breeding back to a period in which a remote taint of outside blood may not have crept into the veins of an animal, or a tribe of animals, which have always passed for thorough-bred, both before and since the year 1822, when the first Herd Book was established. We have made the analysis also to demonstrate the injustice of condemning an animal having a remote taint of impure blood far away back in its English lineage where its pedigree has been admitted into the Herd Books of that country, even when such remote taint can be traced; and we may assert the injustice also of denying purity of blood to animals imported into America without pedigrees at all, both before and since the English Herd Book was established, such animals being certified by creditable breeders' evidence that they were good Short-horns. The names of such originally non-pedigreed animals and their produce have been sent back to England for record in the Herd Books there, and they have been accepted and recorded as *Short-horns;* whether right or wrong, in all individual instances, we do not decide—but there we find them. A short pedigree of but four or five crosses, even at the present day, appears to have no terror to English breeders, as we find bulls recorded, by *name only*, as late as the year 1843, in Vol. 4, by Coates, and in Vols. 6 and 7, in 1846 and 1847, by Mr. Strafford. We also find many bulls in the continuous volumes down to the 19th, published in 1871, which have only two, three, or four *known* crosses in their pedigrees, and no one, either in England or America, appears to question the integrity of their blood as legitimately belonging to the Short-horn race.

THE AMERICAN HERD BOOK.

Having compiled and edited the first volume of this work in the year 1846, and its successive volumes to the eleventh, inclusive, down to the year 1872, we purpose to give a brief notice of its beginning and after continuance.

Although we had seen a few herds in previous years, we began breeding Short-horns in 1833, when our first *experimental* acquaintance was made with them. The importation of Mr. Dun into Kentucky in 1833, and the Scioto valley importation into Ohio in 1834, spread the Western reputation of the Short-horns more widely than any others which had preceded them, and the arrivals which annually followed, for several years continuously, rapidly increased it. The produce of these importations added to the produce of previous introductions in other States, brought out many new pedigrees. The inconvenience and difficulty of sending these American pedigrees to England for record, as well as the importance of having a registry nearer home, suggested to our consideration some time afterwards the policy of establishing an American Herd Book. We had occasional conversations with leading breeders of New York on the subject as early as the year 1843, and also at different times with breeders in other States, and endeavored to enlist them into taking a part in its compilation. But little confidence, however, was expressed in either the possibility or success of such an undertaking, if attempted. Yet impelled by the growing conviction that such a work must of necessity ultimately come, in the year 1845 we ventured to send out a prospectus for the contribution of pedigrees, and assume the compilation of a pioneer volume, as an experiment, if nothing more. Although the prospectus was sent to every then known Short-horn breeder in the country, but few responded to it. Some considered it an act of assumption for one on this side the Atlantic to attempt an *American* Herd Book, when England had one already established to which the American breeders, equally with its own, had access for their records. Another discouraging obstacle was in the way: Short-horns were then very low in value in this country, as they also were and had been for some years past in England. Sales were few, and many breeders felt indifferent either to the propagation of their stock, or recording their pedigrees in a Herd Book anywhere, much less in the United States.

Under these adverse circumstances the pedigrees contributed were comparatively few; yet, under the advice of several zealous breeders whose confidence in the future progress of the Short-horns in our country, and in the importance of establishing and maintaining a domestic record was unflagging, a sufficient number of pedigrees were forwarded within a year to venture the compilation of a first volume. Accordingly the work was done and an edition of six hundred copies printed in the year 1846. It was a meagre book at the best, containing the records of only 190 bulls, and about 350 cows and heifers, with several names of their produce appended. The sales of copies were so few, that the work resulted pretty much in a dead loss, financially, to say nothing of the time and labor spent upon the compilation. With such a result, it may well be supposed that a further enterprise of the kind would not be soon attempted. Perhaps 150 copies of the book had been sold within a year from its issue, and the remaining ones were long stored away in our garret, ultimately, as we anticipated, to find their way among other waste material to the paper mills.

In the course of a few years times changed. The year 1852 had awakened a new impulse in American Short-horn progress. That and the succeeding year had brought some new importations into the country, and the spirit in neat stock improvement had become aroused to further progress, importance, and extension.

Several valuable importations of Short-horns having been made into Kentucky and Ohio during the year 1853, in the succeeding year (1854) many of the spirited breeders in Ohio who had been engaged in late importations, formed an association with a large subscription list for the payment of premiums, and invited the "United States Agricultural Society," then in existence, to hold their annual October meeting at Springfield in that State. The society accepted the invitation; wide publicity was given to it, premiums of most liberal character were offered in the prize lists (confined chiefly to neat cattle of various breeds), and anticipations were indulged—among the Short-horn breeders more especially—that it would be an event of great interest and gratification, as well as drawing a wide attendance; and in its result the public were not disappointed. The Kentuckians came over in strong array, both in person and with the choice of their herds. Ohio was "at home," and furnished, as might be supposed, a full quota of her best cattle, as well as a multitude of spectators. Indiana contributed her share of both; and even New York unexpectedly sent a few of its fine Short-horns and Devons, while the late liberal-hearted Mr. Roswell L. Colt, of Paterson, N. J., some 600 miles away, sent from his home, a nice selection of his unique little Alderneys, which, during some previous

16

years, he had imported and skillfully cultivated. The show of Short-horns was numerous, and unequaled in quality at any previous exhibition which had taken place in the United States, many costly and lately imported ones being on the ground. With a single exception the important prizes were all won and promptly paid.

During the exhibition a copy of the American Herd Book fell into the hands of Mr. Brutus J. Clay, one among the many liberal and large Short-horn breeders of Kentucky. He had never before seen it. On looking it over, and considering the importance of a continuation of the work, after consulting with several of the larger breeders of his own and other States present, he proposed to its editor the publication of a second volume, with a remunerating price attached to it, and urged its prosecution. With this encouragement the second volume was undertaken, a prospectus circulated, and several hundred contributors sent their pedigrees for publication. In the year 1855 the Book was issued, with 980 bull pedigrees, added to those of the first volume, making up the whole number to 1170. In addition to the bulls, a much larger number of cows were recorded, making altogether, with the introductory matter included, a well-sized octavo of about six hundred pages. Thus was promptly established the *necessity* of an AMERICAN Herd Book.

The second volume, it must be recollected, was compiled nine years after the first one of the American, and eleven years after the fourth and fifth volumes of the English Herd Book had been given to the public, in which latter ones the great majority of American pedigrees, published in England, either before or since, were recorded. During so long an interregnum the American pedigrees had remained in the private memorandums of their breeders, or if published at all, were only so in the scattered agricultural papers of the day, with no surety that even there the records would be permanently kept. Meantime, many breeders had given up and sold out their herds; others had died, while a considerable majority of them sedulously held on to their stocks, bred them well, kept their pedigrees correctly, and sent them to the second volume of the American Herd Book for record.

At that time there were not a dozen *full* sets of the English Herd Book in America, aside from the few odd volumes, scattered about in the hands of different breeders. It may, therefore, be supposed that a chaotic mass of material was poured into the hands of the editor for examination, compilation, and revision, a labor of most exacting kind, involving a great amount of toil and investigation, to say nothing of the patience required in dissecting, patching together, and arranging such promiscuous and miscellaneous matter into intelligible shape. But, such as it was, the labor was done. It is but justice to say, however, that very many of the pedigrees were made out by their breeders in admirable order, with a spirit of truth and integrity to have them recorded in a manner challenging the most critical investigation; while others, not familiar with keeping pedigrees, and less methodical in their memoranda, sent in a mass of material incongruous in manner, almost illegible in manuscript, and desperate in the hieroglyphics composing the names of their cattle, as well as wrong figures in their numbers. The compilation of these last was truly a job, and such as under no other circumstances would be again undertaken—at least by the compiler of *that* Herd Book.

As may be supposed, some errors in name, birth, and genealogy, crept into the work. Still, it was welcomed and encouraged by the breeders, with a further wish that it should be continued, and in 1857 a third volume was issued, containing 1298 bulls, and a considerably larger number of cows, swelling the whole number of the former to 2,468, and several hundred more of the latter. This third volume also contained sixty-eight corrections of errors in the pedigrees of bulls, and about one hundred corrections of errors in the pedigrees of cows that were inserted in the second volume. Many of the errors were, however, of a trivial kind, not seriously affecting the integrity of the pedigrees, while some others were important; yet, being thus promptly corrected, the lines of their lineage were not affected, the produce being properly recorded in successive volumes; and thus the work, through varying fortunes, has continued to the publication of its eleventh volume in the year 1872, in all containing more than 30,000 pedigrees; but the issue of the first six volumes *never paid the compiler and publisher a penny of pecuniary profit*—labor and time thrown in.

We have thus detailed at so much length the history of the English and American Herd Books to illustrate the zeal and painstaking labor of the meritorious class of men who, for a century past, have spent their energies to ennoble and improve the valuable race of animals to which their attentions have been devoted; and not alone for the private gains anticipated in their cultivation, for on the other hand many of the breeders have suffered large pecuniary sacrifices in their efforts, through various calamities, from one cause or another, which they encountered in their herds.

CHAPTER XIII.

PROGRESS OF SHORT-HORNS IN AMERICA. HAVE THEY IMPROVED IN BLOOD, QUALITY, OR CONDITION, SINCE THEIR FIRST IMPORTATIONS?

To give a short and decisive answer to the above pertinent question, we say they evidently have improved here, as they also have in England for many years past; and although we may not speak of English Short-horns exclusively by themselves, yet, as we have received various importations almost annually, of some of their choicest animals for the past twenty years—equally good as any which the breeders retained at home, and many of the best of which have passed under our own observation—we shall speak of them in general, both in that country and in this.

We have already shown that late in the last century, and in the earlier years of the present, the English Short-horns recorded by name and having pedigrees of their lineage were few, and in the hands of only a limited number of breeders who sedulously cultivated their better qualities to the highest development which their perseverance and skill could command. They labored in their praiseworthy vocation for more than forty years before they could even establish a record of their pedigrees, and for more than forty years longer before they could gain a *public* recognition of the importance of such a record, although the cattle were thickly distributed in the counties of Northumberland, Durham, York, and Lincoln, as a well-established race. Their reputation had also extended into various adjoining, and even distant counties, both of England, Scotland, and possibly into Ireland, where many reputable animals had been taken and bred with both skill and profit.

It may be supposed that during that period of eighty years the great majority of tenant farmers in the original Short-horn region— less active in new enterprises than men of more widely-varied pursuits—paid some attention to improving the qualities of their herds, when of the Short-horn race, but not so much attention as did the more skillful and thoughtful men whose names we have from time to time mentioned. As a consequence their cattle were less refined in quality than those which had been more highly cultivated and cherished. Yet, we may presume their herds had been enriched by the use of bulls bought from the early popular breeders, and that they had progressed to a degree of excellence much beyond what they were in the days of their remote, or even immediate, ancestors. The extending increase, by their rapidly growing demand, brought into use many cows, and even bulls of but moderate quality, although of good blood, and from them various herds were bred by their enterprising owners with acceptable pedigrees, which found a record in the Herd Book when once established.

There were in those early days occasional animals of wonderful quality, with whose history we have become familiar; but such remarkable ones did not abound in every herd, nor were their excellences so conspicuous as to give them wide notoriety in the annals of their day. Some of the earlier American importations from England were from the herds of the Collings, Mason, Wetherell, Maynard, and other distinguished breeders of the best cattle of the time; and also from several other reputable breeders known to possess blood of excellent quality derived from the ancient well-bred stocks. A very important item, however, entered into these earlier importations: they had to be obtained at prices within the limits which the buyers dared venture on a race of cattle whose success was as yet but an experiment in this country. As a consequence the costliest ones were not purchased and brought to America, but useful, good animals of approved blood and pedigrees, such as would stamp their better qualities on the common classes of our native stock, and satisfactorily propagate their kind with each other. These animals were, no doubt, a full *average* in quality to the stocks of the reputable Short-horn breeders in England at the times they were imported. Favorites, Comets, and their like, were then not common there. Nor have bulls of the very highest distinction, been *common* there since; but we venture the assertion that there have been as good bulls bred both in England and America since their day as was even Comet; yet Dukes of Northumberland and Commanders-in-Chief, in all their striking perfections, may only crop out once in a series of years, while many others equally meritorious in all essential qualities may be, and are produced now-a-days, both in England and America during every successive year.

Although some excellent, even extraordinarily good Short-horns had been imported from time to time into America from England among the earlier ones, their produce have been improving ever since with the American breeders. We venture the assertion that our American average is fully equal in their general qualities to the English. Those of forty, or even thirty years ago, as a rule, were inferior to what they are now. We remember many of the imported ones, and their looks are yet as familiar to our mind, as they were to our eye at the time we saw them. Their *handling* was less elastic; although their heads and necks were good, their chests were not so broad and deep; their shoulders less expanded and smooth; their crops more depressed, and they exhibited a less full and graceful outline generally. Their defects were more striking, and what should comprise their chief excellences were not so fully developed as now. We might name sundry animals, bulls and cows, with which we were familiarly acquainted, winning first prizes in the annual exhibitions of Agricultural Societies, twenty-five years ago, which no owner of such as they would now venture to lead into a show ring; and still, descendants of those animals at the present time take the highest honors; but they do so with fresher and costlier strains of blood in their veins, and by a more skillful attention being paid to their breeding than formerly. Our American breeders have within the past thirty years acquired more skill in the propagation of their herds, and as a consequence improved their stock in a corresponding degree. They are better judges of the qualities of animals than were the breeders of fifty, forty, or even less years ago; yet the older breeders were deserving great credit for their efforts, *for they had it all to learn*, while their successors have had the benefit of their experience and judgment, so far as they had acquired it. Added to these advantages, the later breeders have, with a wise foresight, opened their purses and bought animals at prices which in the days of the earlier ones would have been deemed ruinous, so far as any returns for their outlays could be expected. Such, also, has been the experience in England. Although Comet brought $5,000 at Charles Colling's sale in the year 1810, bulls and heifers equally thorough-bred and begotten by his own sire, sold for less than a fourth of his price. The price paid for Comet was said all over England to be extravagant, and such a sum for a bull was never again reached, so far as we can find, until more than forty years later, when Mr. Thorne, of New York, bought Grand Duke, and 2d Grand Duke, descendants of Comet, at the same bold, and as then considered, exhorbitant prices. One or more bulls have since been sold in England for Australia at still higher figures ($7,500 for one, if we recollect aright), while some remarkable cows have been purchased at prices of about $5,000 or more each, to come to America, or go to Australia.

In these enumerations we do not mention the fabulous sums—much higher than either of those we have mentioned—which Mr. Bates is said to have *refused* for his Duke of Northumberland, as he had many times declared that no price from any other party would obtain him. Three to even six thousand dollars each have been paid by American breeders for several American-bred bulls, mainly, or partially of the same blood as those above mentioned.

Still, *pedigree* has not altogether made those prices. The animals so sold have possessed the highest excellence of quality, superadded. *The excellence endorsed the pedigree, and the pedigree endorsed the excellence.* Such mutualities of character make up the maximum of worth in all blood animals whatever, where the highest points of perfection are sought, or found. Another item should be understood when naming the prices of such animals: *there is a* FASHION *in their blood.* No matter whether the fashion give such *real* increased value or not. When men take a fancy to a thing, be it Short-horn, Horse, or anything else, if their purses can afford it, they are quite apt to indulge in the luxury of its possession. We could name animals, were we so disposed, which thirty years ago one would pass, without notice, only that they were Short-horns, yet descended from imported animals, with good pedigrees, so run down by neglect as to *look* not worth a hundred dollars each. But taken in hand by good breeders, and crossing first-class bulls on them and their produce, in two or three generations they were raised to rank in show competitions with some of the costliest of recent importations. The purchasers of those neglected and inferior animals saw in their pedigrees that good blood was there, and believing in the integrity of *good pedigree* to rest upon, and that proper care and keep would restore the *excellence* that ought to be in the creature, they applied the means, and succeeded.

The fact that our American, as well as the current English herds, have been improved within the last forty or fifty years, to a higher standard of average excellence than they ever before approached, has been questioned by those who say the Short-horns, as a race, are no better than they were in the days of the Collings or Maynard, the elder Booth or Mason. That the old breeders had some remarkably good animals in their herds there can be no doubt; but all the testimony we have found has shown a continuous improvement from their days down to the present; and in the history we have of their herds from other breeders of the time when the points of their animals were closely criticised, their defects were such as would exclude most of them from a modern English or American prize-ring. That the American Short-horns *have* constantly improved in excellence within the last thirty years, and that the average quality of our herds, where skill and care have been bestowed upon them, is now higher than at any previous period, is a fact beyond contradiction in the judgment of accurate observers.

The Qualities of Pedigrees—Their Titles to Record in the Herd Books.

In our history of the English Herd Book we have learned how its pedigrees were originally gathered and admitted to record. We have seen, too, the lack of certainty attending the genealogy of many animals therein registered. The histories and pedigrees of known animals recorded in the first volume, of the year 1822, had been accumulating in the written memoranda, and also in the memories of men, (a good deal of the latter by tradition only,) for more than eighty years.

It is not necessary to repeat the circumstances under which the early pedigrees were admitted into the first Herd Book, nor that the same course of admission was pursued in the succeeding volumes edited by the Coateses, father and son, for the next twenty-two years, until 1844, when the labors of the son terminated with the close of the fifth volume. Down to the latter time the five volumes comprised a large majority, probably, of the pedigrees of the British breeders, and in addition to them many American pedigrees which their breeders had transmitted across the ocean for record. Yet it must be known that a considerable number of American breeders who had just as well bred cattle at home, and with just as good pedigrees as many that were transmitted to the Herd Book, did not send their pedigrees forward, and as a consequence they were not recorded in the English volumes. The rule of admission adopted by the Coateses appear to have been that any animals showing a reasonable evidence of descent from good Short-horn blood were entitled to record in the same manner that blooded horses were admitted to the "Stud Book;" that is, showing a large preponderance of thorough breeding without a known infusion of baser or foreign blood in their veins. Yet there were some exceptions to this rule, as we have seen; still in the contrarieties of opinion—some of that opinion based on certain knowledge, and some of it not—as well as in the different private interests and partisan feeling which existed among many of the breeders, and partialities in favor of particular strains of blood, and equal prejudices against others, perhaps hardly a single breeder could be found who would say that the Herd Book was correct in *all* the particulars of its pedigrees. There were fault-finders then, as well as now, and some who would be content with nothing which did not comport with *their own* ideas of positive correctness. Amid such contrariety of opinion, therefore, the only conclusion could be to accept the records as *mainly* correct, each contributor being satisfied in his own mind that *his own* pedigrees were quite as good, if not better than the average of his neighbors.

The fact may be also understood that the first Herd Book contained only a small minority of the well-bred cattle which had existed for the past fifty years; neither did it embrace anything like the full number of well-bred Short-horns alive at the time of its publication. For instance: Charles Colling had but 59 of all the animals he ever bred recorded in it, although in his thirty years of breeding he had probably bred and sold some hundreds of thorough-breds, and left breeding twelve years before the book was printed. Robert Colling, who bred cattle down to two years of its publication had only 93 of all his extensive herds recorded. The three Booths, Thomas, John and Richard — father and sons — then in the full career of their breeding, had but 52; Major Bower had 56; Mr. Coates had 42; Mr. Compton had 19; Mr. Currier 20; Mr. Donkin 15; Mr. Earnshaw 18; Mr. Gibson 47; Mr. Hutchinson, of Stockton, 54; Sir Henry Carr Ibbetson 28; the two Joblings 30; Mr. Mason 77; the three Maynards 15; Col. Mellish 30; Mr. Ostler 18; Mr. Parker 20; Mr. Parrington 15; Mr. Robertson 23; Major Rudd 35; Mr. Seymour 18; Mr. Simpson 60; Mr. Smith 44; Mr. Spoors 25; Sir Henry Vane Tempest 13; Mr. Chesterfield 27; Col. Trotter 38; Mr. Wailes 15; Mr. Wetherell 45; Mr. Whittaker 46; Mr. Wright 35; *Miss Wright* 35; and they comprised the chief contributors of pedigrees, and were all old breeders. The remainder of pedigrees which the book contained were contributed by the smaller breeders, besides very many animals known by name and tradition only, with no breeder's or owner's name appended to them. Such a record, with much of it so loosely made up, would be utterly condemned at the present day by some who suppose that a well-bred Short-horn should carry its pedigree back for centuries; but others who know that a genealogy among *brute animals* must begin at sometime "when the memory of man runneth not to the contrary," will be content to accept the dates and pedigrees of the Short-horns as they stand in Coates' five volumes, and there leave them.

It may be supposed that the several men engaged in breeding had sold during the anterior years of their labors a large number of well-bred Short-horns, which had not found their way into the first, nor afterwards into either the second or third volumes of the Herd Book; but many of them, and the produce of two or three of their descending generations, may have come into the fourth and fifth, which in the year 1844, at the end of twenty-two years from the publication of the first, embraced an addition of 3,802 bulls, and full as many cows, thus gathering during the last seven years since volume three was printed a large majority of the well-bred Short-horns of England, Scotland and Ireland, entitled to record, besides many additional American pedigrees beyond what were recorded in the previous books.

The fourth volume, containing only bulls, like the first, second and third, had many animals by name simply, some with only a sire, others with but a single sire and dam; many more with not over two or three known crosses, and a large number of them without notice by whom they were bred, or when they were born—whether in the last century or the present—thus gathering the known animals of the race under one legitimate fountain-head where their future produce could be traced into a common genealogy of blood, whether that blood could be definitely traced further back into pure sources, or not. In this general "consolidation"—to use a comprehensive phrase of the present day—the British Short-horn public at large acquiesced and were satisfied. With a very few noted exceptions, everything recorded there was considered by the general consent of English breeders a "Herd Book Short-horn," and as such, its produce was entitled to record in any and every future Herd Book which should be anywhere published.

To an antiquarian in Short-horn genealogy the above summary may seem to arrive at both a sweeping and arbitrary conclusion. Yet the breeding world of Great Britain sustained it, and followed out their own pedigrees in pursuance of the then established records from which there has been little or no appeal; or if appeal were made it was only in personal complaints, to which the breeding public paid no particular attention, falling back on the Herd Book record, after all, as the standard of blood and genealogy, there being no appellate court to set the records aside.

The sixth volume of the Herd Book, under Mr. Strafford's compilation, followed the fifth volume of Coates' within the next two

THE QUALITIES OF PEDIGREES. 251

years, in 1846, and under the same order and system of record the successive volumes have continued at intervals of about two years down to the nineteenth, issued in 1871. Yet the *non*-pedigreed animals became fewer as time progressed; but short pedigrees, with only two, three, or four crosses have been continued down and even into the last volume. A word as to why these short pedigrees have been, and also may in future volumes be so continued. It is well known in England, and ought to be as well known in America, that many herds of well-bred Short-horns exist at the present day in Britain, the owners of which have never kept *written* records of their breeding, and whose pedigrees have never found their way into the Herd Books. We give an instance: When Mr. John R. Page, the well-known American cattle artist, was in England a few years ago, looking over Mr. T. C. Booth's herd with him one day in their pasture, he remarked somewhat on the *short* pedigrees to some of the cattle which Mr. Booth, as well as other breeders of celebrity had in their herds. "Look out on yonder field," said Mr. Booth, pointing to a broad pasture on a hill some half a mile distant where were grazing a fine herd of Short-horns; "do you see those cattle?" "I do," answered Mr. Page. "Well, sir, the owner of that herd is an old dairyman and stock raiser. I have known him, his herd and their history, from my boyhood. His father bred the progenitors of that herd, which were good Short-horns in the days of my grandfather, Thomas Booth, in the year 1780, and the cows have been bred from that day to the present time to bulls belonging to him, my own father, my uncle Richard, and myself. Why are they not good Short-horns, although a pedigree beyond two or three crosses cannot be traced among them?" Mr. A. B. Allen, of New York, related to us that when in England in the year 1841, he saw several herds of good Short-horns, which had been long bred in the same manner to noted bulls of other breeders.

We do not give the above relations to excuse the neglect of recording pedigrees, or to justify short pedigrees which cannot be traced into *thorough-bred* Herd Book parents on both sides; but as a fact showing that there are men in England who are as careful in the blood of their cattle bred only for economical uses as those who rear their stock for the sale of pedigree animals alone; but not breeding for the latter purpose they pay no attention to recording their cattle in the Herd Book. And this may account for many of the short pedigrees of the present day in some English herds, together with many which have been imported to the United States within the last forty or fifty years, with little or no pedigree at all attached to them.

The above explanations have appeared to be necessary in order to understand the exact condition of the English Herd Book, and the principles on which it was founded.

THE PEDIGREES OF THE AMERICAN HERD BOOK.

Assuming the necessity of a Herd Book on this side the Atlantic, there could be no other plan so well adopted for its compilation as that of the English. To the records of the latter the Americans must resort for the lineage of all their pedigrees tracing to animals which found a place in it. In addition to that, Short-horns imported from England to America, together with their descendants, whether recorded in the English volumes or not, *with equal evidences of good breeding as very many others which were recorded in their pages*, had equally good title to enter the American books, particularly when many of their contemporaries had already found a record there.

As has been observed, the year 1844 closed the labors of the Coateses with the fifth volume of the English work, and the several books down to that time contained many pedigrees of American cattle. In the year 1846 the first small volume of the American, and the sixth volume of the English, under Mr. Strafford, were simultaneously published, but neither of them, we believe, known to the compiler of the other, at the time. Of course the two books, or their editors, had no relations with each other. The American was an independent work altogether. Its sole object was to establish a record for *American*-bred animals, without interference with either the past or the future English records, yet upon the same basis of admission.

Questions had arisen among the American breeders as to what bloods, tribes, or pedigrees ought to be admitted into an American book in the event of one being published, for even in the early days of our Short-horn breeding some partisan feeling had arisen as to what pedigrees were or what were not entitled to a record as well-bred Short-horns. About the year 1840, or soon afterwards, as we have learned, the principal Kentucky breeders came to a resolution to get up an American Herd Book, and Capt. Benjamin Warfield, of Fayette, now deceased, together with Dr. Samuel D. Martin, of Clark, and Mr. Robert W. Scott, of Franklin counties—the two last named gentlemen still living—were appointed a committee to receive pedigrees, examine and decide upon their merits and compile the records. Many pedigrees were sent to them; they had several meetings on the subject, but after much consideration the whole matter was indefinitely postponed, and nothing came of it. Nor was it likely that any other *committee* would arrive at any definite conclusions, particularly when conflicting opinions, and possibly interests in the way of blood and pedigrees would interfere. Thus the way was left open to individual enterprise, and insignificant as its first effort promised, the opportunity was ventured.

Opposing questions, if such existed, relating to the authenticity of the pedigrees to be admitted to its pages did not enter into the compilation of the first volume, although many of the elder breeders in several States were consulted. But when the second volume was about to be issued, questions were addressed to them, and the gist of their opinions seemed to be reached in a letter from the late Rev. Dr. Breckenridge, of Danville, Ky., who, aside from his professional labors, was a veteran breeder of Short-horns and other improved stock in Kentucky, to the editor, in which he remarked:

"I think you act wisely in accepting all pedigrees which run back into the English Herd Books; for, right or wrong, that is the fountain of the genealogy of the race at present. But, having taken that apparently inevitable step, it seems to be impossible to refuse to take the next, necessitated by that one, namely, to accept all American pedigrees as good as the average pedigrees of the English Herd Book. These two principles cover the whole ground; and all the rest is merely a question of *truth* in the alleged pedigrees, concerning which, unless the contrary appears, you cannot well avoid recognizing the truth of pedigrees that on their face appear to be true.

"After all, a Herd Book is but a *record office*. It can neither settle the *quality* nor the *title* of the estate admitted to record."

These remarks, so full of sound logic and good sense, were adopted by the editor, and pedigrees admitted to the English Herd Book were taken as a standard for the future records of the American work.

Looking at the condition of the American herds and their pedigrees, let us see how they stood. The early Kentucky and Ohio Short-horn herds had been chiefly founded, first on the Gough or Goff and Miller, or Patton stock, and afterwards commingled with the Sanders importation of 1817, all of them without known pedigrees, as no English Herd Book had then been published; but the 1817's were certified in their bills of purchase to be well-bred Short-horns. Many of the female produce of these herds, after the year 1826, were bred to recorded bulls from the imported herds of Colonel Powel and others, from the Eastern States, and the pedigrees of many of their progeny had been accepted and recorded in the fourth and fifth volumes of the English Herd Book, together with some of the originals from which they sprung. That there may be no misunderstanding of the matter we give a list of some of the bulls of the Patton and 1817 stocks and other originally *non*-pedigreed ones recorded there, to which we might add an equal or larger number of cows of like quality and pedigree also recorded. They are as follows, the numbers of the bulls attached. The words after the numbers are our own:

Florian (6018), bred by C. N. Bement, Albany, N. Y., running back to the Cox importation of 1816.

Paul Jones (4661), got by San Martin (2599), out of Mrs. Motte, Ky. imp. 1817.

Tecumseh (5409), was of the Ky. imp. of 1817, by Col. Sanders.

San Martin (2599), Ky. imp. 1817, by Col. Sanders.

Corwin (3500), bred by M. L. Sullivant, ending in imp. dam Flora, bred by Mr. Mason, of Chilton.

Embassador (3711), a *Hereford bull*, imported by Henry Clay into Kentucky in the year 1816.

Rising Sun (6386), a *Long-horn bull*, imported by Col. Sanders into Kentucky in 1817.

Independence (4070), got by Ajax (2944), no dam, bred by Gen. Van Rensselaer, Albany, N. Y., although known to be descended from imp. Pansy, by Blaize (76), etc.

Shannon (5111), ending in Flora, same as Corwin, above.

Buzzard (3253), of the Gough and Miller Virginia importation in the year 1785, or soon afterwards.

Charles (3344), of Ky. imp. 1817, ending in Buzzard (3253).

Chieftain (3369), ending in the Teeswater cow, Ky. imp. 1817.

Clarke (3394), ending in the Durham cow, Ky. imp. 1817.

Fantastical (3760), ending in Ky. imp. 1817.

Farmer (3763), ending in Buzzard (3253).

Goldfinder (3909), ending in Teeswater cow, Ky. imp. 1817.

Harrison (3979), ending in Buzzard (3253).

Kleber (4165), ending in a son of Rising Sun (6386), and the Teeswater cow, Ky. imp. 1817.

Lannes (4182), ending in the Teeswater cow, Ky. imp. 1817.

Lofty (4245), ending in Buzzard (3253).

Major (4340), ending in Teeswater cow, Ky. imp. 1817.

Mohawk (4492), by Tecumseh (5409), out of Mrs. Motte, both of Ky. imp. 1817.
Mohican (4493), ending in Buzzard (3253).
Priam (4762), ending in Buzzard (3253).
Ranter (4781), ending in the Teeswater cow.
Rufus (5034), ending in the Teeswater cow
Sambo (5073), ending in Buzzard (3253).
Sir Henry (5158), ending in the Durham cow, Ky. imp. 1817.
Superior (5359), ending in same as Kleber (4165).
Andrew (5755), ending in Durham cow, Ky. imp. 1817.
Billy Button (5795), ending in Buzzard (3253).
Goldbud (6042), ending in Teeswater cow, Ky. imp. 1817.
Indian Chief (6090), ending in Durham cow, Ky. imp. 1817
Sultan (6552), ending in Buzzard (3253).
Winfield (6687), ending in Teeswater cow.
Wonder (6689), ending in Teeswater cow.

There are carpers knowing little of the subject, as we infer after reading some of their criticisms, who profess to detect sundry grade or spurious pedigrees in the American volumes, (a few cases of which may possibly be so,) and besides them, condemn in one sweeping clause the pedigrees of the descendants of the "Patton stock," and also those of the Kentucky importation of 1817, together with sundry others, of which they *know* quite as little as they do of them.

Let us look somewhat into these animals and their asserted qualities. The true blood of the Patton stock, we admit, is somewhat cloudy in its origin. But we give the evidence of many of the venerable leading breeders of past days, some of whom years ago passed away, while others are still living. Among the deceased were Col. Lewis Sanders, the importer of the 1817 stock; the brothers Dr. Elisha and Capt. Benjamin Warfield, Capt. John Cunningham, Mr. Walter Dun, Dr. Breckenridge, of Kentucky, together with Gov. Allen Trimble and Mr. George Renick, of Ohio. There were others, also deceased, not now recollected. To these we add the names of the venerables Robert W. Scott, Samuel D. Martin, Jeremiah Duncan, Rev. John Allen Gano, Rev. R. T. Dillard, B. W. and B. T. Dudley, Issacher Fisher, Micajah Burnett, of the United Society of Shakers at Pleasant Hill, together with Ithamer Johnson and Peter Boyd, of the Society of Shakers, Union Village, Ohio, still living. Several of the above named gentlemen, now dead, we personally knew years ago; some of the others yet alive we are well acquainted with, and they who knew the animals, without difference of opinion, have assured us that the early Patton bulls—Buzzard (3253); Pluto, 825; Mars, 1850; and Shaker, 2193—taken into Kentucky and Ohio, had the appearance and characteristics of Short-horns, and good ones; while those of the well-known Kentucky importation of 1817—bulls and cows alike—were, to all appearance, *true* Short-horns, showing purity of blood, with the distinguishing qualities of good breeding, which mark the race at the present day. Yet these animals had no *written* pedigrees, being sent out of England years before a Herd Book was known in that country, and what genealogy they had was only kept in the private notes or memoranda of their breeders, or retained in their memories, or by tradition, except that of the cow Mrs. Motte, whose pedigree has since been traced in our previous account of the particulars of the 1817 importation.

We are not disposed to argue the question of the purity of Short-horn descent in all or any one of these animals, nor of any others which have come into the country *claiming* to be well-bred Short-horns, but without certified pedigrees. We purpose to calmly and plainly state facts, so far as we have been able to obtain them. We are aware that of late there has grown up a prejudice against the blood of the above named tribes of cattle—right or wrong, we do not decide, yet we believe very much of that prejudice to be unfounded.

Let us state the case clearly. When the Patton bulls came into Kentucky, although the blue-grass region at that early day had herds of good native cattle, they were at once recognized as a superior breed to any ever before seen in that locality, and were immediately adopted and encouraged for use in breeding by the most sagacious of the cattle breeders there. In course of time came the 1817 importation of Col. Sanders. They were represented as without taint or blemish of outside blood in their compositions; as true Short-horns from near the river Tees, the ancient, and then best known home of the race. That was five years before the name of a public Herd Book was known in that or any other country. The enterprising cattle breeders of Kentucky at once adopted them, as well as the Hereford bull Embassador, and the Long-horn bull Rising Sun, which were both of good and ancient established breeds, and down to the present day are held in high estimation in England. These two bulls were not much used, the Short-horns having a decided preference with the principal breeders, and after some crosses on the Short-horns they soon run out, leaving but few visible traces of their blood among them. This course of breeding continued several years, and until bulls were bought from Col. Powel, of Philadelphia, who had begun his Short-horn importations in the year 1824, two years after the first English Herd Book was issued, wherein the pedigrees of his stock were recorded.

Philadelphia and Baltimore for many years had been the principal, perhaps the only markets at which the Kentucky and central Ohio breeders and drovers sold their best beef cattle, and they soon found and saw the newly imported Short-horns. Ascertaining that some of them were for sale, they wisely opened their purses and obtained a few choice ones—bulls to cross upon their Patton and 1817 bloods, and cows to rear from them younger and equally pure blooded ones with which to perpetuate their stocks. From that time forward the Kentucky, and such of the Ohio breeders as had adopted them, throve apace with their herds, exhibited them at their domestic cattle shows, took prizes in competition with each other, and sold their surplus animals to their neighbors, and into other States, gave them pedigrees, truly, no doubt, yet the great majority of them ending in the "Durham cow," the "Teeswater cow," "Mrs. Motte," or with the bulls Buzzard, Pluto, Mars, Shaker, of the Patton stock, with the other names of San Martin (2599), Tecumseh (5409), Comet, and Prince Regent (of 1817), occurring in more or less of the pedigrees.* Thus the Patton, the Sanders importation of 1817, and the later Powel stocks were all intermingled in the general class of Short-horns, and many of their pedigrees sent over to the successive volumes of the English Herd Book for record, where they were welcomed and published without reserve or exception. Among them were frequent animals (as related by several of the old breeders who have been mentioned) which would pass creditably in most of the modern herds. Numerous descendants of those stocks have been distinguished as prize winners, even down to the present day, in some of the noted show-rings of the Short-horn localities.

With the array of early animals without known pedigrees, both imported, and American bred, which we find recorded in the *English Herd Book*, it legitimately follows that the breeders of them and their produce were entitled to a continuation of such pedigrees in the American record; and equally entitled to admission by the side of them were like pedigrees of animals of other breeders, which had not been sent to England for record. The proposition needs no argument.

---

* It is proper to state here that the pedigrees of the bulls Pluto, 825; Mars, 1850; Shaker, 2193; Comet, 1382, and Prince Regent, 877, whose numbers are only in the American Herd Book, were not publicly recorded until the 2d and 3d volumes of the latter were published.

There is still another class of imported non-pedigreed Short-horns, or with but a single cross or two of pedigree attending them, which need a like explanation, as the Pattons and 1817's. From the year 1816, (in which the Cox importation into Rensselaer county, N. Y., was made,) and during later years, to 1830, sundry Short-horns were brought over from England, to all appearance well bred, and so certified by the breeders' certificates. Some of these and their produce had also been recorded in the English Herd Book, and of course were entitled to record in the American. Cox's bull is (3513), E. H. B.

Yet a later class of non-pedigreed cows—or with only a single cross or two attached—have been introduced, beginning in 1834, with the first importation of the Ohio Company, and continued during the two or three years of their subsequent arrivals. A few such cows came out with other good pedigreed ones to Kentucky in 1837-9. Some others were also imported into several of the Eastern States and there bred. These short, and non-pedigreed ones, were purchased of the same classes of breeders as were the pedigreed cows, and some of them came over in the same ships with them. They were, apparently, equally well bred, showed as well in quality, and the buyers were assured by their English breeders of whom they purchased them that they were thorough-bred Short-horns, although they gave no *written* evidence of the fact. *Why* the short, or non-pedigreed cows were bought, when those having good pedigrees could be readily obtained, it is now hard to say. But most of them were accepted by our home breeders in their several localities, on their arrival, as pure Short-horns, their produce have been recorded in the Herd Books, and they stand unquestioned in public opinion as well-bred animals. We do not name the cows alluded to, but they and their produce can be readily found by referring to the records. The same state of facts apply to other cows which were imported a dozen or fifteen years later into several States. On looking at the circumstances attending these later non-pedigreed cows of 1834 to 1856, and the like circumstances attending the importations of 1817 to 1830, twenty to thirty odd years earlier, and with equal evidences of good breeding, we fail to discover the equity of reasoning which makes the produce of the later ones *thorough-breds*, and leaves the produce of the earlier ones, with several additional and equally good crosses in their veins, only *grade* animals! All the non-pedigree classes we have named having been admitted to record in the *English* Herd Book, they could not be excluded from the American record without upsetting the entire system on which the

English work had been founded, conducted and sanctioned by the Short-horn public in both hemispheres.

If later breeders objected to these pedigrees, or had little confidence in the blood of the stock which the pedigrees represented, they had only to let them alone, and select their stocks from others more to their liking. It was no detriment to other preferred pedigrees that the objectionable ones were there. Their *supposed* inferior blood could not injure the better blood of others, recorded by the side of them. The idea that an impure pedigree being recorded in the Herd Book, *makes it pure*, is a fallacy of the sheerest kind. Every pedigree rests on its own merits or demerits, and by such they are to be judged.

In this discussion of the admission of past pedigrees in the Herd Books, it is not to be inferred that impure-blooded animals, or grades known and understood as such, should be admitted to record. We simply say in conclusion of this particular topic, that the strains of blood which have been admitted into the English Herd Book are equally entitled to admission into the American. The breeder can either include them in his selection or reject them, as his interests or tastes may determine.

Having summed up at such length the situation of the Herd Books, both English and American, and the question of their pedigrees, we may not have allayed a single prejudice against any tribes, bloods, or strains of blood which may exist in the minds of any breeders; nor have we wished to detract from the merits of others to which they may be partial. We have only aimed to relate facts which may enlighten doubting minds, and satisfy hesitating conclusions as to certain bloods and genealogies. If we have made clear matters which have heretofore been doubtful, our aim has been accomplished; if not, we can only regret that our labor has been in vain.

Fastidious critics may object to the remote taints of Hereford and Long-horn blood which may be traced into some of the early Kentucky pedigrees; but when it is recollected that both these breeds are of ancient descent, and at the present day are highly esteemed in England—preferred, even, in their own localities, to the Short-horns—the 1-128th, 1-256th, 1-512th, or less fraction of these bloods in their veins works no *irreparable* injury, any more than did the distant taint of Charles Colling's Galloway, or the imputed West Highland crosses of nearly a century ago work a deadly objection to many English Short-horns of their own time. We say this not as advocating these outside crosses; on the other hand we object to them; but being adopted in the English Herd Book, which is our standard authority, they cannot be consistently ruled out of the classification.

Another thing should be recollected by the breeders who claim that their own herds are untainted by these remotely questionable pedigrees. Their own superior bulls and cows, as they term them, find frequent and some of their best customers among the breeders of the 1817 and other early non-pedigreed imported stocks, and there need exist no jealousy on the part of the untainted pedigree breeders that their own bloods are to be cheapened by reason of the others being tolerated. There is room and scope for all in our broad and rapidly developing country, and so long as individual choice in bloods and pedigrees is open to the public, *superior merit*, both in pedigree and quality, will assert its claims in the judgment of all who have an eye to the improvement of their stocks.

If it be objected against those far-away slightly tainted stocks that they (as may possibly be the case) throw out an occasional progeny betraying the foreign blood, let it be also understood that an occasional defective product of even the most approved tribes is also witnessed. It is simply nonsense to assert that even the best of blood will, in *every individual instance*, breed its own like in its descendants. Animal nature is always exceptional, more or less, in the production of its kind, from humanity itself, down to the lowest grades of domesticated things, and we must submit to results as we find them, doing the best we can, meanwhile, by proper means and care, to promote the most successful issues to our labors.

Notes on Breeding.

After the exhaustive, and possibly tiresome historical matter we have recorded, the reader and breeder will hardly expect from us an essay on the proper breeding of Short-horns as a basis of instruction to further efforts in the improvement of his stock. Numerous essays have been written, various in theory and opinion—some wisely, and some not—which have been studied by thoughtful physiologists and breeders, frequently with profit, and sometimes without. Our own ideas on this important subject have been given in a work lately issued from the press, entitled "AMERICAN CATTLE, THEIR HISTORY, BREEDING, AND MANAGEMENT," which can be obtained at almost any of the book collections of the agricultural papers in the country. We have little, if anything, to say in addition to what has been written there, and to that work we refer the inquirer, if he wishes to investigate the subject further than what his own previous reading and observation have already done.

The disposition of almost every Short-horn breeder to record his pedigrees in the Herd Book is a testimony of the importance which he concedes to it. He there finds the records of animals by name and pedigree, which public opinion has decided to be of the highest standards of blood and excellence thus far attained, and his own observation (if he has kept up with the progress of the race) must have educated him to know what a good animal should be. If in all these he has yet formed no ideas of guidance for a further improvement in his herd, we fail to know how he can be instructed. If he decide to proceed on the "in-and-in system," (breeding closely together those which are of the same family blood,) he must be cautious in the choice of animals which it may be safe to couple with each other—wise if rightly done, but hazardous if not; or, if out-and-out (breeding with such animals as are not close of kin) be his choice, equal care and consideration must be given that their style, figure, and conformation be such as to blend their good qualities, and exclude the bad, if either one possess them.

A large majority of the American Short-horn breeders, now that the race has been generally adopted as the best and most profitable for flesh-producing purposes, (not only in their fullness of blood, but as instruments for improving the lower orders of our native stock to the most profitable development,) propagate their animals mainly for that object, apparently regardless of the milking faculty of the cow, as the dairy product forms little or no part of the revenue expected from her. Yet, it has been seen in the progress of our history, that the Short-horn, from the earliest account we have of her, has been a good milker, and that quality was fostered by most of the early breeders of which we have an account, and is still encouraged in her use by such as esteem it of any considerable importance. The dairy quality may be partially bred out, if the breeder so desire it, or equally well retained if he so wish it, by the use of bulls descended from cows of like tendencies. It is only for him to choose which course to pursue, and in so doing he need not forget, in view of the examples we have recorded, and his own observation also, that after having done her full duty in breeding, and at the pail, she fulfills her destiny in a profitable carcass at the shambles. He must remember, however, that the cow cannot well carry a full carcass of flesh while yielding generous flows of milk to the dairy, and consequently will show less attractively to the eye than one giving little or no milk in the plenitude of good pasturage, or stall-feeding. But her produce will show equally well, with the same care and keeping, (if that produce be devoted solely to flesh purposes,) as the progeny of the other and fleshier one.

In a past notice we have tried to give the points of a perfect Shorthorn; and the nearer an animal approaches perfection in its anatomy, the more valuable it is for flesh-producing purposes, as such anatomy yields the best product in the choicer parts of the carcass, and of course more profitable to the seller and consumer. Therefore the nearer perfection a breeding bull approaches in his various points, the more valuable he is as a getter. For such a bull, to the breeder of grade stock for the shambles only, it is more economical to pay a round price than to take a defective one at a much lower price, or even as a gift. Such is the reason why experienced breeders sometimes pay enormous prices for extraordinarily good bulls, as we have known; not that such bulls are to be used on native or low-bred cows for grade breeding, but that on good thorough-bred cows they beget a much higher class of bulls than are usually sought for more common uses. It is, therefore, an object for any breeder, and for whatever purpose, to command as good blood in the bulls of his herd as circumstances will admit.

Let *continuous* improvement in *blood, quality*, and *style* of his animals be the aim of every breeder, and never for any trivial purpose lose sight of it. The new breeder in selecting the females to compose his herd, if he have a preference for any particular strain of blood, should determine which he will adopt, and then obtaining the best selections he can from them go on persistently in breeding, still bearing in mind that *uniformity* in the characters of his herd, *when coupled with true excellence*, is a great merit, giving conspicuity and reputation to the breeder, and of course, a superior selling value to his animals. A herd so established, in the present convenient ways of locomotion through our country, need not suffer from the evils—if men so think—of too close interbreeding. There are bulls enough, mainly of the same blood and lineage, scattered over the Short-horn districts of the United States and Canadas, to give fresh crosses in every herd of their own tribes when such crosses become necessary.

Quality and *pedigree* both, should go together; each endorse the virtues of the other. Yet, even defect in the *quality* of a bull may be remedied by the superior excellences of his pedigree, when that pedigree has run through some previous generations of marked distinction. Among many bulls which, without any noticeable characteristics of superior quality in themselves, have proved remarkably good getters, may be named Robert Colling's Lancaster (360), white, calved in 1814; and Thomas Bates' Short Tail (2621), red and white, calved in 1824; both small and inferior *looking* bulls, yet they begat many among the best animals of their day. We mention these not to give any preference to their particular bloods, or families, but because they were comparatively *mean* in appearance. Others and parallel instances of the kind may occur to the recollection of the reader.

Thorough-breds—Full-bloods.

The above terms have been frequently applied, for many years past, among the Short-horn breeders of the Mississippi valley, to designate a difference in the bloods of Short-horns—"thorough-breds" meaning such animals as run their pedigrees back into the Herd Books without taint of *known other blood;* while "full-bloods" mean such pedigrees as run back through many Herd Book crosses into *unknown* lineage. We consider the term "full-blood," thus used, as simply *conventional* with those applying it. *Thorough*-bred and *full*-blood are identical in meaning, if language has any signification. *Thorough* means *full*, and *full* means *thorough*, according to the dictionaries. The manner in which the terms have been used is erroneous, and the practice of it only confuses the inexperienced breeder, is of no service to the matured one, and should be discontinued. If a convention of Short-horn breeders, representing *all* the different sentiments and opinions which prevail relating to bloods and pedigrees could declare, through *unanimity* of opinion, at what fraction of outside or foreign blood, a pedigree should be admitted to, or excluded from a Herd Book record, an important point might be gained; but until such decision can be made, "thorough-bred" and "full-blood" may mean something, or nothing, in the way of distinction, as those who use the terms may decide. The entire pedigree of the animal in question, so far as ascertainable, is the only proof of breeding, and that must be determined by the Herd Book, if no better record can be found.

We here conclude our historical labors. Much collateral matter has, of necessity, been introduced as explanatory to incidents and facts which would appear uncertain or doubtful without it. Much more than has been gathered into these pages we might have written relating to sundry animals in many of the English, as well as our

American herds, but which, had we done so, although it might gratify curiosity, would not change any individual opinions which may exist touching either the merits of their blood, or the authenticity of their pedigrees.

So long as select breeding in any race of animals is followed there will be preferences for particular bloods, tribes and individual animals, with their different strains of genealogy, over others; and there will be more or less party spirit betrayed in discussions which may arise regarding them. No individual judgment can definitely settle those disputed questions, and merit or demerit will have its award mainly in private opinion rather than through acquiescence in any public decision, even if such decision should be attempted; and if attempted, would be simply impossible.

INDEX.

	Page
Agriculture in England—Early Authors,...	17
American Cow, ...	54
Alloy of the Galloway, bred by Charles Colling,......................................	65-68
Althorp, Lord,................................	149
American Short-horns — Their History—	155
Their Improvement,.....................	244
American Pedigrees in English Herd Book,	254
Bulls, Studley bull,........................	28
J. Brown's red bull,..................	29
Other noted early bulls,...........	30
Hubback,............................	36
Foljambe,............................	43
Bolingbroke, Favorite, Comet,.....	44
Belvedere,............................	127
Bakewell, Robert, as a stock-breeder,...	33
Berry, Rev. Henry,........................	61
Bell's (Thomas) Short-horn History,.....	118
Breeding, Charles Colling's mode of,.....	46
Robert Colling's mode of,.........	53
Booth family, as Short-horn breeders—Career during three generations,.......	95-117
Bates, Thomas, his early life, cattle breeding and history,................	118-147
Death,................................	138
Sale of his herd,...................	138
Did he improve the Short-horns,...	144
Breckenridge's (Rev. R. J.) opinion of Pedigrees,................................	253
Breeding, notes on,........................	260
Cow on Durham Cathedral,.............	20-21
Chillingham wild Cattle,..................	24
Colling, Robert and Charles,.............	31
Cows, The Stanwick, or original Duchess,	41
Lady Maynard and Y. Strawberry,.	42
Phœnix,...............................	44
Haughton,............................	57
Duchess, by Daisy bull,............	123
Duchess 1st,........................	123
Duchess 34th,......................	128
Matchem Cow,.....................	129
High prices paid for in early days,..	150
As Milkers,...........................	215

	Page
Colling's (Charles) Sale in 1812,.........	69-76
Colling's (Robert) Sale in 1818 and 1820,..	77-92
Collings' Cattle Improvement,............	93
Colors of Short-horn noses,.............	218
Colors of Short-horn hair,................	219
Carr's (of Stackhouse) History of the Booth Short-horns,...........................	95-117
Color of Bates' herds,.....................	134
Danish Invasions of Northumbria,.......	15
Danish Cattle taken to Northumbria,.....	15
Dutch Cattle said to be introduced into England,................................	24
Duke of Northumberland a cattle-breeder,	24
Durham Ox,................................	51
Duchess Tribe,...........................	125-131
Ducie's (Lord) Sale,......................	141
English People—Their early condition,...	16
Earliest known Short-horn Breeders,....	24-26
Early Colors and Appearance of the Cattle,	27
Elder Short-horn Breeders,...............	148
Etches, J. C., selected Cattle in England,	165
Exportations of Short-horns to England,	222
English Short-horns—Late Improvement,	244
Foggathorpe Tribe,.......................	133
Full-bloods,...............................	263
George III. a Short-horn Breeder,........	33
Galloway Grandson of Bolingbroke,......	61
Gough (or Goff) and Miller Importations,	156
History, First Period,.....................	13-18
Second Period,.....................	18-27
Herd Book, English,......................	231-239
American,...........................	240-243
Improvement in Short-horns—When began,......................................	23
In later years,.....................	244-254
Improvers in Breeding—The Collings,	56-61-93
Importations of 1815 and 1816,.........	160
Importations of 1817 to Kentucky,......	161
Importations of 1817 to 1830 by various parties,................................	172-177

INDEX.

	Page
Importations of 1833 to 1840, by various parties,	178-188
Importations of 1849 to 1871, by various parties,	193-212
Importations into Canada,	212-214
Killerby Short-horns—Booth,	108
Kirkleavington described,	124
Matchem Cow,	129
Mason, Christopher,	148
Miller Importation,	156
Oxford Tribe,	130-132
Perfect Short-horn described,	225
Pedigrees,	230
Pure Short-horns,	230-235
Pedigrees, English,	235
English, their qualities, etc.,	248
In American Herd Book,	252
Diagram of,	49-50
In Vols. 4 and 5, English Herd Book,	254

	Page
Pedigrees, American authorities for,	255
Absence of,	258
Patton Stock,	158
Red Rose Tribe,	133
Short-horns, Early characteristics of,	19
As a flesh-producing animal,	216
Storer on Colling's Breeding,	47
Studley Short-horns—Booths,	102
Sanders' (Col. Lewis) importation of 1817,	161
Produce of,	168
Short-horns imported without pedigrees,	258
Teeswater Cattle,	31
Thorough-breds,	263
White Heifer that Traveled,	52
Warlaby Herd—Booth,	113
Waterloo Tribe,	132
Wild Eyes Tribe,	133
Youatt's Cattle History,	62